THE CURTI LECTURES

The University of Wisconsin–Madison
1988

To honor the distinguished historian Merle Curti,
lectures in social and intellectual history
were inaugurated in 1976 under the sponsorship of the
University of Wisconsin Foundation and the
Department of History of the University of Wisconsin–Madison

PUBLISHED BY THE UNIVERSITY OF WISCONSIN PRESS

Christopher Hill, *Some Intellectual Consequences of the
English Revolution* (1980)

Carlo M. Cipolla, *Fighting the Plague in
Seventeenth-Century Italy* (1981)

James Willard Hurst, *Law and Markets in United States History:
Different Modes of Bargaining among Interests* (1982)

Gordon A. Craig, *The End of Prussia* (1984)

Michael Kammen, *Spheres of Liberty: Changing Perceptions of Liberty in
American Culture* (1986)

Paul Conkin, *Cane Ridge: America's Pentecost* (1989)

Power and Persuasion in Late Antiquity

Towards a Christian Empire

PETER BROWN

THE UNIVERSITY OF WISCONSIN PRESS

The University of Wisconsin Press
114 North Murray Street
Madison, Wisconsin 53715

3 Henrietta Street
London WC2E 8LU, England

Printed in the United States of America

Library of Congress Cataloging-in-Publication Data
Brown, Peter Robert Lamont.
     Power and persuasion in late antiquity: towards a Christian
empire / Peter Brown.
     192 pp.   cm. — (The Curti lectures ; 1988)
     Includes bibliographical references and index.
     ISBN 0-299-13340-0   ISBN 0-299-13344-3 (pbk.)
     1. Rome—Politics and government—284–476.   2. Rome—Social
conditions.   3. Upper classes—Rome—History.   I. Title.
II. Series.
DG311.B76   1992
937'06—dc20   92-50245

Contents

Preface

It was a great honor for me to have been invited to deliver the Curti Lectures for 1988 and an undiluted joy to find myself once again in Madison, Wisconsin, beside quiet waters and among friends, colleagues, and heroes of long standing. Not the least of these pleasures was to make the acquaintance of Merle Curti and to offer, through this narrative of a distant age, some tribute to the humane values which he has always maintained in the study of modern America.

The reader should know that these four long chapters grew out of the three lectures delivered at that time and that the three lectures themselves marked only the beginning of a process of self-education which, I very much hope, will continue for many years beyond the publication of this book. The book must be read in this light. It is an essay, with all the tentativeness, even the lopsidedness, that goes with such an endeavor. And it is an essay written largely to help myself, my readers, and future students of the later Roman Empire to catch up on certain themes in the political, cultural, and religious history of the time, on which a large body of modern scholarship now exists.

The exciting consequences of much of this scholarship have not been appreciated as fully as they might be. For this reason, I have chosen to write this essay in the form of a synthesis. It is an account of certain aspects of the period between A.D. 300 and A.D. 450, written in the light of recent advances in the field. I have tried to place the traditional culture of the upper classes in a social and political context which gives somewhat greater weight than has been given hitherto to its continued relevance and implicit goals. I have also attempted to link the increased persuasive power of the Christian bishops not only to the emergence of a novel, Christian image of society—for which we have abundant evidence—but also to social developments in the late Roman cities, whose outlines we can trace only in a fragmentary manner.

Readers must know the tentativeness of some of the connections that are advanced in this book between various cultural, religious, and social phenomena. But they should also take heart. For almost every aspect of this period, newly discovered sources, the exploitation of sources hitherto ignored, and the skillful reinterpretation of evidence long taken for granted have opened the way to a new view of the period that saw the final triumph of Christianity in the Roman Empire, the foundation of the Byzantine Empire, and the decline and fall of the empire in the West. It is profoundly reassuring to work in a field among scholars who have questioned and replaced so many standard generalizations and familiar narratives in recent years.

If I were to sum up in a nutshell the changes in the historiography of the late Roman Empire that have affected my own presentation in these chapters, I would say that we are better informed about and also considerably more sensitive to the religious and cultural expectations with which late Roman persons approached the political, administrative, and social developments of their time. It is as if a lunar landscape whose outlines once stood out with unearthly clarity in standard accounts of the political and administrative changes of the age has taken on softer tints, because it is now bathed in an atmosphere heavy with hopes and fears rooted in the religious and cultural traditions of the participants. If my account has recaptured some of the ways in which educated contemporaries reacted to, exploited, and presented to themselves the many dramatic developments that took place in the fourth and fifth centuries A.D., I will be content. If it persuades others that this can be done, and done better than in this essay, I will be delighted.

For these reasons, I have tried wherever possible, in my footnotes, to do justice to the most up-to-date scholarship on the subjects that I consider. I have cited sources that are difficult of access or little known with full references to editions, whether these are the most modern or, as is frequently the case, the most widely available standard editions. Most notable are the *Patrologia Graeca* and *Patrologia Latina*, edited by J. P. Migne in his *Patrologiae cursus completus* (Paris, 1844 onwards). To support my arguments, I have deliberately chosen, whenever possible, to cite passages from works of authors for which translations and commentaries in English or French exist. This is particularly the case with the extensive works and letters of Libanius of Antioch, whom I cite from the edition of R. Förster,

Libanius: Opera, vols. 1–11 (Leipzig: Teubner, 1903–22), giving, between parentheses, the volume number of that edition in roman and the page in arabic numerals. Other well-known authors I have cited in references that are standard in most works on ancient history. The reader should have little difficulty in tracing these to standard editions and to reliable translations. The *Res gestae* of Ammianus Marcellinus, in particular, is edited and translated in the Loeb Classical Library, by J. C. Rolfe, *Ammianus Marcellinus* (Cambridge, Mass.: Harvard University Press, 1952–56). W. Hamilton, *Ammianus Marcellinus: The Later Roman Empire (A.D. 354–378)* (Harmondsworth, Eng.: Penguin, 1986), provides a more recent, slightly abridged, translation.

In this process of self-education, I have been more than fortunate in the help I have received. The John Simon Guggenheim Foundation enabled me to travel throughout the late Roman sites of Turkey and Syria. I would not like it to be forgotten that the absorption of whole landscapes once central to the history of early Christianity and of the eastern empire was only possible because of those innumerable persons—Turks, Syrians, and exiles from Palestine—whose rare courtesy, skill, and, at times, high-spirited courage made travel possible in remote regions. The few days that I spent at Aphrodisias in Caria remain, in a way, the imaginative core of the book. A late classical city was brought alive to me—as to so many scholars in this generation—through the rare generosity of a uniquely vivid and uncompromising host, the late Kenan Erim. I would wish him to be remembered as he lies now in the city that he loved, whose unequaled riches he has unlocked for so many.

Colleagues at Princeton University, especially those in the history department, contributed at almost every stage to the slow and difficult process by which the insights of the first draft of these lectures became chastened and gathered weight, through an increasing sense of the complexity of the social and political life of the later empire. The meetings of the Shelby Cullom Davis Center, then under the directorship of Lawrence Stone, gave me almost weekly food for thought throughout 1988–89 on issues tantalizingly close to those with which I found myself forced to grapple. But ultimately, the manuscript owes most to fellow scholars in my own field. Charlotte Rouché and Garth Fowden read and reread drafts in such a way as not only to add a wealth of further information, such as only they were able to provide, but also to alter, quite decisively, the perspectives and the balance of the study as a whole. At the end, Judith Herrin's apposite criticisms helped me to bring greater cohesion to a story which could easily have fallen apart into its constituent themes, handled as they are in separate chapters. With candor, generosity, and patience, these readers have made the book what it is on a far deeper level than merely providing erudite information or removing superficial blemishes: the constant challenge of their friendship stands between it and earlier, less satisfactory drafts.

The manuscript would not have been prepared so quickly or with such ease if I had not turned to Olga Savin, who proved to be not only adept at word processing but also an exceptionally alert reader of my text. The index I owe to the intelligence and industry of Beatrice Caseau.

Last of all, I would like to thank my wife, Betsy. She has shared, with unfailing cheerfulness about their outcome, both the disruptions of travel and the tiresome and quotidian dislocations occasioned by the work that turned three lectures, delivered with an easy heart and in good company, into a book whose efforts to survey a complex and rapidly changing field may be of some use, I hope, to students of the later empire and so prove worthy of a lecture series delivered in the university where none other than Michael Rostovtzeff began his American career.

Power and Persuasion
in Late Antiquity

CHAPTER ONE

Devotio: Autocracy and Elites

This is a book about one aspect of the control of power in the later Roman Empire. It attempts to describe the expectations with which upper-class subjects approached the emperor and his representatives, to ward off the cruelty and fiscal rigor that characterized the government of the Roman Empire in the fourth and fifth centuries A.D. It will not describe all the mechanisms by which such approaches were made, nor all the strategies employed: rather, it will concentrate on the cultural and religious elements that were thought to have played a role in making the imperial power, for all its domineering majesty, amenable to persuasion.

The first chapter will offer a brief sketch of the social and administrative setting within which the power of the emperor normally made itself felt among those who wished to temper its impact. It will stress the extent to which the imperial administration, though greatly strengthened in comparison with previous centuries, still needed to make sure of the collaboration of the upper classes in the cities and provinces if its demands were to be effectively implemented. The structural weakness of the central government made it essential that the *devotio,* the loyal support, of a wide and varied constituency of local notables should be actively engaged. This led to the elaboration of a language of power and to occasional gestures of grace and favor that kept a place, in the midst of a hard-dealing system of government, for expectations that the emperor and his local representatives could be persuaded to act according to norms upheld by spokesmen of the upper classes.

The second chapter will examine the traditional culture of the upper

3

classes, as this was imparted to them through the system of education that went by the name of *paideia*. It will attempt to measure the role of this culture in creating common ground among all members of the upper classes, the rulers and the ruled alike, and in elaborating exacting codes of courtesy and self-control, linked to the ideal of a benevolent, because cultivated, exercise of authority.

The prevalence of ideals associated with *paideia* explains a further feature of the political imagination of the age—the repeated references to a persuasive role exercised by the philosopher. In reality, philosophers tended to be peripheral figures on the political scene in late antiquity; some, indeed, were fierce recluses, proud of their ability to avoid all contact with public life. Yet the late antique philosopher had been empowered by long tradition to act as the disinterested adviser, even as the critic, of the powerful. He had been assigned a clearly written character-part in the drama of persuasion, even if this part was frequently left unplayed or was played only by ceremonious yes-men of little real authority.

The third chapter will consider the social changes within the late Roman cities that led to the emergence of representatives of Christianity in an arena that had previously been considered the exclusive preserve of the traditional upper classes. In the last decades of the fourth century, bishops and monks showed that they could sway the will of the powerful as effectively as had any philosopher.

They were, in many ways, disturbingly new protagonists. But they had been able to make their debut on the stage of late Roman politics because contemporaries needed them to act according to scripts that had been written, in previous centuries, by men of *paideia*. An upper-class bishop such as Ambrose, at Milan, and even a wild man of the Syrian hilltops such as the hermit Macedonius, at Antioch, acted as effectively as they did because they found roles into which they could step with confidence. They were "true" philosophers. They played the ancient part of the courageous and free-spoken man of wisdom, but in playing this ancient role they invested it with a heavy charge of novel meaning. The strong religious overtones associated with their interventions brought a new world of values, characterized by belief in supernatural sanctions, into a system of control that had, until then, remained resolutely profane. The most urgent concern of those who "had been formed through *paideia*" had been with the self-grooming of a governing class according to classical notions of deportment.[1] The bishops and monks, by contrast, spoke of the wrath and mercy of a new, high God.

The intrusion of the supernatural betrayed the presence of more than

1.   Libanius, *Ep.* 994.2 (XI.124).

new beliefs: another element had entered the politics of the empire. The emperor's willingness to listen to bishops, as he had once listened to philosophers, implied his recognition of new forms of local power. This power could wear a sinister face: its non-Christian victims spoke of it, accurately enough, as a "usurped authority."[2] The unauthorized demolition of major shrines of the old religion, unpunished attacks on Jewish synagogues, and, finally, the lynching of a leading member of the prestigious town council of Alexandria, the woman philosopher Hypatia, in 415, were acts of violence that showed that the cities themselves had changed. They had fallen, in part, into the hands of new, nontraditional leaders, and their inhabitants sought redress for their grievances in novel, frequently more threatening, forms of direct action.

The fourth chapter, therefore, concludes the book with a description of the elaboration, in Christian literature, of a new language of power and, so, of a new rationale for its control that reflected the balance between imperial autocracy, civic notables, and the Christian church in the fifth-century eastern empire.

Throughout the book, the eastern provinces of the Roman Empire will hold the center of attention. From the Danube to the Euphrates, and from the Black Sea to as far south as the upper Nile and westward to Cyrenaica, in an area that now embraces the territories of no less than ten modern states (Greece, Bulgaria, and Romania south of the Danube, in Europe, along with Turkey, Syria, Jordan, Lebanon, Israel, Egypt, and Libya, in the Middle East), the ruling classes of what was, in the last analysis, a mighty confederation of regions prided themselves on sharing a common Greek culture and were expected to exhibit strenuous loyalty to a theoretically undivided Roman Empire. This last was hardly ever the case. For thirteen years, between Constantine's conquest of the eastern provinces in 324 to his death in 337, and then for only another seven years in all, from that time to the death of Theodosius I, in 395, the eastern and western parts of the empire were united under the rule of a single emperor. Usually, up to 395, and invariably from then onwards, the eastern provinces were ruled by an emperor who, either by agreement or because he had no option, allowed a western colleague to control the Latin-speaking provinces of the empire, from Britain to the present-day frontiers of Greece, Bulgaria, and Romania.

By concentrating on the eastern provinces, the book will do no more than respect the contours of a division within the Roman world that was already transparent in the fourth century and that became definitive in the

2.   Eunapius, *Lives of the Sophists* 472, in *Philostratus and Eunapius,* ed. and trans. W. C. Wright, Loeb Classical Library (Cambridge, Mass.: Harvard University Press, 1952), 422.

fifth with the collapse of the western empire and the emergence of a specifically East Roman state, the predecessor of what we call the Byzantine Empire.

The decision to deal principally with the eastern provinces inevitably involves viewing the Roman world from a single and, in many ways, peculiar viewpoint. It is easy to overlook the limitations that such an angle of vision imposes. Late Roman people lived in a wider world than our neat divisions between East and West, Latin and Greek, would imply. Many of them possessed surprisingly wide areas of peripheral vision.

To take a crucial example: the evidence for the eastern parts of the empire in the fourth and fifth centuries is overwhelmingly written in Greek. The "Greek East" is as good a shorthand term as any to describe the distinctive cultural world that we meet in the majority of the sources. Yet there was always more to it than that. We are dealing with a political system that embraced a variety of ancient regions. In many areas, members of the ruling classes and their clients combined respect for Greek culture with an ability to express themselves in languages that derived from the leading tongues of the ancient Near East: in Syriac, the lineal descendant of Aramaic, long the *lingua franca* of the Fertile Crescent, from Gaza to southern Mesopotamia, and, in Egypt, in a Coptic that was the last, most flexible version of a language once spoken by the pharaohs. Above all, these regions were held together by an imperial system that was staunchly, even aggressively, Roman. No educated or influential Greek—not even a professor of Greek rhetoric, such as Libanius of Antioch—could afford the tunnel vision necessary to deny this fact. Latin was the native language of almost all the emperors of the age. In the crucial upper reaches of the imperial service, traditional cultural boundaries meant little. High-ranking imperial servants moved with ease from one half of the empire to the other. A knowledge of Roman law and an ability to speak to the great in their own Latin tongue remained a *sine qua non* for success at the court, and in the provinces, a command of Latin conferred priceless advantages on Greek speakers faced with the perpetual, intrusive presence of a Mediterranean-wide Roman state.

Two western Mediterranean provinces, Italy and North Africa, also appear occasionally in our account. They provide abundant evidence for themes that were common to the late antique Mediterranean as a whole, in both its Greek-speaking and its Latin parts. The vigor of an analogous form of urban life; the continued attraction to easterners of Rome as a traditional soundingboard for their restless talents; and above all, the strategic logic that made Milan—standing as it did at the center of the road system that led from Gaul through northern Italy to the Balkans, and thence to

Constantinople — the pivot of repeated attempts by eastern emperors to assert themselves as sole, or dominant, rulers of the entire Roman world: these factors ensured that Milan, Aquileia, Rome, and, to a lesser extent, Carthage never faded entirely from the field of vision of leading inhabitants of Constantinople, Antioch, and Alexandria.

The reader should labor under no illusion. Power, not persuasion, remains the most striking characteristic of the later Roman Empire in all its regions. The fourth-century empire that we find described in the work of its principal Latin historian, Ammianus Marcellinus, was frankly authoritarian. Ammianus found it unusual, and praiseworthy, that the emperor Valentinian I did not attempt to "bend the necks of his subjects by menacing prohibitions."[3] It was more normal to impose obedience by imperial fiat, in religious as well as in secular matters. In the words of John Matthews' masterly study: "Imperial government in Ammianus' time was unmatched in Graeco-Roman history in its scale and complexity of organization, in its physical incidence upon society, the rhetorical extravagance with which it expressed, and the calculated violence with which it attempted to impose its will."[4]

When pitted against so formidable a system, the language of persuasion most commonly deployed by educated persons in the later empire seems out of touch with reality. Greek gentlemen were still taught to "install Demosthenes in their souls," just as their Latin equivalents absorbed the works of Cicero.[5] They brought into the fourth century A.D. a political language that had been perfected in the days of the free city-states of Greece and in the Roman Republic. Yet Demosthenes and Cicero themselves already spoke under the shadow of impending tyranny, and by A.D. 300 politics of the kind that a historian of the classical world might recognize, in Athens and in republican Rome, were a thing of the remote past.[6] It is, indeed, tempting to dismiss the bulk of our evidence for the political views of the educated classes as no more than out-of-date verbiage. The conceit that the politics of a vast, despotic empire could be represented

3. Ammianus Marcellinus, *Res gestae* 30.9.5; John Matthews, *The Roman Empire of Ammianus* (London: Duckworth, 1989), 256.
4. Matthews, *Roman Empire of Ammianus,* 253.
5. Libanius, *Ep.* 1261.2 (XI.339).
6. M. I. Finley, *Politics in the Ancient World* (Cambridge: Cambridge University Press, 1983); Fergus Millar, "The Political Character of the Classical Roman Republic," *Journal of Roman Studies* 74 (1984): 1–19; idem, "Politics, Persuasion and the People before the Social War (150– 90 B.C.)," *Journal of Roman Studies* 76 (1986): 1–11; J. A. North, "Democratic Politics in Republican Rome," *Past and Present* 126 (1990): 3–21.

in terms of the life of classical Athens; the continued emphasis placed on the practice of classical political virtues, such as freedom of speech, respect for legality, clemency, and the ability to display deliberative eloquence; the obligatory, flattering comparisons between contemporary emperors and the great statesmen of Greece and Rome: all this has been characterized as "completely conscious and completely artificial,"[7] "tedious" and "jejune."[8] It is assumed, by most scholars, that the intellectual baggage of classically educated persons can be safely ignored in any description of "real" politics in the fourth and fifth centuries A.D.

In the opening chapters of this book I will attempt to find another way around the dilemma posed by the seeming dissonance between late Roman upper-class culture and late Roman political reality. Without giving classical rhetoric undue weight in the decision-making of the later empire, it can, at least, be suggested that we are not dealing with a total split between "language" and "reality." Rather, the persistent recurrence of appeals to ideals of behavior derived, through education, from the classical past was one aspect, among many, of a late Roman political practice that was more complex than we might at first suppose. The nuances of the late Roman political imagination, and the complexity of the ground rules of late Roman politics, deserve closer attention than they have received in many recent accounts. It is to these that we must now turn.

In his lecture on the constitution of the later Roman Empire of 1910, J. B. Bury remarked that little attention had been paid to "the forms of government which are commonly classified as absolute monarchies. . . . Probably the reason lies in the apparent simplicity of a constitution, by which the supreme power is exclusively vested in one man. When we say that the monarch's will is supreme, we may seem to say all that there is to be said."[9] There is, in fact, much more to be said, even on the topic of the theoretical basis of the imperial office. Recent studies have stressed the fact that the later Roman Empire remained a *Rechtsstaat.* There is sufficient evidence to suggest that Ammianus Marcellinus was not out of touch with late Roman reality when, at the end of the fourth century, he propounded his own, workaday definition of the imperial power under which he and his contemporaries expected to live: "There were properly instituted courts of law and regular procedures, and in the observance of these

---

7.   Ramsay MacMullen, "Some Pictures in Ammianus Marcellinus," *Art Bulletin* 46 (1964): 437, now in *Changes in the Roman Empire* (Princeton: Princeton University Press, 1990), 81.

8.   Ramsay MacMullen, *Corruption and the Decline of Rome* (New Haven: Yale University Press, 1988), 113.

9.   J. B. Bury, *The Constitution of the Later Roman Empire,* Creighton Memorial Lecture, University College London (Cambridge: Cambridge University Press, 1910), 1–2.

was the essence of what Ammianus . . . called a 'civil and rightful empire,' *civile iustumque imperium.*"[10]

Other scholars have stressed the manner in which even the theorists of imperial autocracy, precisely because they still drew on a long tradition of Hellenistic treatises on the ruler as philosopher-king, continued to spell out, to the recipients of praise, an insistent antithesis between the self-will of the tyrant and the civilized adherence to law that distinguished a legitimate ruler.[11] Recently, the density and the permanence of this normative system has been studied, as a rallying point for opposition and as a grid on which contemporaries mapped their criticism of individual emperors, up to and beyond the reign of Justinian.[12]

It is, perhaps, time to add a further dimension to these considerations. Studies of late Roman law and political theory have tended to concentrate almost exclusively on the role of the emperor. By so doing, such studies run the risk of taking at its face value the vast "institutionalized egotism"—the conviction that all power and all political initiative should reside in the person of the emperor—which characterized the imperial office in the fourth century in much the same way as it characterized the claims to absolute sovereignty made by Louis XIV. Yet in neither case did the ruler truly stand alone. Absolute monarchy, in late antiquity as in late seventeenth-century France, was as effective as it was because its servants had learned—over many centuries, in the case of the Roman Empire—"the limits within which the practice of absolutism was possible."[13] These limits of the possible can be sketched briefly.

The emperor's vast notional power had to be mediated through his representatives in the provinces. For we must always remember that the emperor lived at an almost insuperable distance from the majority of his subjects. When at Trier, for instance, or at Sirmium, in the Balkans, the emperor was over a month's journey away from Rome and as much as a quarter of a year away from petitioners in North Africa. If at Constantinople, he was a month away from Antioch, and a further six weeks of travel, by land, from Antioch to Alexandria, and three weeks from An-

10. Matthews, *Roman Empire of Ammianus,* 252.

11. J. Karayannopoulos, "Der frühbyzantinische Kaiser," *Byzantinische Zeitschrift* 49 (1958): 369–84, now in *Das byzantinische Herrscherbild,* ed. H. Hunger, Wege der Forschung 341 (Darmstadt: Wissenschaftliche Buchgesellschaft, 1975), 235–57.

12. I. Čičurov, "Gesetz und Gerechtigkeit in den byzantinischen Fürstenspiegel des 6.–9. Jhts.," in *Cupido Legum,* ed. L. Burgmann, M. T. Fögen, and A. Schminck (Frankfurt: Löwenklau, 1985), 33–45; Christian Gizewski, *Zur Normativität und Struktur der Verfassungsverhältnisse in der späteren römischen Kaiserzeit,* Münchener Beiträge zur Payrologie und Rechtsgeschichte 81 (Munich: C. H. Beck, 1988).

13. P. J. Coveney, Introduction to *France in Crisis, 1620–1675,* ed. P. J. Coveney (Totowa, N.J.: Rowman and Littlefield, 1977), 43, 56.

tioch to Edessa. Even with the advantages conferred by the *cursus publicus*—
the system of rapid transport made available to imperial officials and mes-
sengers—the speed with which the emperor's edicts reached their destinations fluctuated widely with the seasons. Difficult enough in any period
of imperial history, communications appear to have become slower towards
the end of the fourth century as barbarian inroads disrupted the overland
routes in western Europe and the Balkans.[14]

The maintenance of an autocratic imperial system involved a perpetual
battle with distance. The wielders of power were only too easily isolated
from the world they claimed to control. In the words of A. H. M. Jones,
"in view of the slowness of communications, the administration of the
empire was centralized to a fantastic degree."[15] The central nucleus of the
imperial government—the emperor, with his praetorian prefects, commanders
in chief, heads of the bureaucracy, palace officials, and personal advisers—
kept for itself as many final decisions as possible. At meetings of the *consistorium,* generals and heads of government departments were summoned
ad hoc, to stand in the presence of the enthroned emperor—hence its name.
Vigorous discussions, marked by raised voices and sweeping gestures, might
ensue. But the emperor could bring the debate to a close at any moment
simply by rising from his seat. He was expected to listen to his ministers,
and he often participated in their discussions. But once he had heard them
out, his decision was final.[16]

This was the world of the *celsae potestates:* it was a chill peak, which
few provincials scaled, and then only at their peril. Little was known to
the outside world of discussions in the *consistorium.* Even so important a
figure as Ambrose, bishop of Milan, was deliberately kept ignorant of the
debate that had led to Theodosius I's decision to impose a punitive massacre on the inhabitants of Thessalonica.[17] This inner circle "played" with
the destinies of distant cities and regions.[18] Delegates from the provinces
could be ignored or subjected to savage punishments: one group, sent by
the city of Sardis, emerged from the presence of the praetorian prefect feeling their heads, to make sure they were still on their shoulders.[19]

14. A. H. M. Jones, *The Later Roman Empire* (Oxford: Blackwell, 1964), 1:402–3;
R. Duncan-Jones, *Structure and Scale in the Roman Economy* (Cambridge: Cambridge University Press, 1990), 7–29.

15. Jones, *Later Roman Empire* 1:403.

16. Ibid., 1:331–41, 403–6; Matthews, *Roman Empire of Ammianus,* 267–69, is ex-
cellent on such meetings.

17. Ambrose, *Ep.* 51.2.

18. Ammianus Marcellinus, *Res gestae* 28.6.9.

19. Eunapius, *Fragment* 72.1, in *The Fragmentary Classicising Historians of the Later Roman
Empire,* ed. and trans. R. C. Blockley, ARCA 10 (Liverpool: Francis Cairns, 1983), 119.

The resolute and fortunate few, of course, had less reason to complain. By approaching the *celsae potestates* directly, they gained the kind of advantage that so centralized a system made peculiarly precious: they came away with direct authorization, which bypassed the slow-moving and unreliable process of appeal and correspondence that normally linked provincials to the centers of power. In A.D. 245 a group of villagers from the Euphrates was quite prepared to wait for eight months in Antioch, in order to bring home a ruling from the prefect himself.[20] This remarkable document — from a recently discovered collection of parchments and papyri from Roman Syria — illustrates the fact that the centralization of the imperial system was as much wished upon the emperors and their higher officials as it was created by them. Litigants wanted direct access to the only truly authoritative courts — those closest to the emperor. The reduction in the sizes of individual provinces, under Diocletian, which virtually doubled the presence of Roman government throughout the empire, increased the availability of courts to which to appeal. Hence the importance of the title of *métropolis.* In previous centuries, this title had been a mark of honor. It had singled out one city from among the many that might aspire to preeminence within the province. It assumed competition among roughly equal centers. From the late third century onwards, the title of *métropolis* was held by the provincial city at which a governor resided. The *métropolis* became the undisputed legal and administrative capital of the region. This change was quickly followed by the foundation of an imperial capital at Constantinople and by prolonged imperial residence in a major eastern city, Antioch. Both developments are not only a tribute to the centralizing tendencies of the late Roman state, but they also reflect the insistence of the notables of the Greek East that they should have, at best, an emperor, or at least one of his representatives, within comfortable traveling distance.[21]

Most litigants, however, did not wish to linger at the court. Those who, like Ammianus Marcellinus, found themselves involved in the murderous politics surrounding the emperor, the generals, and the higher officials wrote of their experiences as a *venatio,* as an enclosed arena where they had been forced to pit their skill against exotic and ravenous beasts.[22] The tales of violence and cruelty that have had the most decisive effect in forming mod-

20.   D. Feissel and J. Gascou, "Documents d'archives romains inédits du Moyen-Euphrate (iii. siècle après J.C.)," *Comptes rendus de l'Académie des Inscriptions et Belles Lettres 1989* (July–Sept. 1989): 547–48.

21.   Charlotte Roueché, *Floreat Perge, Images of Authority: Papers Presented to Joyce Reynolds,* ed. M. M. Mackenzie and C. Roueché (Cambridge: Cambridge Philological Society, 1989), 218–21; Fergus Millar, *The Emperor in the Roman World* (London: Duckworth, 1977), 40–57.

22.   Ammianus Marcellinus, *Res gestae* 15.5.23, 28.1.10; cf. 15.3.3, 29.1.27.

ern views of the workings of the late Roman autocracy usually relate either to events that happened near the emperor or to deeds that were committed in the provinces by those few who felt certain, at the time, that they enjoyed the full support of the emperor and his inner circle.[23]

Terrifyingly active and peremptory at the center, the imperial system of government found itself becalmed on a Sargasso Sea once it reached the provinces.[24] The overwhelming bulk of the evidence discussed in this book is provided by the writings of those who lived at a safe distance from the court. It shows local notables scanning the last tentacles of an imperial system, as these worked their way from the emperor and his entourage into provincial society. This evidence inevitably determines the shape of the present study. We usually find ourselves viewing the centers of power in the late Roman state from a series of more or less peripheral regions. There is the Antioch of Libanius (314–393), a gigantic city by late Roman standards, with two hundred thousand inhabitants and a town council of six hundred members. Though visited more frequently by the emperors in the fourth century than any other city, Antioch remained very much a world of its own. A showpiece of Greek urbanism on the edge of a less-urbanized Syria, it was set back half a day's journey from the Mediterranean, in the rich valley of the Orontes. Its splendid isolation was heightened by the winding mountain passes over which the land-roads reached the city, from Asia Minor to the northwest, and from Phoenicia to the south.[25] The Cappadocia revealed in the letters of Basil of Caesarea (330–377 or 379) and Gregory Nazianzen (329–389) was a very different region, isolated on the high plateau of Anatolia and less securely centered on a single, highly populated city.[26] Different again was distant Cyrenaica (in modern Libya), the discontents and vigorous infighting of whose notables are revealed to us by the correspondence of Synesius of Cyrene.[27]

It is difficult to generalize about a world made up of so many distinctive landscapes. Its cities still prided themselves on their cultural diversity and self-reliance. Many of these cities are now known to historians only from

23.   Ibid. 28.1.12ff., on Maximinus as *vicarius* of Rome for Valentinian in 370; 29.1.27, on the trials for sorcery when Valens was resident in Antioch in 371–377. Matthews, *Roman Empire of Ammianus,* 258–62.

24.   Jones, *Later Roman Empire* 1:407–9.

25.   Paul Petit, *Libanius et la vie municipale à Antioche au ive. siècle après J.C.* (Paris: P. Geuthner, 1955); J. H. W. G. Liebeschuetz, *Antioch: City and Imperial Administration in the Later Roman Empire* (Oxford: Clarendon Press, 1972).

26.   Ramon Teja, *Organización económica y social de Capadocia en el siglo iv.,* Acta Salamanticensia: Filosofía y Letras 78 (Salamanca: Universidad de Salamanca, 1974).

27.   Denis Roques, *Synésios de Cyrène et la Cyrénaïque du Bas-Empire* (Paris: C.N.R.S., 1987); J. H. W. G. Liebeschuetz, *Barbarians and Bishops: Army, Church and State in the Age of Arcadius and Chrysostom* (Oxford: Clarendon Press, 1990), 228–35.

the most vividly local of all sources—from their tumbled stones, bearing late antique inscriptions, and from excavations of their buildings.[28] Even if we knew more about each individual region, our picture would remain lopsided. Those who claimed to be able to persuade (even if their efforts were frequently futile) have remained voluble for us in the surviving evidence. Those who exercised power, by contrast, are virtually mute. We know about the imperial laws, largely as they were collected in the *Theodosian Code* in A.D. 438, but next to nothing of the day-to-day problems of those who were charged with their administration. The frank letters of Pliny, while governor of Bithynia, to the emperor Trajan have no late Roman equivalents. We need only read the abundant letters in which the royal servants of Louis XIII and Louis XIV wrote of their difficulties, fears, and proposed strategies, when reporting back to their masters at court, to realize the extent of the area of silence that lies at the heart of our own evidence.[29] Yet the resilience of the common culture shared by educated notables in each region, combined with the relatively uniform methods and limitations of the imperial government, make it possible to reconstruct a tentative model of the manner in which persuasion was brought to bear on many occasions. The rest of this chapter, therefore, will be devoted to sketching briefly some of the rules of the game that governed the relations between representatives of the emperor's power and those groups of provincial notables whose expectations, at least, are fully documented in our evidence.

It is best to begin with the ceremony of *adventus,* the solemn entry of the emperor or his representatives into a city. This was an event central to the political imagination of the age. A little group of notables, dressed in the ceremonial white robes that marked them out as town councillors, would line up outside the gates of their city. Behind them, in carefully ordered ranks, stood the representatives of other professional groups—the

28.   Hence the model epigraphic study of Charlotte Roueché is centrally important: *Aphrodisias in Late Antiquity,* Journal of Roman Studies Monographs 5 (London: Society for the Promotion of Roman Studies, 1989). See also Clive Foss, *Byzantine and Turkish Sardis* (Cambridge, Mass.: Harvard University Press, 1976); idem, *Ephesus after Antiquity* (Cambridge: Cambridge University Press, 1979); Alison Frantz, *The Athenian Agora xxiv: Late Antiquity* (Princeton: American School of Classical Studies at Athens, 1988); Garth Fowden, "The Athenian Agora and the Progress of Christianity," *Journal of Roman Archaeology* 3 (1990): 494–501; J. Ch. Balty, "Apamée au vie. siècle: Témoignages archéologiques de la richesse d'une ville," in *Hommes et richesses dans l'Empire byzantin: ive.–viie. siècles* (Paris: P. Lethielleux, 1989), 79–89.

29.   I have learned most from the documents edited by A. A. Lyublinskaya in *Vnutrennaya politika Francuskogo absolyutizma* (Moscow: Izdatelstvo Nauk, 1961), ably exploited in W. Beik, *Absolutism and Society in Seventeenth-Century France* (Cambridge: Cambridge University Press, 1985).

guilds, clergy, and circus factions.[30] The populace crowded behind these, in the streets of the city itself, scrambling on the roofs and perching on the rubbish heaps to get a better view of the new arrival as he rolled up the main avenue in a high coach.[31] The notables would receive provincial governors with acclamations and solemn speeches of welcome. They rarely had to deal with a higher official, and hardly ever with the emperor himself. Even major centers seldom saw an emperor or a praetorian prefect. Antioch was the only city in the East, outside Constantinople, in which emperors resided for long periods, spending a decade in all between 337 and 377. After 378 they left for Constantinople, never to return.[32] The great palace, built on an island in the Orontes to house the emperor and his court, became an empty shell, on the steps of which a hermit pitched his tent.[33]

Yet by the simple fact of arriving in full state, the governor's *adventus* punctuated the life of every city and region with a reminder of a distant authority brought, for a moment, within reach.[34] The notables who gathered to welcome the representatives of their rulers would estimate, from generations of experience, where, in the greatly overextended chain of communication that brought the power of the central government to their locality, a weak point might be found. Much of what we know of the politics of the later empire, as viewed from the provincial cities, was concerned with those points where the imperial system could be turned to the advantage of the local elite and where precisely it might be expected to "give."

There was, indeed, every expectation that the system would "give." The initiatives of the central government invariably became subject to a mysterious loss of momentum. Fear of distance; an awareness of the difficulties involved in maintaining rapid communication with the emperor; and above all, continued uncertainty about the strength of the pressure groups at the imperial court in favor of any one course of action: all these considerations began to weigh upon the bearers of imperial authority, even as they made their way to their destinations. For all the imposing ceremonial accompaniments of their arrival in state, provincial governors, as we shall

30. Sabine G. MacCormack, *Art and Ceremony in Late Antiquity* (Berkeley: University of California Press, 1981), 17–89; MacMullen, *Corruption and the Decline of Rome,* 62.

31. E. A. Wallis Budge, *Miscellaneous Texts in the Dialect of Upper Egypt* (London: British Museum, 1915), 586.

32. Benjamin Isaac, *The Limits of Empire: The Roman Army in the East* (Oxford: Clarendon Press, 1990), 437–48.

33. John Rufus, *Plerophoriae* 88: *Patrologia Orientalis* 8:142.

34. Raymond Van Dam, *Leadership and Community in Late Antique Gaul* (Berkeley: University of California Press, 1985), 9–24.

see, were notoriously wary persons, anxious to seek allies among the local elites. Even more authoritative representatives of the emperor were also thought capable of wavering.

We know of this most clearly from an unusual source—from a vivid incident of fifth-century ecclesiastical history. As we were not supposed to know about this incident at all—for the information relating to it was "leaked" by opponents of the main protagonist—we must linger over it for a moment, to catch the flavor of a rarely documented, yet crucial aspect of the workings of the imperial system. In a secret memorandum, Cyril, the patriarch of Alexandria, laid down the measures to be taken by his agents at Constantinople in A.D. 431. A commissioner sent from Constantinople to Antioch, with a mandate directly from the emperor, had to be reassured that his original authorization to act in the interests of a policy favored by Cyril still carried the full weight of imperial approval when the commissioner arrived at Antioch a few weeks later. It was a common enough problem. Cyril's correspondence and especially his secret memorandum show very clearly how the problem first arose, how it was faced, and how Cyril thought it could be resolved.

The document shows Cyril in action at a crucial moment in his career and, as it turned out, at a decisive stage in the history of Christian doctrine. At the council assembled at Ephesus in June 431, Cyril, acting swiftly and on his own initiative, had pushed through the condemnation of Nestorius, then patriarch of Constantinople, in the name of a Christological formula: the human and divine natures in Christ had been indissolubly and instantly linked at the very moment of his conception in the womb of the Virgin Mary. Mary must henceforth be called Theotokos, "she who gave birth to God." To deny the formula, as elaborated by Cyril in singularly intransigent terms, was to incur the anathema of all orthodox Christians.

At Ephesus, distance had favored Cyril. He had sailed directly over a calm summer sea, disembarking at Ephesus with a formidable retinue. The potential allies of Nestorius, John of Antioch and the bishops of the East, by contrast, had made their way slowly by land, along the mountainous shores of southern Turkey, as the hottest season of the year approached. After thirty days of travel, marked by delays due to sickness, the bishops of the East had still not reached Ephesus. Cyril seized the opportunity presented by this delay. When John and the bishops of the East finally arrived on June 26, they found that Cyril had acted: Nestorius had already been condemned in a tumultuous assembly.

John and his retinue returned, aggrieved and unconvinced, to Antioch. It was now the duty of Theodosius II, as emperor, to command John to accept the condemnation of Nestorius and its theological corollary, the anathema declared by Cyril against all who opposed his own views. The tribune Aristolaos was, accordingly, despatched to Antioch in the fall of 431, with instructions to impose the decision of the council.

Now, however, distance worked against Cyril. In the month required for Aristolaos to reach Antioch, Theodosius II might change his mind. If Aristolaos knew of this or even guessed that it might happen, his zeal for Cyril's cause would evaporate. This thought was enough to cause Cyril to take to his bed with illness.[35] He had to act. Aristolaos must be made to feel that he still had support in Constantinople.

To this end, Cyril authorized his agents in Constantinople to mobilize the major figures of the court and city. The emperor must not waver or even be thought capable of wavering. The empress Pulcheria and her ladies-in-waiting were to renew their pressure on Theodosius. Dalmatius, the leading holy man in Constantinople, was to bind the emperor by oath to maintain a policy of no compromise. As for the officials of the palace, they were to be paid "whatever their greed demands." The eunuch Chryseros was to be either bribed out of his opposition or, better still, replaced by the chamberlain Lausus. As for the faraway Aristolaos, his wife and his favorite holy man were to write to him, assuring him that all was well at home.[36]

These instructions were accompanied by a detailed list of sums of money and *de luxe* articles of furniture to be distributed as "blessings" from Cyril. One thousand eighty pounds of gold (77,760 gold pieces, the equivalent of the annual stipends of 38 bishops or of a year's food and clothing for 19,000 poor persons) passed hands, along with 24 carpets, 25 woolen tapestries, 14 hanging carpets, 24 silken veils, 18 curtains, 28 cushions, 60 stools (8 of ivory), 14 ivory high-backed thrones, 36 throne covers, 12 door hangings, and 22 tablecloths. A hundred pounds of gold (the equivalent of a year's support for 4 bishops or for 1,800 members of the poor), for instance, went to the wife of the praetorian prefect, and fifty pounds went to his legal adviser. As for the recalcitrant Chryseros: "That he might cease from opposing us, we have been forced to send him double amounts: that is, six large woolen tapestries, and four medium-sized, four large carpets, eight cushions, six table-cloths, six large woven hangings, six small hangings, six stools, twelve throne covers, four large curtains, four thrones of ivory, four stools of ivory, six Persian drapes, six large ivory plaques, six

35. *Collectio Casinensis* 293.3, ed. E. Schwartz, in *Acta Conciliorum Oecumenicorum* 1.4 (Berlin: de Gruyter, 1932–33), 222; see Lionel R. Wickham, ed. and trans., *Cyril of Alexandria: Select Letters* (Oxford: Clarendon Press, 1983), xxii.

36. *Collectio Casinensis* 293.3–5, ed. Schwartz, pp. 222–23; see esp. Pierre Batiffol, "Les présents de Saint Cyrille à la cour de Constantinople," in *Etudes de liturgie et d'archéologie chrétienne* (Paris: Picard, 1919), 159–73.

ostrich-eggs, and . . . if he helps us, he will receive, by the hand of the Lord Claudianus, two hundred pounds of gold."[37]

It was a small price to pay for the peace of the church. A man passionately committed to using the sovereign power of the emperor Theodosius II in order to ensure the victory of his own theological views, Cyril had no illusions about the limits of that power. "Distance, the First Enemy" of all extended empires, worked ineluctably to produce faction at the center and a perpetual wavering along the fringes of the imperial system.[38]

Yet for all its enduring structural weaknesses, we should never underestimate the sheer vigor and self-confident intrusiveness of the imperial system that had emerged, after the crisis of the third century, in the reigns of Diocletian (284–305) and Constantine (306–337). Modern research has made plain that, far from being a melancholy epilogue to the classical Roman Empire, a fleeting and crudely conceived attempt to shore up a doomed society, the first half of the fourth century witnessed the long-prepared climax of the Roman state.[39] Even in distant western provinces such as Spain and Britain, recent studies have shown the extent to which local society came to depend on the continued working of an ambitious tax system and on the military and bureaucratic structures established by the reformed empire.[40] The constant demands of the imperial administration for taxes and for the transport of provisions were decisive factors in determining the economic life of Gaul, Sicily, and North Africa.[41]

The impact of a reinvigorated imperial government is most fully documented in the Greek East.[42] We begin, in the second century A.D., with

37. *Collectio Casinensis* 294, ed. Schwartz, p. 224, trans. John I. McEnerney, in *St. Cyril of Alexandria: Letters 15–110,* Fathers of the Church (Washington, D.C.: Catholic University of America Press, 1985), 151–52; see also Wickham, *Cyril of Alexandria,* 66, n. 8.

38. Fernand Braudel, *The Mediterranean and the Mediterranean World in the Age of Philip II* (London: Collins, 1972), 1:355.

39. C. Wickham, "The Other Transition: From the Ancient World to Feudalism," *Past and Present* 103 (1984): 8–14.

40. S. J. Keay, *Roman Spain* (London: British Museum Publications, 1988), 179–201; A. S. Esmonde-Cleary, *The Ending of Roman Britain* (London: Batsford, 1989), 41–161.

41. Aline Rousselle, *Croire et guérir: La foi en Gaule dans l'Antiquité tardive* (Paris: Fayard, 1990), 60–63; D. Vera, "Aristocrazia romana ed economia provinciale nell'Italia tardoantica: Il caso siciliano," *Quaderni Catanesi di Studi classici e medievali* 10 (1988): 160–70; C. Wickham, "Marx, Sherlock Holmes and Late Roman Commerce," *Journal of Roman Studies* 78 (1988): 191–93.

42. A. H. M. Jones, *The Greek City from Alexander to Justinian* (Oxford: Clarendon Press, 1940), 192–210; idem, *Later Roman Empire* 2:737–63; see, most recently, G. L. Kurbatov, "Gorod i gosudarstvo v Vizantii v epokhu perekhoda ot antichnosti k feodalizmu," in *Stanovlenie i razvitie ranneklassovikh obschestv,* ed. G. L. Kurbatov et al. (Leningrad: University of Leningrad, 1986), 100–37.

a Greek world which could plausibly see itself as consisting of a "common-wealth of cities." Each city enjoyed a measure of autonomy. Each fostered its own vivid and highly localized religious and cultural life, by means of repeated and spectacular ceremonial occasions, paid for by local leaders.[43] The visceral loyalty which a civic notable was expected to show for his hometown bordered on the comic: in a third-century joke book, a well-to-do little boy asked his father if the moon rising above his own city was, indeed, more splendid than the moon of any other town![44] Status gained in the wider world of imperial service supplemented and did not as yet eclipse status conferred by the local community; imperial service brought with it no privileges that excluded the claims of the cities on the lives, the enthusiasm, and the fortunes of their leading citizens.[45]

By the fourth century A.D. it was obvious that all this had changed. In the second and early third centuries the autonomous mints of the cities of Asia Minor had issued coins which dwelt lovingly on the particularities of local cult sites and on the honors paid by the emperors to local deities.[46] With the rise of the Sassanian Empire and its rapid conquests throughout the eastern provinces, these delightfully old-fashioned scenes gave way to a single, brutally simplified image: the emperor now stood alone on the coins of the cities, triumphing over Persian barbarians. By A.D. 275 the civic mints of the Greek world had ceased to function.[47] Nor could these cities any longer consider themselves as roughly equal to each other. Only those cities which won a favored place as *métropolis* of their province, that is, as centers of imperial power in the new administrative geography of the empire, were certain to enjoy continued prosperity. The others sunk perceptibly in status and in self-esteem.[48]

All cities of the eastern provinces came to take second place to Constan-

43.   R. Lane Fox, *Pagans and Christians* (New York: A. Knopf, 1987), 12–14, 53–61, 82; M. Wörrle, *Stadt und Fest im kaiserzeitlichen Kleinasien* Vestigia 39 (Munich: C. H. Beck, 1988), 254–57; Stephen Mitchell, "Festivals, Games and Civic Life in Roman Asia Minor," *Journal of Roman Studies* 80 (1990): 183–93.

44.   *The Philogelôs; or, Laughter-Lover* 49, trans. B. Baldwin (Amsterdam: J. C. Gieben, 1983), 9.

45.   Fergus Millar, "Empire and City, Augustus to Julian: Obligations, Excuses and Status," *Journal of Roman Studies* 73 (1983): 87–90; Wörrle, *Stadt und Fest*, 62–66.

46.   Kenneth Harl, *Civic Coins and Civic Politics in the Roman East, A.D. 185–275* (Berkeley: University of California Press, 1987), 52–70, plates 22–29; David S. Potter, *Prophecy and History in the Crisis of the Roman Empire* (Oxford: Clarendon Press, 1990), 195–96; Peter Hermann, *Hilferufe aus römischen Provinzen: Ein Aspekt der Krise des römischen Reiches im 3. Jht. n. Chr.,* Sitzungsberichte der Joachim-Jungius Gesellschaft der Wissenschaften, Hamburg, 8 (1990), no. 4 (Göttingen: Vandenhoeck and Ruprecht, 1990).

47.   Harl, *Civic Coins and Civic Politics,* 89–92, plate 16.

48.   Roueché, *Floreat Perge,* 218–21.

tine's new city, Constantinople. Although the court did not reside there on a permanent basis until after 395, the inauguration of Constantinople in 330 and the rapid expansion of an eastern senatorial order, recruited from among the notables of Greek provincial cities, in the subsequent reign of Constantius II ensured that even a *métropolis* with the prestige of Antioch no longer offered to those who served on its own town council status and privilege equal to that now obtainable at Constantinople. All over the Greek East, success at the court of the emperor meant escape from the demands of one's hometown: "In the end, the Empire and its constituent cities were in direct and continuous competition for the same human and financial resources."[49]

Constantine's condemnation of sacrifice and the closing and spoliation of many temples further undermined the cultural autonomy of the cities.[50] The local notables found themselves denied the right to resort to precisely those religious ceremonials that had once enabled each city to give public expression to its own sense of identity. It was no longer considered advisable to sacrifice, to visit temples, or to celebrate one's city as the dwelling-place of particular gods bound to the civic community by particular, local rites. Instead, the Christian court offered a new, empire-wide patriotism. This was centered on the person and mission of a God-given, universal ruler, whose vast and profoundly abstract care for the empire as a whole made the older loyalties to individual cities, that had been wholeheartedly expressed in the old, polytheistic system, seem parochial and trivial.[51]

On the local level, the most obvious result of this abrupt centralization of power was a fracturing of the elite. For as long as the empire had been a distant presence, it had been possible to delegate the business of government in each city to a relatively homogeneous class of urban notables: they alone were considered to be in control of their little world. The fourth century saw increased infighting among members of the local elites. Different groups derived their status in the locality from differing sources. We see this most clearly in the case of Antioch. No longer the sole patrons of the peasantry, urban landowners found that they had to compete with military men for the obedience of the prosperous villages of the Orontes valley.[52] In Antioch itself, retired imperial officials allied with leading no-

49. Millar, "Empire and City," 96.

50. T. D. Barnes, *Constantine and Eusebius* (Cambridge, Mass.: Harvard University Press, 1981), 211–12, 246–47; Kenneth Harl, "Sacrifice and Pagan Belief in Fifth- and Sixth-Century Byzantium," *Past and Present* 128 (1990): 7–26.

51. G. Dagron, "L'Empire romain d'Orient au ive. siècle et les traditions politiques de l'Hellénisme: Le témoignage de Thémistius," *Travaux et Mémoires* 3 (1968): 35–82.

52. Peter Garnsey and Greg Wolf, "Patronage of the Rural Poor in the Roman World," *Patronage in Ancient Society,* ed. A. Wallace-Hadrill (New York: Routledge, 1990), 163–64;

tables, who owed their status to collaboration with the imperial government, in order to victimize their less fortunate colleagues on the town
council.[53] Many notables flouted the traditional Greek culture of their city
by leaving Antioch to learn Latin and Roman law in the schools of Beirut.[54] A town council whose original unity had been splintered was challenged by the rise of a new pressure group associated with the Christian
bishop and with the violent monks of Syria.[55]

Not surprisingly, such developments forced the rhetor Libanius, a man
whose ancestors' portraits still hung in the town hall of Antioch, to wax
"tiresome" in his old age.[56] It is a tribute to Libanius' skill as a writer
that his vivid narrative of the discontents of his beloved Antioch has been
accepted, by most scholars, as conclusive evidence for the sure operation
of an irreversible decline of urban life throughout the eastern empire.[57]
"L'avènement du byzantinisme,"[58] the emergence of a "Byzantine" style
of government centered on the person of the emperor and based on the
outright social dominance of Constantinople over all other cities, is accepted by almost all scholars as the most clearly documented, indeed, as
the most inevitable, development in the Greek East in the fourth and fifth
centuries A.D.[59] In the long run, the effect on the cities of the changes
that we have described was as drastic as that which accompanied the absorption of former Italian *communes* into the absolutist, territorial states
of post-Renaissance Italy: what sense of local identity remained in these
cities came to be maintained in profoundly different circumstances.

Yet if we are to study the expectations of those who lived through such
changes, we must avoid the temptation of hindsight. It is important to recap-

---

J. M. Carrié, "Patronage et propriété militaires au ive. siècle," *Bulletin de correspondance
hellénique* 100 (1976): 159–76.

53.   Libanius, *Oratio* 48.41 (III.448), in *Libanius: Selected Works 2,* ed. and trans. A. F.
Norman, Loeb Classical Library (Cambridge, Mass.: Harvard University Press, 1977), 456;
Petit, *Libanius,* 269–94; Liebeschuetz, *Antioch,* 174–92.

54.   Libanius, *Oratio* 2.44, 49.29 (I.253, III.466), in Norman, *Libanius 2,* 34, 484; Petit,
Libanius, 363–66; A. J. Festugière, *Antioche paienne et chrétienne,* Bibliothèque des écoles
françaises d'Athènes et de Rome 194 (Paris: E. de Boccard, 1959), 410–12; Liebeschuetz,
Antioch, 242–55.

55.   Libanius, *Oratio* 2.32, 30.8–11 (I.249, III.91–93), in Norman, *Libanius 2,* 26, 106–
10; Liebeschuetz, *Antioch,* 224–42.

56.   Libanius, *Oratio* 2.10 (I.242), in Norman, *Libanius 2,* 14.

57.   Petit, *Libanius,* 291–93, 356. M. Forlin Patrucco and D. Vera, in "Crisi di potere
e autodifesa di classe: Aspetti del tradizionalismo delle aristocrazie," in *Società romana e
impero tardoantico 1: Istituzioni, ceti, economie,* ed. A. Giardina (Bari: Laterza, 1986), 252–59,
suggest an alternative interpretation.

58.   Petit, *Libanius,* 293.

59.   Peter Brown, *The Making of Late Antiquity* (Cambridge: Mass.: Harvard University Press, 1978), 32–33.

ture a little of the contingent nature of local politics in the fourth-century empire. Let us conclude, then, with sketching some of the advantages which the local elites still expected to enjoy, even in the changed circumstances of the fourth century.

The eastern empire remained an urban civilization. To enter a late Roman city in the Greek East was an impressive experience. The city was a place of "delights" whose ancient monuments continued to amaze and charm the visitor.[60] In Ephesus, for example, the theater, where Saint Paul had once stood, still towered at the end of the carefully maintained arcade leading up from the harbor; its "immense circle" radiated civic "delight" at the actions of a late Roman governor who had built retaining walls to support its venerable fabric.[61] Access to imperial funds and to transport facilities and the ability to impose forced labor on the peasantry ensured that it was the governor, not local notables, who did most to bring "the many veins of glistening stone" into a fourth-century city.[62] Imperial officials replaced private benefactors in fulfilling the ancient urge to act as "founder" of public buildings and as the "benefactor" and "savior" of one's city.[63] But the governors' activities affected only the ancient monumental facade of the city. They were more than balanced, in the fourth century, by the splendid development of new private palaces. As we can see from the case of Antioch, the mosaics of these palaces still spoke of the civic generosity of their owners, and their facades (especially if decorated with columns appropriated from public buildings, such as temples[64]) contributed to the beauty of the city quite as effectively as did work undertaken by a governor.[65]

In normal times, the city continued to be the preferred place of residence for the notables of the province. When Libanius described his own life as a man about town — exchanging courtesies with shopkeepers on his way through the market, keeping up his bedside visits to sick friends despite attacks of the gout, and dutifully attending their funerals[66] — he took for granted that he shared with his readers an urban style of sociability that did not, as yet, admit an imaginative alternative, even in a considerably less urbanized region such as Cyrenaica.[67]

60. *Expositio totius mundi et gentium* 26, 32, 38, ed. J. Rougé, Sources chrétiennes 124 (Paris: Le Cerf, 1966), 160, 164, 174, with commentary on pp. 245–46.

61. Foss, *Ephesus after Antiquity,* 61; Louis Robert, *Hellenica* 4 (1948): 87–88.

62. *Codex Theodosianus* 10.19.2; Libanius, *Oratio* 48.38, 50.16–23 (III.447, 478–81), in Norman, *Libanius* 2, 454, 72–78.

63. Petit, *Libanius,* 291–93; Liebeschuetz, *Antioch,* 132–36; Foss, *Ephesus after Antiquity,* 27–29; Roques, *Synésios de Cyrène,* 134.

64. Libanius, *Ep.* 724.1 (X.650).

65. Petit, *Libanius,* 381–82.

66. Libanius, *Oratio* 2.6, 22, 50 (I.240, 246, 255), in Norman, *Libanius 2,* 12, 22, 38.

67. Roques, *Synésios de Cyrène,* 135–38; see esp. J. Ch. Balty, "Notes sur l'habitat

Installed in their cities, the upper echelons of provincial society met arriving governors less as inferiors than as equals. Precisely because of the centralization of the empire, the local governors, sent out at regular intervals to the 104 provinces of the empire, enjoyed relatively little prestige and could show little initiative. They held office for short periods, frequently, as in the case of the *consularis* of Syria, resident at Antioch, for less than a year.[68] They wielded a minimum of coercive power. The armies were stationed on frontiers far from most civilian provinces and were subject to an independent, military chain of command. Despite imperial laws to the contrary, the governor's permanent staff, his *officium,* was run by locals.[69] A governor was as effective as his staff allowed him to be, and the venality and inertia of the *officia* were legendary. Any attempt to ensure that governors obeyed laws issued by the emperors included sanctions against their *officia* for conniving at abuses and for disregarding imperial edicts.[70] A member of the governor's *officium* enjoyed far less status than did an average town councillor. Notables might be browbeaten by a governor, but Libanius expected his readers to agree that it was an intolerable failure to inspire deference on the notable's part if he gave way to a mere governor's official.[71]

Furthermore, the very process by which the imperial government had altered the social structure of the local elites undermined the power of the emperor's representatives. Even in small cities, imperial honors, obtained directly from the court, conferred protection on their holders. The eccentric Count Joseph, settled at Scythopolis in Palestine, weathered the disapproval of a powerful Arian bishop, under Constantius II, on the strength of an honorary countship granted by Constantine.[72] In a great city such as Antioch, the governor would have confronted residents, many of whom held court titles, had themselves served as governors, and had been frequent visitors to the imperial court. The rapid turnover of governorships ensured that major cities throughout the eastern provinces had many such persons resident in them. They were firmly established as the leaders of local society, to which they had returned as *honorati,* as bearers of exemptions and privileges associated with their short spells of service in the imperial administration. For this crucial group, the borderline between "cen-

romain, byzantin et arabe d'Apamée," in *Rapport de Synthèse, Apamée de Syrie: Actes du Colloque Apamée de Syrie, 29–31 mai 1980* (Brussels: Centre belge de recherches archéologiques d'Apamée de Syrie, 1984), 494.

68. Liebeschuetz, *Antioch,* 111; Roques, *Synésios de Cyrène,* 174.
69. Rouché, *Aphrodisias in Late Antiquity,* 74–75.
70. *Codex Theodosianus* 16.10.10.
71. Libanius, *Oratio* 35.8 (III.213), in Festugière, *Antioche,* 486.
72. Epiphanius, *Panarion* 1.2.30.5: *Patrologia Graeca* 41:413A.

tral" and "local" government had been obliterated. Members of an empire-wide system, even when resident in their hometown, they felt entitled to treat the incoming governor as a junior colleague. They shared the same bench with him when he heard cases. They watched him jealously for any sign of undue pretensions to superiority. Lucianus, when *consularis* of Syria, had propped himself up on pillows so that he sat with his head and shoulders above the local *honorati*.[73] It proved to be a fatal mistake. If such men turned against him, a governor had little chance of survival.

Governors might even be subject to boycott. Direct criticism of the emperor and his policies was out of the question. On the surface, at least, the elites of the empire appeared caught in the grip of a "contagion of obedience" as powerful as that which affected the provincial aristocracies of the France of Louis XIV.[74] But the discreet and persistent withdrawal of collaboration by the local notables was always possible. What happened in many modern colonial regimes happened also in the later empire. Unpopular policies were met by a slackening of zeal that amounted to a "go-slow" in the conduct of government.[75] The failure of the emperors to impose their religious policies on large regions of the empire is a measure of the silent powers of resistance of which a late Roman provincial society remained capable. As the emperor Honorius once complained, his laws against Donatists and pagans in Africa continued to be ineffective because of the "evil sloth of the governors . . . the connivance of their office staffs and the contempt of the municipal senates."[76]

Governors lived in constant fear of isolation. To arrive in a province such as Cappadocia was to enter a region cut off from Constantinople for at least two months of the year by heavy snows.[77] The town councillors of Caesarea owned great fortified villas in the Anatolian countryside.[78] If disaffected, they would withdraw from town, leaving the governor to his own devices.[79] The prospect that an unpopular governor might find a city empty of its upper-class residents, who had retired to the countryside, "leaving the doors [of their palaces] hanging open," was a possibility with which contemporaries frequently toyed, in letters and in cautionary

73. Libanius, *Oratio* 56.4 (IV.133).

74. Beik, *Absolutism and Society*, 31.

75. Dale Eickelman, *Knowledge and Power in Morocco: The Education of a Twentieth-Century Notable* (Princeton: Princeton University Press, 1985), 153.

76. *Sirmondian Constitution* 12 (A.D. 407), trans. C. Pharr, in *The Theodosian Code* (Princeton: Princeton University Press, 1952), 483.

77. Basil, *Ep.* 48, in *Saint Basil: The Letters*, ed. and trans. R. Deferrari, Loeb Classical Library (Cambridge, Mass.: Harvard University Press, 1961), 1:314.

78. John Chrysostom, *Ep.* 9.2f, in *Jean Chrysostome: Lettres à Olympias*, ed. A. M. Malingrey, Sources chrétiennes 13 (Paris: Le Cerf, 1947), 146.

79. Basil, *Ep.* 88, in Deferrari, *Saint Basil* 2:116.

tales.[80] Even the bishop might take to his bed with a politic illness.[81] Altogether, like the royal agents of Louis XIV in the far smaller compass of the kingdom of France, each governor "faced a distant territory and an awesome governing prospect."[82]

Above all, no representative of the imperial majesty could be certain that his authority would be upheld by those who had sent him. The huge distance that opened up between him and the centers of power became a place of ambush. The process by which the imperial government had come to permeate the upper echelons of the civic notables, by recruiting them to serve outside their cities, ensured that networks of patronage and friendship linked each locality to powerful figures at the court itself. The intervention of such persons, on behalf of clients and fellow provincials, might overturn a governor's decisions, effect his removal from office, or, worse still and more predictably, expose him to the vengeance of highly placed enemies once he returned to private life. As in any large administration (and especially in an administration where no office carried with it the security of tenure), survival counted for more than efficiency. It was wiser not to leave a province, after a short term of office, having incurred lasting enmities through undue zeal and severity. It could be said of Severianus, a provincial governor of the fifth century, that a few ill-advised executions during his term of office dogged him with misfortune for the rest of his career.[83] The letters of Basil of Caesarea and Libanius on behalf of retired governors embroiled in retributive investigations explain the need felt by officials to ensure against the future by using their powers, when in office, to create a favorable "constituency" among those whom they had governed.[84] Nor surprisingly, fear of the long reach of the provincial nobility and the risk of vengeance once out of office acted on most governors as an exacting

80.   Libanius, *Ep.* 1351.3 (XI.400); cf. 1392 (XI.433). *Martyrdom of Conon* 1, in *The Acts of the Christian Martyrs,* ed. H. Musurillo, (Oxford: Clarendon Press, 1972), 186.

81.   Basil, *Ep.* 94, in Deferrari, *Saint Basil* 2:148. Basil's theological opponent, Eunomius, was less flattering: he wrote of the bishop shivering with fear behind the closed doors of the "hovel" to which he had retreated; Gregory of Nyssa, *Contra Eunomium I: Patrologia Graeca* 45:288B. Ambrose withdrew to the countryside, on the excuse of illness, when Theodosius came to Milan after the massacre at Thessalonica; Ambrose, *Ep.* 51.5.

82.   Beik, *Absolutism and Society,* 99. Raymond Van Dam, "Emperors, Bishops and Friends in Late Antique Cappadocia," *Journal of Theological Studies,* n.s., 37 (1986): 60, is a model study of the working out of an incident in the politics of Cappadocia in terms of the structural features that determined "the equilibrium between a remote and undermanned central administration and locally influential elites."

83.   Damascius, *Vita Isidori,* fragment 280, ed. C. Zintzen (Hildesheim: G. Olms, 1967), 221.

84.   Basil, *Ep.* 96, in Deferrari, *Saint Basil* 2:158; Basil was writing to Sophronius, a Cappadocian, to protect the former governor Elias. See A. H. M. Jones, J. R. Martindale, and J. Morris, *The Prosopography of the Later Roman Empire* (Cambridge: Cambridge

school of courtesy in their day-to-day dealings with the leading men of the region.

In the fourth century, courtesy was still necessary. In the all-important matter of taxation, the Roman Empire had remained a "commonwealth of cities." The eastern half of the empire was covered with a grid of some nine hundred cities.[85] It was through these cities that the emperor gained access to the taxable wealth of the countryside. Each city was held responsible for collecting the taxes of its territory.[86] These territories varied greatly in size and prosperity. Antioch controlled a rich and well-disciplined plain of some thirty-five square miles.[87] Cyrrhus, by contrast, a small city some seventy-five miles northeast of Antioch, was responsible for the taxes of a stretch of rugged countryside, forty square miles in area, that flanked the rich valley of the 'Afrin in northern Syria. It included "many high mountains, some wholly bare and some covered with unproductive vegetation," among which perched inaccessible and frequently refractory villages.[88]

It was in these relatively manageable, traditional units that the tax system of the Roman Empire became a reality. A yearly tax budget, first written out in the emperor's own hand for his praetorian prefects, was passed on by them to each provincial governor.[89] The town councils of the various cities of each province were summoned to the governor's palace. There, they would have had read out to them, by the governor's herald, a complicated list of specific demands, that took the form of levies in kind for the army—grain, clothing, horses, fodder, even recruits.[90] The legal designation of a person's status as attached to a town council, a *curia* or *boulé*—not the more flattering and imponderable advantages of birth and culture which so many notables flaunted when justifying their status in the locality—determined who was a *curialis,* a *bouleutés.* Finally, what the government needed were persons of sufficient wealth for their property to act as surety for any shortfall in the taxes. Women, merchants, members of

University Press, 1971), 1:847–48, Sophronius 3; and Basil, *Epp.* 147–49, in Deferrari, *Saint Basil* 2:352–60. On behalf of Maximus, see *Prosopography* 1:585, Maximus 23; Libanius, *Ep.* 1456 (XI.491); on behalf of Alexander of Heliopolis, see *Prosopography* 1:41, Alexander 5.

85.   Jones, *Later Roman Empire* 2:712–18.

86.   Ibid., 1:456–60.

87.   Liebeschuetz, *Antioch,* 40–41, 61–73.

88.   Theodoret of Cyrrhus, *Ep.* 42, in *Théodoret de Cyr: Correspondence 2,* ed. Y. Azéma, Sources chrétiennes 98 (Paris: Le Cerf, 1964), 110; trans. B. Jackson, in *Library of the Nicene and Post-Nicène Fathers* (Oxford: J. Parker, 1892), 3:264. Theodoret, *Historia Religiosa* 21.15: *Patrologia Graeca* 82:1444BC; idem, *Ep.* 81, ed. Azéma, pp. 192–94, trans. Jackson, p. 277.

89.   Jones, *Later Roman Empire* 1:448–56.

90.   See the vivid scene described in a Latin-Greek phrase book: A. C. Dionisotti, "From Ausonius' Schooldays? A Schoolbook and Its Relations," *Journal of Roman Studies* 72 (1982): 104.

the urban *plebs,* and even illiterates might find themselves enrolled as *curiales,* as town councillors, provided that they had the money.[91]

Yet the administration's concern could never be purely financial. It needed the authority of well-established local figures to bolster its own authority in the collection of taxes and in the maintenance of law and order. The central government might assess the taxes, but officers chosen by each town council gave reality to the tax registers, by collecting the taxes and transferring the proceeds of this collection — whether as levies in kind or money — to imperial depots.

The encounter of the emperor's representatives with the town councils, which opened the tax campaign of the year, was a solemn occasion. At one and the same time it displayed both the absolute power of the emperor to demand taxes and the intimate dependence of the imperial government on the collaboration of local groups for their collection. The emperor fixed the tax amounts. On that issue, there was no room for negotiation. When the demand for a special levy of 1,600 pounds of gold was read out to the Senate of Rome in A.D. 383, "a vast silence" descended on the stunned assembly.[92] But there was considerable room for shifting the weight of taxation. The town councillors were generally able to ensure that the main burden of taxes was paid by others, not themselves. We are dealing with a situation characterized by "collusively low valuation on the elite's own property, early collection of other people's taxes, and late payment of taxes by the rich."[93] As in seventeenth-century Languedoc, the position of the leaders of late Roman provincial society was "shored up, not levelled" by imperial taxation.[94] It was they who retained the ability to turn tax collecting into a source of profit and a basis for local power.

Accompanied by their local bureaucracy, the *susceptores,* the town councillors held responsible for collecting taxes, descended on the countryside. Every year, the authority of the city notables in their locality was put on display. Usually, the representatives of a great city such as Antioch felt sure that they came to "their" villages, to groups of peasants who had been effectively cowed, over generations, into paying taxes and rents promptly and without question. They arrived in the villages in their double capacity as agents of the imperial tax system and as dominant landowners. In Libanius' words, the peasants had learned "to cringe at the sight of a tax-

91.   Jones, *Later Roman Empire* 2:737–40; P. J. Sijpesteijn, "A Female *Bouleutés,*" *Bulletin of the American Society of Papyrologists* 24 (1987): 141–42.

92.   Symmachus, *Ep.* 2.57.

93.   Keith Hopkins, "Taxes and Trade in the Roman Empire (200 B.C.–400 A.D.)," *Journal of Roman Studies* 70 (1980): 121, n. 60.

94.   Beik, *Absolutism and Society,* 334.

collector's uniform."[95] Taxation, like the collection of rents and debts, meant yet another visit from their masters. Only on a few occasions did the notables meet their match, as when villagers resorted to the protection of more powerful patrons, such as local military men. Then, memorably shocking incidents took place. A personal display of authority on the part of the notables ended in vivid personal defeat: the collectors "present their demands, nicely at first and in a tone of restraint, but, being met with contempt and ridicule, with increasing anger and raised voice, as is to be expected when people do not receive their proper due. . . . Then they threaten the village headmen . . . lay hands on them to arrest them, but the villagers reveal their armory of stones. So the gatherers . . . make their way back to town, revealing what they have suffered by the blood on their clothes."[96]

These few failures were portrayed with verve by spokesmen of the offended notables.[97] But we should remember that they were the exception to the rule. More usually, collectors were only too successful. The life of a village holy man describes one such notable, Letoius (from a well-known family in Antioch), arriving to claim the crops of "his" village, "with more severity than was needed." Pleas for mercy were in vain. The grain was loaded up. Only a miracle prevented Letoius from riding back to town in his coach (as so many must have done) with his levy successfully collected at the expense of the early harvest of the peasants.[98] Writing in fifth-century Gaul, Salvian of Marseilles spoke of the *curiales* as the "tyrants" of their region: "What place is there where the wealth of widows and orphans has not been gnawed to the bone by the leading men of the cities?"[99] The emperor Justinian even declared that *curiales* should not be made priests: they were, he wrote in 531, "bred in harsh exactions . . . to carry out the cruellest acts."[100] They were, in fact, persons whose ruthless qualities were far too useful to the imperial tax system to be wasted in the milder duties of clergymen. In the later empire, taxes continued to come in with surprising regularity, given the weaknesses of the imperial administration.[101] This was due in no small part to the ferocity with which the members of the city councils collected the taxes of those less able to protect themselves.

95. Libanius, *Oratio* 30.15 (III.95), in Norman, *Libanius 2,* 114; Liebeschuetz, *Antioch,* 63–69; A. H. M. Jones, "The Roman Colonate," *Past and Present* 13 (1958): 1–13.
96. Libanius, *Oratio* 47.7 (III.407–8), in Norman, *Libanius 2,* 507.
97. Carrié, "Patronage et propriété militaires," 169–72.
98. Theodoret, *Historia Religiosa* 14: *Patrologia Graeca* 82:1413B.
99. Salvian, *De gubernatione Dei* 5.18.
100. *Codex Justinianus* 1.3.52.1.
101. Jones, *Later Roman Empire* 1:406.

The *quid pro quo* of the brusque treatment of the vast majority of tax-payers, that is, of the peasantry, was the ease with which the rich could allow their tax arrears to accumulate. The handling of arrears was the stuff of local politics. The exaction of arrears marked the uneasy borderline between the privilege of the few and the exposure to official violence that haunted the many. It is significant that the office of *exactor,* that is, of the person responsible for the collection of arrears, usually fell to a senior member of the town council. It was an office worth going to some effort to obtain.[102] The *exactor* knew how to make the most of the leverage that such a post placed in his hands. As a result, the town councils became divided. A small and clearly defined group of town councillors were able to manipulate the tax system to their advantage. They could allow their fiscal debts to coast along, while other, less well-placed notables found that tax arrears pushed them over the precipice that separated their class from the mass of the populace. Failure to meet demands for arrears of taxes exposed even town councillors to the shameful, lower-class punishment of flogging.[103] Relative leniency and harshness in calling in fiscal debt, therefore, played a decisive role in bringing about the split, within the notable class itself, between a minority of privileged leading citizens, the *prôteuontes* or *principales,* and the rank and file of the town council, the *decuriones,* that was the most blatant feature of urban life of the late Roman Empire.[104]

By the same token, outstanding arrears provided the emperor with a much-needed reserve of political capital. The cancellation of fiscal debts enabled him to give clear gestures of favor to the upper classes. For as Salvian made plain, it was the unpaid taxes of the rich that were written off through imperial edicts of indulgence. The less fortunate had been given no opportunity, in the first place, to amass arrears: "The rich divide up among themselves alone the relief given to all."[105]

The more closely one studies the actions of an emperor—those of the emperor Julian the Apostate are a case in point—the clearer it becomes that no emperor wished to frame a revolutionary fiscal policy.[106] The tax system of the empire was too firmly set in place to admit any but the most

102. H. I. Bell et al., eds., *The Abinnaeus Archive* (Oxford: Clarendon Press, 1962), no. 58, pp. 118–20, Arsinoe, A.D. 348; A. Chastagnol, *L'album municipal de Timgad,* Antiquitas 3.22 (Bonn: R. Habelt, 1978), 28.

103. *Codex Theodosianus* 12.1.126.

104. G. E. M. de Sainte Croix, *The Class Struggle in the Ancient Greek World* (London: Duckworth, 1981), 465–76; Claude Lepelley, *"Quot curiales, tot tyranni:* L'image de décurion oppresseur au Bas-Empire," in *Crise et redressment dans les provinces europeénnes de l'Empire,* ed. E. Frézouls (Strasbourg: A.E.C.R., 1983), 144–56.

105. Salvian, *De gubernatione Dei* 5.35.

106. Edgar Pack, *Städte und Steuern in der Politik Julians: Untersuchungen zu den Quellen eines Kaiserbildes,* Collection Latomus 194 (Brussels: Latomus, 1986).

superficial adjustment of its structures. What Julian and his advisers had before them, rather, was a list of the fiscal debts of individual cities. By remitting some of these, with "adroitness and sophistry,"[107] in the opening year of his reign, through a series of well-publicized *beneficia* (acts of imperial favor), Julian spoke directly, not to the general tax structure of the empire, but to the interests of the well-to-do representatives of those cities and regions in the Balkans and the East that had recently fallen unexpectedly under his authority.[108] In the same way, almost a century later the emperor Theodosius II was able to bring the upper-class residents and clergy of Constantinople to heel, by reminding them that he might look into the tax arrears of anyone who opposed the theological views of his favorite, the monk Eutyches.[109]

The process of taxation highlighted, every year, one of the principal points at which the imperial system — seemingly so implacable in its workings — could be expected to "give." It underlined the permanent importance of the group with which the imperial government had to collaborate if it was to succeed in its main objective, the collection of its taxes. The lesson was plain. To be effective in his post, a provincial governor had to know with which notables he should ally himself.

For this reason, it is frequently misleading to read the speeches of Libanius and the letters of Synesius of Cyrene as if governor and provincials invariably faced each other in "an endless war, with the provincials inevitably the losers."[110] Whenever we can recapture it, the reality is more complex. In normal conditions, the representative of the central government was one participant among many in a shifting local situation. Neither he nor any group could be certain of outright victory. A governor worked most effectively through alliances with local factions. When Andronicus, a local figure, returned to Cyrenaica as governor in 411, he promptly allied himself with Julius, the head of a faction opposed to Synesius. Julius had first thwarted Synesius a decade previously. Although obliged to Synesius for protection against a charge of treason, Julius had clashed with him again in 407, in the fully public forum of a general gathering of provincial notables. Now Julius found himself powerful, due to the support of Andronicus, at the moment when Synesius became bishop in Ptolemais. It

107. G. W. Bowersock, *Julian the Apostate* (Cambridge, Mass.: Harvard University Press, 1977), 76.

108. Pack, *Städte und Steuern*, 113; see also Stephen Mitchell, "Maximinus and the Christians: A New Latin Inscription," *Journal of Roman Studies* 78 (1988): 122.

109. Nestorius, *Bazaar of Heraclides* 2.2 [467] in *Le Livre d'Héraclide de Damas,* trans. F. Nau, (Paris: Letouzey and Ane, 1910), 299.

110. Roger A. Pack, "Studies in Libanius and Antiochene Society under Theodosius" (Ph.D. diss., University of Michigan, 1935), 30.

was an irritating prospect for Synesius. He had only one consolation: Julius had already become as overbearing to his new ally, the governor, as he had been to everyone else. Perhaps the alliance might not last.[111]

For no governor could be certain that any one alliance would endure. There were so many groups whom he might offend. Lucianus, governor of Syria, ended miserably after he had alienated influential former officials resident in Antioch, by attempting to sit higher than they did on the judge's bench, in the manner described. Another governor, though the son of a powerful Roman aristocrat, had to leave his post in a hurry for having imposed a flogging on a member of the town council of Ephesus.[112] The fear of isolation and of subsequent vengeance were real factors in the life of a late Roman governor.

The labile situation that we have described created a strictly delimited, but constant, role for the use of a language of persuasion. Far from being rendered unnecessary by the autocratic structure of late Roman government, rhetoric positively throve in its many interstices. For rhetoric transposed the creaking of an unwieldy political organism into elevating, classical music. It presented educated contemporaries with the potent image of a political world held together, not by force, collusion, and favoritism, but by *logoi,* by the sure-working, ancient magic of Greek words. Emperors and governors gave way, not because they were frequently unsure of themselves, ill-informed, or easily corrupted; rather, they had been moved by the sheer grace and wisdom of carefully composed speeches. Governors did not seek allies or respect vested interests out of fear of isolation or from an instinctive sense that the late Roman tax system worked best through collusion with the rich. They did so because their own high culture enabled them to see, in the local notables, men of *paideia,* their "natural" friends and soul mates.

Above all, rhetoric enabled successful factions to celebrate their victories. Libanius of Antioch and Synesius of Cyrene produced justifiably famous denunciations of a whole range of contemporary abuses. It is highly unlikely that these brilliant performances ever played a significant role in bringing about the changes that their authors advocated. That would be to expect too much of the late Roman political scene. And this was not because late Roman rhetors were any more servile than their predecessors had been in previous centuries. It is rather because their speeches now served the in-

---

111.   Synesius, *Epp.* 95, 79, in *Synesii Cyrenensis Epistulae,* ed. A. Garzya (Rome: Istituto Poligrafico, 1979), 157–63, 140; A. Fitzgerald, trans., *The Letters of Synesius* (Oxford: Oxford University Press, 1927), 180–84, 170. See Roques, *Synésios de Cyrène,* 178–79.
112.   Libanius, *Oratio* 28.5, 42.15–16 (III.49, 314–15).

terests of a political system where change happened, if at all, not through
the effect of persuasive oratory, but through the manipulation of factions
and the creation of networks of patronage. The successful rhetor was the
one who lent momentum, through the dazzle of his words, to the slow
working of those factors. He was most effective when wise after the event.
To take a small example: on the advice of friends who knew the state of
factions in the palace at Constantinople, Libanius of Antioch kept back
a speech that he had composed against a certain law. Only when "Fortune
herself" had decided the issue "on my behalf" and the law was rescinded
did the old rhetor commit himself to a full public reading of his invec-
tive.[113] Libanius was no coward. A man in his sixties by that time, he
knew that in late Roman conditions political objectives were best served
by careful attention to the state of parties at court and by the memorable
celebration, in educated circles, of only those victories whose success was
already certain. There was no point in alienating powerful persons through
a mistimed display of free speech.

Major speeches against political abuses and unpopular governors were, of
course, rare events. The day-to-day politics of the provinces, rather, took
place in a fine dust of ancient phrases that settled heavily, in the form of
eulogy, petitions, and advice, on the main protagonists — the governors.
Faced by what was often an insecure situation, where their continued popu-
larity with influential groups of local notables was essential for their survival, late Roman governors had every reason to wish their actions to be perceived against a golden haze of old-world values. Appeals to the ideal of a
harmonious, because persuasive, style of rule were frequent. Persuasion, indeed, remained part of the living language of late Roman politics. For the
devotio of the well-to-do had to be wooed by gestures of respect if the com-
pliance of the remainder of the population (or of the less fortunate members
of the notable class itself) was to be extorted, if need be by force.

For this reason, the good governor was careful to show honor to the
local elite. Libanius of Antioch described how the *consularis* of Syria would
make a point of dismounting from his coach on approaching the town
hall of Antioch, in order to advance on foot to greet the town council,
drawn up on the steps to receive him: even those with gout had done so.[114]
Libanius himself expected to receive personal honors: the governor would
send a special herald to summon him to the palace, and when the aging
sophist fell ill, the governor was expected, indeed anxious, to pay him a
bedside visit. Not to agree to receive such a visit was a sign, on Libanius'

113. Libanius, *Ep.* 916.2–3 (XI.63).
114. Libanius, *Oratio* 46.40 (III.398).

part, of disapproval of the governor.[115] Likewise, it was shocking when a governor gave a kiss to only one member of the council at his reception for New Year's Day.[116]

Acts of courtesy, indeed, were a means of government. When backed by the chilling alternative—the threat of public acts of dishonor—they were expected to win conformity. When Bishop Phileas of Thmuis, a civic notable from Alexandria, refused to sacrifice, in the reign of Diocletian, the governor professed to be nonplussed. He had gone out of his way to respect the "honor" of Phileas: "Remember that I have honored you. I could have dishonored you in your own city. . . . I have done a favor (*befinecium*) for your brother; do me this favor. . . . Now, if you were a peasant. . . ."[117]

It was a lesson that any governor had to learn. Almost sixty years after the Great Persecution of Diocletian, Libanius wrote to the *consularis* of Syria, Alexander of Heliopolis, about how to deal with Eusebius, a recalcitrant Christian town councillor of Apamea. An appointee of Julian the Apostate's and a staunch polytheist, Alexander had a reputation for bad temper and high-handedness.[118] He must learn how to control himself: "Consider this—whether it is better to show gentleness and get your job done, or to show yourself a hard man and to make things hard for yourself."[119]

Libanius' advice to Alexander and his frequent interventions on behalf of well-to-do Christians at the time of Julian the Apostate—despite his own polytheistic beliefs—have long endeared him to modern scholars: "Such letters are an oasis of humane tolerance."[120] But we should not forget that they sprang from a solid bedrock of political wisdom. It was difficult enough for a governor to strike the right balance between the selective wooing of influential notables and the occasional display of force against others, without this delicate equilibrium being upset by the righteous anger of a true believer. In this, Libanius was a realist rather than a liberal. He had a clear estimate of the many incentives a well-placed local figure had to remain loyal. Alexander should not feel unduly alarmed by Eusebius' pro-

115. Libanius, *Oratio* 54, 30–36 (IV.84–86). See Libanius, *Oratio* 2.9 (I.241–42), in Norman, *Libanius 2,* 14, where Libanius refuses such visits.

116. Libanius, *Oratio* 27.12 (III.28–29).

117. *Acts of Phileas,* Latin 5, Greek 11, in Musurillo, *Acts of the Christian Martyrs,* 348, 340, 342. In a vividly imagined martyrdom, the hero is offered imperial donations, *legata,* for his hometown and the promise to succeed to the governorship; H. Halkin, "Deux Passions inédites des saints Eutrope, Climaque et Basilisque," *Analecta Bollandiana* 104 (1986): 20.

118. Ammianus Marcellinus, *Res gestae* 23.2.3.

119. Libanius, *Ep.* 1351.3 (IX.400).

120. A. F. Norman, "Libanius: The Teachers in an Age of Violence," in *Libanios,* ed. G. Fatouros and T. Krischer, Wege der Forschung 621 (Darmstadt: Wissenschaftliche Buchgesellschaft, 1983), 362.

fession of Christianity. Eusebius was a man that he did not need to browbeat: "He is not the sort of man to be unaware of the prevailing climate of the regime, and is guided by calculation rather than by daring."[121]

The effective governor, therefore, was the one who maintained the reputation of being open to persuasion, because capable of persuading. The ultimate test of a governor's courtesy and of his skill in manipulating local alliances was the smooth functioning of the tax system over which he presided. Each group in every locality treasured the memory of its "good" governors. Synesius of Cyrene wrote of Gennadius the Syrian: "Administering his office with moderation and persuasiveness, he has without anyone realising it brought more money to the public treasury than those of his predecessors, who were most cruel and notorious for harshness. . . . One might justly term this a pious contribution, which neither violence nor the lash compelled."[122] In the opinion of his supporters, at least, Gennadius had known how to distill from a distant province the precious elixir of *devotio.*

It was in these concrete, largely unheroic circumstances that the articulate members of the local elites of the later empire, whose ample writings have come down to us, learned the exact scope and limits of persuasion in their dealings with the representatives of the emperor's power. *Devotio* was elicited by persuasion and, in turn, created a continued expectation on the part of privileged groups of notables that they could persuade those who wielded power. In the words of an edict of Valentinian I, carved on stone in a southern Italian city, "concord" and "gracious favor" were supposed to reign in the relations between the governor and the leading figures of each region.[123] This expectation, in itself, was nothing unusual. Nor did it represent an old-world idyll, at odds with reality. Despite the more drastic assertion of state power that characterized the fourth century, a system of government based upon collusion with the upper classes had continued to idle under a centuries-old momentum. Nor was such "concord" invariably artificial. In the words of Edward Thompson: "Once a social system has become 'set,' it does not need to be endorsed daily by exhibitions of power. . . . What matters more is a continuing theatrical style."[124]

In order to understand the discreet persuasive power still associated with the "theatrical style" favored by the elites of the fourth century, we must

121. Libanius, *Ep.* 1411.2 (XI.452).

122. Synesius, *Ep.* 73, ed. Garzya, pp. 132–33, trans. Fitzgerald, p. 165.

123. A. Giardina and F. Grelle, "La Tavola di Trinitapoli: Una nuova costituzione di Valentiniano I," *Mélanges de l'école française de Rome: Antiquité* 95 (1983): 260.

124. E. P. Thompson "Patrician Society, Plebeian Culture," *Journal of Social History* 7 (1974): 389.

turn, in the next chapter, to the system of grooming, to the *paideia,* that had remained a distinguishing feature of the Greek and Latin worlds. We must consider what options in public behavior and, hence, what ideals for a style of rule and what strategies of persuasion were first internalized and in later life propounded by those sons of good families who could boast of having received the benefits of a traditional education, "as if by the gift of heaven to the fortunate few."[125] For it is only by comparing the widely accepted codes of political behavior, linked to the *paideia* of the civic notables, with the emergent Christian culture of the bishops and the monks that we can measure the extent and the significance of the change in "theatrical style" that came about in the last decades of the fourth century. In that crucial generation, Christian spokesmen, representing the needs of Christian congregations in the cities, began to intervene in the politics of the empire. As we shall see, however, they frequently did so by taking on roles, in their confrontation with those in power, that had originally been elaborated by men of *paideia.*

125.   Ammianus Marcellinus, *Res gestae* 29.2.18.

CHAPTER TWO

Paideia and Power

Paideia

At some time around 258–259, Lollianus, a grammarian of Oxyrhynchus in Egypt, petitioned the emperors Gallienus and Valerian for back payments of his salary: "Your heavenly magnanimity and your fellowship with the Muses (for *Paideia* sits beside you on the throne) have given me confidence to offer a just and lawful petition."[1] Lollianus was a little man, hoping to cling to the great through the delicate osmosis of a shared culture: he had already written twice to his friend at court, to no effect.[2] Yet the wording of the petition was a sign of the future. The more effectively the imperial government brought its power to bear in the eastern provinces, from the reign of Constantine onwards, the greater the emphasis which came to be placed, in inscriptions set up for imperial governors, on their ability to combine justice with devotion to the Muses. These inscriptions took the form of poems, elegantly carved on stone.[3] They were not addressed to a wide public. Written in idiosyncratic characters in an esoteric Greek, whose composition required a mastery of ancient forms,[4]

1. Peter J. Parsons, "The Grammarian's Complaint," in *Collectanea Papyrologica: Texts Published in Honor of H. C. Youtie,* ed. A. E. Hanson (Bonn: R. Habelt, 1976), 2:420.
2. R. A. Kaster, *Guardians of Language: The Grammarian and Society in Late Antiquity* (Berkeley: University of California Press, 1988), 304–5.
3. L. Robert, "Epigrammes du Bas-Empire," *Hellenica* 4 (1948): 35–114.
4. Charlotte Roueché, *Aphrodisias in Late Antiquity,* Journal of Roman Studies Monographs 5 (London: Society for the Promotion of Roman Studies, 1989), xxii–xxiii, 68–70.

the inscriptions signaled to a small circle of *cognoscenti* the harmonious alliance between the governor and the local elite. They were the comment of a highly educated group of notables on the forbidding image of a late Roman administrator that would have stood, in the form of a life-size statue, above the elegant writing.[5] In the late fourth century, Oikoumenios, governor of Caria, received one such statue. A professional servant of the reformed empire, Oikoumenios had learned Latin and, doubtless, Roman law; but in the opinion of the "friendly council," who inscribed his praises on the statue base, he had "blended the Italian Muse with the sweet-voiced honey of [an] Attic" Greek. Oikoumenios would be remembered in Aphrodisias as a governor who wielded power "pure in mind and hand."[6] In the Latin West, also, a governor could be praised for having been "a guardian of legal science and the laws, a fostering father of all humane studies, a friend alike of culture and of justice."[7]

These inscriptions are no more than the tip of an iceberg. They proclaimed the existence of a common culture that was held to be the distinguishing mark of the diffused governing class of the empire, shared alike by the notables of each region and by the personnel of the imperial government.

Within this common culture, we inevitably know most about those who followed the Muses as a vocation: the professional poets who were the "Wandering Scholars" of the eastern empire;[8] the "sophists" of Athens and the province of Asia, vividly portrayed by Eunapius of Sardis (345/6–414 +);[9] and, especially, the rhetor Libanius of Antioch, whose 64 surviving speeches, innumerable model declamations on classical themes, and 1,544 letters inevitably dominate our picture of fourth-century Greek culture.[10]

5. J. Inan and E. Rosenbaum, *Roman and Early Byzantine Sculpture in Asia Minor* (London: British Academy, 1966), 181, plate clxxviii, 3; Roueché, *Aphrodisias in Late Antiquity,* 102–4.

6. I. Ševčenko, "A Late Antique Epigram," in *Synthronon: Recueil d'études par André Grabar et un groupe de ses élèves* (Paris: Klincksieck, 1968), 30; Roueché, *Aphrodisias in Late Antiquity,* 54–55.

7. *Corpus Inscriptionum Latinarum* 6.1722; see Kaster, *Guardians of Language,* 18, n. 19; V. Neri, "L'elogio della cultura e l'elogio delle virtù politiche nell'epigrafia latina del iv secolo d.C.," *Epigraphica* 43 (1981): 175–201.

8. Alan Cameron, "Wandering Poets: A Literary Movement in Byzantine Egypt," *Historia* 14 (1965): 470–509; idem, "The Empress and the Poet," *Yale Classical Studies* 27 (1982): 217–89.

9. Robert J. Penella, *Greek Philosophers and Sophists in the Fourth Century A.D.: Studies in Eunapius of Sardis,* ARCA 28 (Leeds: Francis Cairns, 1990).

10. A. J. Festugière, *Antioche païenne et chrétienne,* Bibliothèque des écoles françaises d'Athènes et de Rome 194 (Paris: E. de Boccard, 1959); Bernard Schouler, *La tradition hellénique chez Libanius* (Paris: Belles Lettres, 1984).

But there is no doubt that, throughout the Greek East, the leaders of society as a whole stood out as the possessors of a high degree of literary culture. They maintained the services of professional teachers—first of grammarians and then, for older boys, of rhetors—so that their sons might acquire a high degree of competence in classical Greek[11] at a time when general literacy, never widespread, may well have begun to shrink.[12]

It goes without saying that this culture was not widespread. In each locality, it tended to be the possession of a few leading families. It was possible to be a town councillor, a *curialis,* in a major city and yet to be illiterate.[13] Nor was it spread equally over all areas of the empire. The culture of late antiquity was based on "an archipelago of cities."[14] In this archipelago, the islands still clustered significantly in the areas of densest urban life and of longest exposure to Greek civilization—that is, around the Aegean and along the eastern seaboard of the Mediterranean. Hence the sons of the gentry of less-privileged provinces (such as Armenia, Arabia, and Cappadocia) engaged in vigorous "island-hopping," making their way to major centers—Athens, Antioch, Gaza, and Alexandria—in order to complete their education.

But there is no doubt that, in every major province with which the imperial administration had to deal, its representatives met a group of persons who claimed, on the basis of their high culture, to be the natural leaders of society. If aristocracy can be defined as "a distinctive kind of power exercised by a distinctive kind of people,"[15] then those local notables, whose *paideia* was held to be the cultural concomitant of their innate good birth and fortunate circumstances, could convincingly claim to be the aristocracy of the eastern empire. They considered themselves to be persons "initiated" into *paideia,* with all that the phrase still conveyed to ancient men of sharing with a select company the ineradicable imprint of a privileged, and hard-won, experience.[16] Even largely non-Greek provinces maintained such elites. When we study regions of the Roman empire, such as Egypt and Syria, where literatures other than Greek emerged in late antiquity, we are impressed by the tenacity of the groups of notables who

11.   Kaster, *Guardians of Language,* 3–6, 20–51.
12.   William V. Harris, *Ancient Literacy* (Cambridge, Mass.: Harvard University Press, 1990), 285–322. See also K. Hopkins, *Conquest by Book, Literacy in the Roman World,* ed. J. H. Humphrey, Journal of Roman Archaeology, Supplementary Series 3 (Ann Arbor: University of Michigan Press, 1991), 133–58.
13.   Kaster, *Guardians of Language,* 39.
14.   Ibid., 21.
15.   Mark Motley, *Becoming a French Aristocrat: The Education of the Court Nobility, 1580–1715* (Princeton: Princeton University Press, 1990), 6, citing Jonathan Powis, *Aristocracy* (Oxford: Blackwell, 1984), 2.
16.   Libanius, *Ep.* 285.2 (X.270); Kaster, *Guardians of Language,* 16, n. 7.

retained Greek forms of *paideia* and by the vigor of the professionals who emerged from their ranks or were supported by their patronage.[17]

The more the Roman government invaded local society, the more effectively it was colonized by representatives of Greek culture. The few cases of successful careers by lowborn, uneducated persons in the higher reaches of the bureaucracy, recorded with disgust by Libanius,[18] should not blind us to the cumulative success of educated civic notables in obtaining governorships and higher offices in the course of the fourth century.[19] The *paideia* which sons of notables had absorbed as late adolescents in the schools of the rhetors was held to be permanently relevant to their subsequent careers. Only a young man who had "installed Demosthenes in his soul" at an early age could be trusted to behave correctly when governing a province: "He will think that his duty is to make the cities happy; he will rejoice when the executioner's sword lies idle; he will make the citadels beautiful with buildings; and he will remain throughout a servant of the Muses."[20]

The ideal of the cultivated governor, the carefully groomed product of a Greek *paideia,* was a commonplace of the political life of the eastern empire. Being a commonplace, the phenomenon does not lend itself to precise analysis. Apart from a few, well-studied cases of men of letters who came to exercise power in the Greek and Latin parts of the empire,[21] it is difficult to measure the exact relationship between the widespread expectations that governors should be cultivated persons and the political practice of the age. Even in better-documented periods (as in Renaissance Europe), the relation between a formal education and the social and political activities which this education claimed to support remains elusive.[22] The evidence from late antiquity is inevitably one-sided. It reflects the views of those with a vested interest in *paideia,* that is, of teachers of rhetoric,

17.   L. S. B. MacCoull, *Dioscorus of Aphrodito: His Work and His World* (Berkeley: University of California Press, 1988): G. W. Bowersock, *Hellenism in Late Antiquity* (Ann Arbor: University of Michigan Press, 1990), 29–33, 61–68.

18.   Libanius, *Oratio* 42.23–24 (III.318–19).

19.   Paul Petit, *Les étudiants de Libanius* (Paris: Nouvelles éditions latines, 1956), 166–88; John Matthews, *Western Aristocracies and Imperial Court: A.D. 364–425* (Oxford: Clarendon Press, 1975), 102–6; Kaster, *Guardians of Language,* 124, n. 133; J. H. W. G. Liebeschuetz, *Barbarians and Bishops: Army, Church and State in the Age of Arcadius and Chrysostom* (Oxford: Clarendon Press, 1990), 135–40.

20.   Libanius, *Ep.* 1261.2, 4 (XI.339).

21.   Notably, Keith Hopkins, "Social Mobility in the Later Roman Empire: The Evidence of Ausonius," *Classical Quarterly* 11 (1961): 239–49; Petit, *Etudiants de Libanius,* 165–86; F. S. Pedersen, "On Professional Qualifications for Public Posts in Late Antiquity," *Classica et Medievalia* 31 (1975): 161–213; D. Nellen, *Viri litterati: Gebildetes Beamtentum und spätrömisches Reich im Westen* (Bochum: Studienverlag Brockmeyer, 1981).

22.   A. Grafton and L. Jardine, *From Humanism to the Humanities* (Cambridge, Mass.: Harvard University Press, 1986), 7.

such as Libanius. The actual level of culture in the majority of pupils and the role of this culture in their lives are less well known to us. All that we can do is point to some of the factors which help to account for the prominence of *paideia* in the political expectations of the later empire.

The social background of this system of education has long been obvious: "In a very important sense, the function of this culture was precisely to define an elite over against the ordinary run of mankind."[23] Only the sons of notables had the wealth and leisure to travel long distances from all over the Greek East to linger in the classrooms of a teacher such as Libanius, at Antioch, or Prohaeresius, at Athens.[24] They emerged from an expensive and intellectually taxing experience with no mean opinion of themselves: they were convinced that "the square-set soundness of [their] speech and its polished brilliance produced by skill" made them as superior to the uneducated as human beings were superior to mere cattle.[25]

Paideia was a means of expressing social distance. Its skills were difficult to acquire and, once acquired, could only be displayed within rigid, traditional conventions. Education, therefore, controlled "unstructured" social mobility.[26] At the same time, it offered an acceptable avenue of promotion to a few men of talent from less-privileged backgrounds. Sons of petty notables, such as Augustine, at Thagaste, were enabled, through great effort and the patronage of wealthy friends, to enjoy successful careers as teachers, rhetors, and poets. These careers might even be crowned by posts in the bureaucracy and by a provincial governorship.

The few examples of social mobility through education have appealed to modern commentators on the later empire. What probably mattered more at the time, however, was that *paideia* united potentially conflicting segments of the governing class. It joined imperial administrators and provincial notables in a shared sense of common excellence. A late Roman education produced remarkable cultural homogeneity. A few great authors (Virgil and Cicero in the West, Homer and Demosthenes in the East) were "burned into the memory" at an early age in the schools of the grammarians.[27] Ever since the early empire, a common culture had provided a language that enabled members of the educated classes from as far apart as Arles and Arabia to meet as equal devotees of Greek rhetoric. The very standardization of this rhetoric, which is so tedious to a modern reader,

23.   John Matthews, *The Roman Empire of Ammianus* (London: Duckworth, 1989), 78.
24.   Petit, *Etudiants de Libanius*, 112–35; Kaster, *Guardians of Language,* 26–27; Penella, *Greek Philosophers and Sophists,* 2–5.
25.   Kaster, *Guardians of Language,* 17, citing Diomedes, *Ars grammatica,* preface to *Grammatici latini,* ed. G. Keil (Leipzig: Teubner, 1857), 1:299.
26.   Kaster, *Guardians of Language,* 23–30.
27.   Orosius, *Historiae adversus paganos* 1.18.1; Kaster, *Guardians of Language,* 44–50.

explains its attraction in the first and second centuries A.D. Formalized, elevated, reassuringly predictable, and invariably fulsome, rhetoric provided a permanent background music to the consensus in favor of Roman rule skillfully fostered among the civic notables of the Greek world.[28]

After the drastic changes of the third century, the schools provided "reassurance that nothing basic had shifted" in the relation between the cities and the central government.[29] Even if they represented a far more intrusive imperial system than before, governors could still expect to meet, in the local elite, men who enjoyed the same *paideia* as themselves. They could carry this mark of status with them to distant cities, as they could not carry the more tangible and localized evidences of their standing in their own hometowns — the buildings they had lavished on their cities, the quality of their private mansions. Through a shared *paideia,* they could set up a system of instant communication with men who were, often, total strangers to them. They signaled, above all, that they were approachable and that they knew the rules of the game. As a "fellow servant of the Muses," no administrator could mistake a compliment or ignore a challenge posed to him as a classical reminiscence. Confronting the legal advisers of a newly arrived governor (who may have grown up in Rome), Libanius posed the crucial question: "How did Odysseus rule when king of Ithaca?" "Gently as a father" was the instant reply. The classical phrase set the tone for the relations between governor and town council in the months that followed.[30]

On the local level, education provided the one common tradition that could be shared by all notables, splintered though they had come to be by increasing factionalism and by diverging criteria of status.[31] The rhetorical culture provided by a teacher such as Libanius amounted to nothing less than the patient re-creation, in every generation, of the "collective memory" of the urban upper class. Through it, they relived, in a highly condensed, almost proverbial form, the religious, social, and political history of the Greek city.[32]

Nor should we underestimate the ability of this culture to maintain a

28.   Fergus Millar, "P. Herennius Dexippus: The Greek World and the Third-Century Invasions," *Journal of Roman Studies* 59 (1969): 13; Averil Cameron, *Christianity and the Rhetoric of Empire: The Development of Christian Discourse* (Berkeley: University of California Press, 1991), 76–79.

29.   Kaster, *Guardians of Language,* 29.

30.   Libanius, *Oratio* 46.3 (III.380), referring to Homer, *Odyssey* 2.233.

31.   Kaster, *Guardians of Language,* 31.

32.   M. Forlin Patrucco and D. Vera, "Crisi di potere e autodifesa di classe: Aspetti del tradizionalismo delle aristocrazie," in *Società romana e impero tardoantico 1: Istituzioni, ceti, economie,* ed. A. Giardina (Bari: Laterza, 1986), 245–72, esp. 256–59, 265.

sense of local pride. Despite the changed conditions of the fourth century, the educated man could still feel that he lived in a "commonwealth of cities." The "lens" of Hellenic high culture continued to bring into sharp focus the particularity of local civic traditions. What public ceremonies had once displayed in the streets of the cities, the verses of fourth- and fifth-century poets now brought to a more restricted audience of "servants of the Muses." Myths of the gods related to specific landscapes and attached by immemorial tradition to proudly remembered hometowns; legends that traced the links which joined the native towns of provincial governors to the Greek cities that they came to rule; fulsome descriptions of cities, of their antiquities and works of art: these were matters of loving concern for men of *paideia* in late antiquity, quite as much as they had been in the second century A.D.[33]

The Magic of Words

It is relatively easy to describe the manner in which a shared *paideia* bridged the distances of a vast empire. It provided a shared imaginative landscape for those whose careers took them, increasingly, far from their native cities. Yet with the exception of Robert Kaster's remarkable examination of the social ideals implied in the respectful and orderly work of the grammarian,[34] insufficient attention has been paid to the ethical and social message conveyed by the methods of teaching practiced in a late Roman schoolroom and by the forms of speaking that were valued by educated contemporaries. It was not enough to provide the notables with a badge of social superiority. The young men assembled in the classroom of Libanius took their social position for granted. Their rowdiness in the streets of Antioch—beating up shopkeepers and tossing a teaching assistant in a blanket—showed that they had their fair share of upper-class arrogance.[35] What mattered was the far more delicate task of making this social superiority appear "natural" because rooted in the personal skills appropriate to superior persons.

Those who passed through the school of a rhetor were considered to have developed a more lively intelligence, a more refined speech, and a more harmonious and impressive bearing than anyone else. This would mark them out for the rest of their lives. In the later empire a rhetorical training that had flourished in the Greek world since the fourth century B.C. re-

---

33.   Pierre Chuvin, *A Chronicle of the Last Pagans* (Cambridge, Mass.: Harvard University Press, 1990), 117–18; Bowersock, *Hellenism in Late Antiquity,* 43–48, 61–68; Roueché, *Aphrodisias in Late Antiquity,* 38.

34.   Kaster, *Guardians of Language,* 206–7.

35.   Libanius, *Oratio* 58.4–5 (IX.183), in Festugière, *Antioche,* 468.

tained unabated importance.[36] Rhetoric remained the "Queen of Subjects" because it dealt with what still mattered in the public life of late antiquity— with the manner in which notables related, face to face through the spoken word, with their official superiors, with their peers, and with those subject to their power and protection.

This rhetorical training suffered from all the limitations that have been observed to constrict codes of highly formalized speech in modern traditional societies. Like these, late Roman rhetoric was "polite, respectful, holy, but from the point of view of the creativity potential of language, impoverished."[37] The choice of words was limited by the need to maintain an Attic purity of diction. Compared with the complexity of late Roman life, the themes on which Greek rhetoric usually touched were reduced to a mere handful of issues, backed by a highly restricted body of illustrations, tags, and historical and mythological references.[38] Yet as with modern codes of formalized speech, it was precisely its "arthritic" quality that accounted for the continued authority of rhetoric in late Roman life. It was an eminently predictable form of speech. Delivered by a person whose status and grooming entitled him to use it, rhetoric might be deployed with great skill and vivacity on a variety of occasions—from the most formal public addresses to letters and extemporaneous interventions. But it was a form of speech that left little room for surprises. Allusive, steeped in the vocabulary and examples of a distant age, the formalized speech of the upper classes was not designed to express sudden challenges and novel sentiments, and still less to indulge in unwelcome plain-speaking. This was its principal social and political advantage, for "if the utterance of a speaker predicts what sort of thing he will say, it also predicts the answer of the other person so long as this other person is also accepting the code."[39]

Hence we see the immediate political significance of the fact that, among the upper classes of the later empire, rulers and ruled alike persistently claimed to know how to speak to each other as "fellow servants of the Muses." For both sides drew on the same code to maintain their authority. If petitions and advice would be listened to if conveyed in the correct manner, so a command, if framed in the same tone, must be obeyed.

Politics and *paideia* were so strenuously linked in the fourth and fifth

36. H. I. Marrou, *A History of Education in Antiquity* (Madison: University of Wisconsin Press, 1982), 194–205.

37. M. Bloch, "Why Oratory?" in *Political Language and Oratory in Traditional Society,* ed. M. Bloch (London: Academic Press, 1975), 17.

38. Bloch, "Why Oratory?" 15; H. I. Marrou, *Saint Augustin et la fin de la culture antique,* Bibliothèque des écoles françaises d'Athènes et de Rome 145 (Paris: E. de Boccard, 1949), 125–27.

39. Bloch, "Why Oratory?" 19.

centuries because there was no guarantee that the tacit agreement which ensured the effectiveness of rhetoric would remain operative. Once there was a danger that the common code of formalized speech, and all that this stood for, might be brushed aside, the notables of the Greek world had to face a degree of vulnerability to the power of the emperor and his servants to which they had no intention of allowing themselves to become habituated. They would maintain their own way of speaking for as long as possible. In a social and political system where power came to be brought to bear in a violent and domineering manner against an ever-widening circle of persons, those who claimed to wield a "natural" authority in their cities and regions based this authority on a training that emphasized the antithesis to such abrasive qualities — restraint, self-discipline, poise, and harmonious utterance.

Bearing these general considerations in mind, let us examine briefly what exactly the notables learned at school and how they expected to apply it to their political situation. Above all, they internalized a fierce sense of verbal decorum. A teacher of rhetoric set to work with a small class of upper-class boys, personally entrusted to him by their parents and often bound to him by intense personal loyalties. He was as exacting with them as a star opera singer holding a master class: "No word alien to Attic usage escaped him, nor a train of thought that wandered for a moment from the aim of the speech; not a single syllable that jarred against due rhythm, nor the placing of any word in a phrase, that went against the harmony required by a trained ear."[40]

In this way, young men learned to "cleanse their tongues" through "associating with the rhetors of old."[41] Exercises in pleading improbable cases or devising imaginary courses of action developed more than verbal skills. These exercises demanded a precision and an ability to analyze the pros and cons of a case that were worthy of a medieval schoolman.[42] But mental acrobatics were only part of a training designed to produce, in the end, "gracefulness and smoothness of speech."[43] It was an education for public performance. Its high point took the form of a miniature anticipation of the forum and the town hall. "Dressed in a little toga, with hair smoothed back," the boys would declaim on classical themes.[44] Rhetoric was seen as a preparation for public life to such an extent that Libanius' classroom

40.   Choricius of Gaza, *Oratio* 7.8, ed. R. Förster and E. Richtsteig (Leipzig: Teubner, 1929), 112.

41.   Libanius, *Oratio* 35.17 (III.219), in Festugière, *Antioche,* 488.

42.   Schouler, *Tradition hellénique,* 1004.

43.   Ps.-Clement, *Recognitiones* 1.25.1.

44.   Jerome, *Contra Rufinum* 1.30; Augustine, *Confessions* 1.17.27; Libanius, *Declamatio* 8.7 (VII.85) in Festugière, *Antioche,* 444; cf. Dale Eickelman, *Knowledge and Power in Mo-*

was separated by only a narrow corridor from the town hall of Antioch. In moments of crisis, the shouts of distressed notables formed a background to his lectures.[45]

We should never forget that Libanius taught a skill which, ever since the days of Gorgias in Athens, carried with it something of the ancient thrill of sorcery. Words were supposed to exercise power over people. His pupils, even if they did not become star performers like himself, were expected to carry into the public world an uncanny ability to "charm," even to "overawe," through speech.[46] A man of *paideia* was a man who knew how to command respect, not by violence (as those who wielded official power might do), but through the potent "spell" of his personal eloquence.[47] He had "come to possess a magical device stronger than the resources of any mere administrator."[48] Ancient words came from his mouth, "beautiful, flowing and with lightning speed."[49] It was these that enabled him "to oppose to the loud voice of official power the authority of persuasive counsel, to gain, through skill in rhetoric, the ability to instill alarm, rather than to cringe in fear."[50]

Not surprisingly, the stories that late Roman enthusiasts for education treasured most were those that showed masters of the art of rhetoric exercising their spell on the most refractory of all possible subjects — a "stern and implacable" imperial governor.[51] In Athens in the late 330s, the proconsul of Achaia, a man from the Latin West, had arrested a group of students and their professors for rowdyism. At the last moment, the young Prohaeresius, a tall Armenian of striking demeanor, was allowed to come forward. "He . . . first delivered a proemium. . . . It launched out and soon slid into a pitiable account of the sufferings [of the students], and he inserted an encomium of their teacher. In this proemium he let fall only one allusion to

rocco: The Education of a Twentieth-Century Notable (Princeton: Princeton University Press, 1985), 65–66, 98–100.

45.   Libanius, *Oratio* 46.16 (III.386); Paul Petit, *Libanius et la vie municipale à Antioche au ive. siècle après J.C.* (Paris: P. Geuthner, 1955), 64; Schouler, *Tradition hellénique,* 894.

46.   Libanius, *Oratio* 48.41 (III.448), in *Libanius: Selected Works 2,* ed. and trans. A. F. Norman, Loeb Classical Library (Cambridge, Mass.: Harvard University Press, 1977), 456; see esp. J. de Romilly, *Magic and Rhetoric in Ancient Greece* (Cambridge, Mass.: Harvard University Press, 1975), 16–43, 78–85.

47.   Libanius, *Oratio* 11.141 (I.483–84), in "Libanius' Oration in Praise of Antioch," trans. G. Downey, *Proceedings of the American Philosophical Society* 103 (1959): 668.

48.   Libanius, *Oratio* 11.141 (I.483–84), in Downey, 668.

49.   Libanius, *Oratio* 35.19 (III.219), in Festugière, *Antioche,* 488.

50.   Libanius, *Oratio* 35.3 (III.211), in Festugière, *Antioche,* 484–85.

51.   Eunapius, *Lives of the Philosophers* 483, in *Philostratus and Eunapius,* ed. and trans. W. C. Wright, Loeb Classical Library (Cambridge, Mass.: Harvard University Press, 1952), 468.

a grievance [concerning the proconsul's high-handed behavior]. . . . At this the proconsul was overcome by the force of his arguments, his weighty style, his facility and sonorous eloquence." Prohaeresius ended with a rousing phrase, whose exact words were still remembered by those present forty years later. Fortunately for the cowed professors, the proconsul "was not uneducated or bred in a boorish and illiberal fashion." He knew what to do next. "Then up jumped the proconsul, and shaking his purple edged cloak (the Romans call it a *tebennos* [or toga]), that austere and inexorable judge applauded Prohaeresius like a schoolboy."[52] The vivid scene is set at a slight distance from reality. It was an anecdote from a venerable university city, where improbable things could still happen. But by representing a man of *paideia* in his most triumphantly persuasive role, it summed up the hopes of notables all over the Greek East.

What mattered, of course, was that the proconsul had played the game correctly. Faced by a relatively trivial incident, he could allow himself to succumb to the "spell" of Prohaeresius without losing face. To give way to such persuasion, indeed, heightened his authority in Athens. For *paideia* was not simply a skill in persuasive speech; it was a school of courtesy. Verbal decorum assumed, and fostered, an equally exacting sense of decorum in personal relations. It taught a man how to give way graciously, as if to a friend. Indeed, it helped him to recognize such friends. *Paideia* showed itself through *philia,* through a carefully nurtured art of friendship, that aimed to recapture, in the midst of the cares of public life, some of the light-hearted enthusiasm of an upper-class adolescence. *Charis* and *hémerotés,* graciousness and gentle courtesy, with their all-important accompaniment, a willingness to grant favors to men of similar background, were the hallmark of the educated person.[53]

The notion of friendship provided a language with which to speak, in acceptable terms, of the hard facts of patronage and alliance that enabled the emperor's representatives to exercise effective power in the provinces. Friendship, based on the mutual admiration that sprang up quite naturally between educated persons, was held to characterize the relations of the elites to those in power. For such a friendship blurred unwelcome asymmetries. It rendered the exchange of requests and favors, by which representatives of the emperor wooed and controlled the provincial notables, innocent, even, indeed, natural. No one was compromised by political transactions that took place in the name of friendship. Writing to a governor of unknown intentions from Constantinople in A.D. 371, Basil, as bishop

---

52. Eunapius, *Lives of the Philosophers* 483, ed. Wright, pp. 470–74.
53. Petit, *Libanius,* 259; Bernard Schouler, *Libanius: Discours Moraux* (Paris: Belles Lettres, 1973), 63–78.

of Caesarea, was careful to co-opt him first as a "friend." Ever since a common acquaintance had praised his "prowess with words," Basil could not but think of him in such terms: *"The wise man, e'en though he dwell in a distant land, though I may never behold him with my eyes, I account my friend,* is a saying of the tragic poet Euripides. . . . Accept, therefore, admirable sir, the appellation of 'my friend,' which is applied to you out of a friendship that is true and genuine."[54] In fact, Basil could not allow himself to think of any governor who arrived in Cappadocia other than as a natural "friend." To have treated him in any other manner would have been to admit that the governor was a superior to whom he must ingratiate himself, and "our character is far removed from adulation."[55] Petitions to governors, if framed in terms of spontaneous friendship, carried with them no admission of dependence. Requests for favors were no more than the weightless shadows that followed two friends as they conversed together in a timeless, Attic world created by their common love of the Muses.[56]

Students of the workings of patronage in Mediterranean societies would not be unduly impressed by such letters: appeals to friendship have been dismissed as "secondary accretions . . . a protective coloring imposed by the powerless to mitigate their dependence."[57] But as we have seen, the balance of power was not as heavily tilted against the men of *paideia* as is usually the case in the type of client-patron relations most often studied by Mediterranean anthropologists. Appeals to a shared love of the Muses tactfully disguised the weakness of the provincial governor's own position. It was considered appropriate for late Roman men to approach those in authority with veiled hands: any other behavior would seem grasping.[58] In the same manner, what was politely veiled in Basil's letters was the open secret of his own considerable power in Cappadocia. By speaking of friendship to a succession of administrators sent out to the distant and inhospitable province of Cappadocia, Basil treated these men as his equals and discreetly yet insistently designated himself as a member of that crucial group of local notables whom it was more prudent to woo, as natural "friends," rather than to attempt to browbeat.

Friendship could ramify, enabling local notables to bridge the great distances of the empire. We should not judge the letters written by men of *paideia* solely by their immediate effects. High officials frequently ignored

54.   Basil, *Ep.* 63, in *Saint Basil: The Letters,* ed. and trans. R. Deferrari, Loeb Classical Library (Cambridge, Mass.: Harvard University Press, 1962), 2:19.
55.   Basil, *Ep.* 63, in Deferrari, *Saint Basil* 2:20.
56.   Basil, *Ep.* 84, in Deferrari, *Saint Basil* 2:104.
57.   J. Davis, *People of the Mediterranean* (London: Routledge and Kegan Paul, 1977), 148.
58.   Ammianus Marcellinus, *Res gestae* 16.5.11.

Libanius' requests.[59] Yet his letters were more than "brief notes . . . distinguished [only] by a tireless facility in manipulating the cliches of polite intercourse."[60] What mattered was the cumulative impression of "conductivity" conveyed by this correspondence. It was impossible for the imperial government to adopt a policy of divide and rule, to treat the individual cities and provinces as isolated cells of a honeycomb, with each of which it could deal separately. The code of friendship ensured that every region was crisscrossed by a web of contacts, which reached to all neighboring cities and extended as far as the capital itself.[61]

What was exchanged on these occasions can never be limited to requests for favors. Friendship meant information and in the later empire, as in the great empires of the age of Philip II, news was "a luxury commodity . . . worth more than its weight in gold."[62] Even if a friend can do nothing else, wrote Theodoret, bishop of Cyrrhus, to a courtier in Constantinople, he can at least show his "benevolence" by passing on news of doings at court.[63] In late antique conditions, letters were merely the occasion for an exchange of news. They were as formal as visiting cards, but their arrival assumed a network of kinsmen, mutual friends, and trusted dependents who acted as their carriers. Such a network of bearers of news, constantly traveling throughout the empire, heightened the alarming "conductivity" of the educated classes. Notables could always threaten to bring their own version of the actions of a provincial governor to the knowledge of highly placed "friends" in the imperial government.[64]

59.   Libanius, *Epp.* 1317, 1463 (XI.376, 497), to Decentius, *magister officiorum* in 364; 1435, 1456 (XI.473, 491–92), to Caesarius, prefect of Constantinople, in 368.

60.   Roger A. Pack, "Studies in Libanius and Antiochene Society under Theodosius" (Ph.D. diss., University of Michigan, 1935), 36.

61.   J. F. Matthews, "The Letters of Symmachus," in *Latin Literature of the Fourth Century,* ed. J. W. Binns (London: Routledge and Kegan Paul, 1975), 80–89; J. H. W. G. Liebeschuetz, *Antioch: City and Imperial Administration in the Later Roman Empire* (Oxford: Clarendon Press, 1972), 17–19. For a later period, see M. Mullett, "Writing in Early Medieval Byzantium," in *The Uses of Literacy in Early Medieval Europe,* ed. R. McKitterick (Cambridge: Cambridge University Press, 1990), 172–85; cf. Eickelman, *Knowledge and Power,* 137, on the manner in which the French in Morocco failed to isolate the elites of individual communities by reason of the strong horizontal ties that bound together the notables of the region.

62.   Fernand Braudel, *The Mediterranean and the Mediterranean World in the Age of Philip II* (London: Collins, 1972), 1:365.

63.   Theodoret of Cyrrhus, *Ep.* 80, in *Théodoret de Cyr: Correspondance 2,* ed. Y. Azéma, Sources chrétiennes 98 (Paris: Le Cerf, 1964), 188.

64.   Synesius of Cyrene, *Ep.* 73, in *Synesii Cyrenensis Epistulae,* ed. A. Garzya, (Rome: Istituto Poligrafico, 1979), 130–31; A. Fitzgerald, trans., *The Letters of Synesius* (Oxford: Oxford University Press, 1927), 163–64.

Anger and Decorum

The emphasis placed on friendship, though it inevitably bulks large in our evidence, was only part of the story. Friendship lent an old-fashioned dignity to the manner in which successful notables manipulated the power of the new imperial system, by forming alliances with governors and by persistent lobbying through well-placed supporters. The education of a notable, however, provided the basis for dealing with a grimmer aspect of late Roman politics—with the increased impingement of official violence, directed against members of the upper class. The ideals associated with *paideia* were invoked, with great urgency, to check such violence.

We should not neglect this aspect of late Roman *paideia*. Rhetoric was never regarded simply as a literary accomplishment, nor was it deployed solely as a mode of address whose solemn tones extorted deference. Formalized speech was held to be, in itself, a form of self-control. The measured speech of a cultivated speaker of Greek or Latin was "a small spot of coherence in a sea of noise."[65] It carried with it a sense of quiet triumph over all that was slovenly, unformed, and rebellious in the human voice and so, by implication, in the human person. It was a fragile speck of order in a violent and discordant world.

Contemporaries were on the alert for those moments when the poise made manifest by formal speech gave way. Some such incidents were memorably awesome. Unhinged by grief at the sudden death of two deeply loved adopted daughters who had been struck by lightning when traveling in the Balkans, Herodes Atticus, the highly cultivated Athenian millionaire, lost control of himself. Immediately after the tragedy, he had to plead before the emperor Marcus Aurelius at Sirmium, in A.D. 173 or 174, against a serious charge of overreaching his authority in Athens: "Driven frantic by this misfortune . . . he was not in his right mind but longed for death. For when he came forward to speak he launched into invectives against the emperor . . . with an aggressive and unguarded tongue." It was manifestly suicidal behavior. An imperial tribunal, sitting in judgment on a serious case, could not afford an explosion of plain-speaking that was all the more pathological for having come from a man accustomed to rising to the height of his talents on ceremonial occasions. Only the "philosophical" serenity of Marcus Aurelius saved the day: throughout the incident, the emperor "never frowned or changed his expression." Philostratus tells us this story with little sympathy. A star rhetor, Herodes Atticus should have known better than to abandon the one sure resource of a cultivated man under strain: "He did not even deploy elaborate circumlocution in

65. Kaster, *Guardians of Language,* 18.

his speech; one would have thought that a man drilled in this style of speaking would have kept his temper under control."[66]

In this respect, the education offered by a man such as Libanius represented a triumph of "paedagogic reason." In the apposite words of Pierre Bourdieu, we are dealing with a system which "extorts the essential while seeming to demand the insignificant."[67] By the meticulous self-vigilance and the striving for harmony associated with the magic of a well-tuned voice, the potentially brutish sons of the gentry were subjected to a discreet but insistent training in order and self-restraint.[68] Direct physical violence was to be as unbecoming to them as incoherent speech.[69] They learned a careful mastery of balanced phrases. Their rhetorical exercises reenacted scenes of dignified interchange and fostered the controlled expression of emotions.[70] A virtuoso rhetorical performance, "in an elevated chanting tone, with carefully planned gestures," was expected to work on the sensibility much as great music was held to do in the Victorian age.[71] The quality of the voice itself fascinated late antique persons. A recent study by Aline Rousselle has shown how much attention was devoted to the medical problems of voice production by Quintilian and his successors.[72] Behind the medical advice, we can glimpse a clear image of the public man. The careful control of breathing and the avoidance of inappropriate stances and discordant gestures were designed to transform an educated person into a tranquil figure whose voice and poise radiated harmonious authority. Ever since the second century, *eutaxia, euschémosuné, semnotés*— terms that conjured up the ideal of a self-controlled, even awesome, bearing—were those most current on grave inscriptions and in laudatory accounts of leading citizens.[73]

Loss of control of the voice was instantly noted. A newly edited letter shows a small-town African lawyer berating his colleague: it was not for a man of culture, he wrote, to give way in a lawsuit to the *fremitus inertis,*

66. Philostratus, *Lives of the Sophists* 561, in Wright, *Philostratus and Eunapius,* 170–72; for the last passage, I have used the translation in Graham Anderson, *Philostratus* (London: Croom Helm, 1986), 2.

67. Pierre Bourdieu, *Outline of a Theory of Practice* (Cambridge: Cambridge University Press, 1977), 94.

68. Festugière, *Antioche,* 217–25, remains the best characterization.

69. Libanius, *Oratio* 58.5 (IV.183), in Festugière, *Antioche,* 468.

70. George A. Kennedy, *Greek Rhetoric under Christian Emperors* (Princeton: Princeton University Press, 1983), 66–73.

71. Ibid., 147.

72. Aline Rousselle, "Parole et inspiration: Le travail de la voix dans le monde romain," *History and Philosophy of the Life Sciences* 5 (1983): 129–57.

73. Peter Brown, *The Body and Society: Men, Women and Sexual Renunciation in Early Christianity* (New York: Columbia University Press, 1988), 11–12.

to the menacing roar of the ignoramus.[74] It was equally unbecoming for a governor's official to shout at Synesius of Cyrene "with untrained mind and voice" when the cultivated bishop attempted to intervene to stop a flogging.[75]

Rather than give way to incoherent rage, public figures were expected to compose themselves as carefully as they composed their speeches. Advising a potentially violent military man to keep a low profile in the city, the Christian priest Isidore of Pelusium drew on his classical *savoir faire:* "*Rhythmize sauton:* Bring harmony to yourself. Tune yourself to adopt the stance appropriate to a well-meaning man. Let no look of your eyes, no flicker of your brows, no cadence of your voice, or tread of your walk allow a single trace of the disease of haughtiness to appear."[76] In late antique culture, *logoi,* dignified words carefully composed and delivered, were expected to work their way into the heart like bars of ancient, reverential music, an intimate Orpheus lulling the beasts whose disruptive power lay so close to the surface of late Roman life.[77] "With measured words," wrote Gregory Nazianzen, "I learn to bridle rage."[78]

So much alert attention to deportment betrays a fact almost too big to be seen. We are in a world characterized by a chilling absence of legal restraints on violence in the exercise of power. This was not a situation that had begun only with the later empire. For centuries philosophers and teachers had grappled with the intensely personal nature of power in ancient society. Ethical writers of the early empire were obsessed by scenarios of acute dependence. From wives and slaves in the household to the abject courtiers of tyrannical rulers, the lives of so many persons in so many situations appeared to depend on the whim of their superiors. A lurking fear of arbitrary violence, untrammeled by legal and political constraints, insensibly shifted the weight of philosophical discussion towards ethical issues, involving self-formation and control of the passions. The emphasis on the "care of the self" that flourished in the first two centuries A.D. was in many ways the reaction of thinking persons to their own bleak percep-

74. Sulpicius Severus, *Opera, Appendix, Ep.* 6.1, *Corpus Scriptorum Ecclesiasticorum Latinorum* (Vienna: C. Gerold, 1866), 254; see Claude Lepelley, "Trois documents méconnus sur l'histoire sociale et religieuse de l'Afrique romaine tardive, retrouvés parmi les *spuria* de Sulpice Sévère," *Antiquités africaines* 25 (1989): 240–41.

75. Synesius, *Ep.* 58, ed. Garzya, *Ep.* 42, p. 74, trans. Fitzgerald, p. 142.

76. Isidore of Pelusium, *Ep.* 2.292: *Patrologia Graeca* 78:721C.

77. Marrou, *History of Education*, 194–205; Sister Charles Murray, *Rebirth and Afterlife: A Study of the Transmutation of Some Pagan Imagery in Early Christian Funerary Art*, B.A.R. International series (Oxford: B.A.R., 1982), 56–60.

78. Gregory Nazianzen, *Oratio* 6.6: *Patrologia Graeca* 35:728.

tion of Roman society, as one in which heightened self-control was the only, frail guarantee of humanity to others.[79]

Despite the rise of intensely metaphysical and otherworldly systems of thought associated with the Neoplatonic school, whose writings bulk so large in our surviving evidence, this recurrent ethical concern, with its insistence on self-mastery and its extreme scrupulosity on issues of deportment, continued unchanged in late antiquity. It formed the solid groundwork of all philosophical systems and was responsible for the continued production of manuals for nonphilosophical readers, manuals written, that is, by professional philosophers for men of *paideia* preoccupied with problems of correct behavior.[80] When late Roman persons spoke of "philosophy" or turned for advice to philosophers, it was these issues, not the mystical ascent of a Plotinus, that they wished to be told about. It comes as no surprise, therefore, that in a fifth-century anthology the Neoplatonic philosopher Iamblichus, the austere exponent of occult methods of ascent to the One, should appear, cited between none other than Demosthenes and Cato the Elder! The extract is a fragment from an exhortation to a provincial governor. It offered the usual, ever-pertinent banalities to a man entrusted with power: "When the severity and majesty of supreme authority is blended with good nature and humane concern, this power becomes as it should be—harmonious, courteous, gentle and approachable."[81]

There was good reason why so much emphasis should be placed on harmony and self-control in the exercise of power. Violence surrounded men of the elite at every level of their lives. They grew up in households where slavery had remained a domestic school of cruelty. An institution maintained by the lash, slavery generated a distinctive pathology of power.[82] When the doctor Galen wrote on the illnesses of the soul in the second century, the passion that bulked largest in his treatment was anger, exemplified by the blind rage of the slave owner. He knew of a landowner in Crete, "in other respects an estimable person," who would fall on his ser-

79. M. Foucault, *The Care of the Self* (New York: Pantheon Books, 1986), 81–95; Aline Rousselle, "Gestes et signes de la famille dans l'Empire romain," in *Histoire de la famille,* ed. A. Burguière (Paris: A. Colin, 1986), 258–62.

80. A. M. Malingrey, *Philosophia* (Paris: Klincksieck, 1961), 101–5, 225–27, 280–83; P. Hadot, *Plotin,* 2d ed. (Paris: Etudes augustiniennes, 1972), 89–101; I. Hadot, *Le problème du néoplatonisme alexandrin: Hiéroclès et Simplicius* (Paris: Etudes augustiniennes 1978), 160–65.

81. Johannes Stobaeus, *Florilegium* 46.76, ed. T. Gaisford (Oxford: Clarendon Press, 1822), 2:279.

82. K. R. Bradley, *Slaves and Masters in the Roman Empire: A Study of Social Control,* Collection Latomus 184 (Brussels: Latomus, 1984), 118–23, 130–34; B. D. Shaw, "The Family in Late Antiquity: The Experience of Augustine," *Past and Present* 115 (1987): 23–24.

vants "with his hands, and even sometimes with his feet, but more frequently with a whip or any piece of wood that happened to be handy."[83] By the fourth century the endemic domestic violence of the upper classes forced itself on the attention of Christian bishops. In Basil's Cappadocia, the deaths of slaves through beating were frequent enough to be cited as usual examples of manslaughter: "It is involuntary also if a person with a desire of punishing another should beat him with a strap or a pliant rod and he should die from the beating. For . . . he wished to improve the offender, not to kill him."[84] Imperial laws had to make plain that certain forms of cruelty were the monopoly of public justice: they were not to be inflicted by a master on his slaves.[85]

Outside the house, young men could view the exemplary violence inflicted on their inferiors in every law court.[86] Even a school textbook for Latin boys learning Greek included scenes of torture as part of a day in the life of a well-to-do Roman: "The governor's seat is set up. The judge ascends the tribunal. . . . A guilty brigand is brought in. He is interrogated according to his deserts. He is put to the torture: the torturer lays into him, his chest is constricted; he is hung up, racked, beaten with clubs. He goes through the full cycle of torture. He denies his crime. He is sure to be punished. . . . He is led out and executed."[87]

Thus, a tide of horror lapped close to the feet of all educated persons. Not surprisingly, legal exemption from corporal punishment was a tenaciously defended mark of special status for even the most humble member of the class of notables. In a newly discovered letter of Augustine, we meet a young man who had been subjected to a flogging by the local clergy for having eloped with a nun. Furious that such an indignity had been inflicted on him as a *curialis,* a civic notable, this small-town Casanova ap-

---

83. Galen, *De cognoscendis animi morbis* 1.4, ed. C. G. Kühn, *Galeni Opera Omnia* (Leipzig: K. Knobloch, 1823), 5:18; P. W. Harkins, trans., *On the Passions and Errors of the Soul* (Columbus: Ohio State University Press, 1963), 38–39. Cf. Porphyry, *Ad Marcellam* 35, ed. A. Nauck, *Porphyrius: Opera Selecta* (Leipzig: Teubner, 1886), 296.

84. Basil, *Ep.* 188, in Deferrari, *Saint Basil* 3:30; cf. Council of Elvira (in Spain, a little before A.D. 303), canon 5, in *Acta et symbola conciliorum quae saeculo quarto habita sunt,* ed. E. J. Jonkers, (Leiden: Brill, 1974), 6.

85. *Codex Theodosianus* 9.12.1.

86. Ramsay MacMullen, "Judicial Savagery in the Roman Empire," *Chiron* 16 (1986): 147–66, now in *Changes in the Roman Empire* (Princeton: Princeton University Press, 1990), 204–19, and *Corruption and the Decline of Rome* (New Haven: Yale University Press, 1988), 137–42; Matthews, *Roman Empire of Ammianus,* 256–57. See T. P. Wiseman, *Catullus and His World* (Cambridge: Cambridge University Press, 1985), 5–9, for similar cruelty, if less indiscriminately applied, in the early empire.

87. A. C. Dionisotti, "From Ausonius' Schooldays? A Schoolbook and Its Relatives," *Journal of Roman Studies* 72 (1982): 105.

pealed all the way to Pope Celestine in Rome to seek reparation. His sexual misdemeanor—a heinous matter for fifth-century persons—was pushed aside in the bitter battle to defend the integrity of his body from a dishonoring punishment.[88]

We see the effect of corporal punishment on the sensibilities of the notable class most clearly in the writings of Libanius. For example, in 384 the governor Icarius shocked Libanius by showing favor to a member of the lower classes for whom (in Libanius' opinion) a beating was entirely appropriate while ordering the public executioner to lay into a young man from a family of notables. Libanius described the incident, which took place at Berroea (modern Aleppo), in all its vivid details. Wielded with vigor, the swinging whip smashed a hanging lamp and drenched those beneath it with oil. The young man's lawyer and his supporters crowded into the courtroom with cries of horror at such a scene. They begged the governor to recognize "the noble birth, the *paideia,*" of the victim.[89] The event marked the end of Libanius' friendship with Icarius, a governor he had once hailed as a "nursling of the Muses."[90] Writing a few years later to the governor Cyrus, who also had flogged a civic notable in a minor Syrian city, Libanius made plain that such an action was not to be expected from a man "formed in *paideia.*"[91] Cyrus had not only failed to show respect to a "fellow servant of the Muses," but he had also incurred loss of respect for himself for having behaved in a violent and indecorous manner. His reputation would suffer accordingly.

By the time that Libanius wrote to Cyrus, in A.D. 390–391, the flogging of town councillors had become a frequent and disturbing occurrence. They were increasingly held responsible for tax arrears and punished accordingly. The widening division, within the class of notables, between those leading figures who collaborated with the imperial government and derived their status from imperial service and the rank and file of *curiales* meant that many notables found themselves treated in the same violent and high-handed manner as were members of the lower classes. Such minor notables were numerous in the Greek East. A great city such as Antioch had a town council consisting of six hundred members. Not all of these were wealthy

---

88. Augustine, *Ep.* 9*.1–2, ed. J. Divjak, in *Corpus Scriptorum Ecclesiasticorum Latinorum* 88 (Vienna: W. Tempsky, 1981), 43–44; *Bibliothèque augustinienne: Oeuvres de Saint Augustin 46B: Lettres 1*–29** (Paris: Etudes augustiniennes, 1987), 158–60; R. B. Eno, trans., *Saint Augustine: Letters VI (1*–29*),* Fathers of the Church (Washington, D.C.: Catholic University of America Press, 1989), 71.

89. Libanius, *Oratio* 28.13–14 (III.52–53).

90. Libanius, *Oratio* 1.225 (I.182), in *Libanius' Autobiography,* ed. and trans. A. F. Norman, (London: Oxford University Press, 1965), 118; see also p. 214.

91. Libanius, *Ep.* 994.2 (XI.124).

or highly educated men. But the more the category of *curialis* was expanded for fiscal reasons, to provide the government with persons who could be held responsible for the payment of taxes, irrespective of their family backgrounds and culture, the more the subtle prestige of those who combined the status of town councillor with good birth and *paideia* was in danger of becoming devalued. The threat of loss of status made such persons all the more acutely aware of their judicial privileges. Cases of flogging and torture imposed upon them were vividly remembered by defenders of the city, such as Libanius.[92]

Once town councillors were considered vulnerable to official violence, there was no telling what might happen. Even the more well-to-do might find themselves exposed, and by losing face in their dealings with governors, the notables would themselves lose the respect of their inferiors. They would no longer be able to act as patrons and protectors of the lower classes.[93] In a vast and murmurous city such as Antioch, law and order themselves were threatened once an urban populace that "knew its place" sensed that their natural leaders, the town council, could be treated with disrespect.[94]

Corporal punishment was a fearsome thing. It was well known that certain kinds of beating, administered with lead-tipped whips, were tantamount to a death sentence.[95] Even when less severe, beating inflicted crushing dishonor on a notable. He would be "stripped and thrown down" to be beaten, as if he were a member of the lower classes; his "free body" would be sullied, from henceforth, by the marks of punishment.[96] By imposing so brutal and shameful a punishment, a governor showed in a peculiarly public manner that he did not feel bound by the tacit agreement which linked him to upper-class subjects.

Yet even after so crass a demonstration of insouciance for the "spell" of *paideia,* a governor might still be persuaded to regret his actions. Harsh punishments could be presented as momentary lapses due to ill-temper. "Anger" was the antithesis to a harmonious and controlled mode of public action. Anger, indeed, emerged as a central component in the language of late Roman politics. It meant, on occasion, the sudden, shameful collapse of self-restraint, associated with a public outburst of rage. But it more usually denoted the morose resentment of a man who would not allow

92. J. H. W. G. Liebeschuetz, *Antioch,* 166, 173; M. A. Wes, "Gesellschaft und Literatur in der Spätantike," *Ancient Society* 18 (1987): 186–87.

93. Libanius, *Oratio* 35.7 (III.213), in Festugière, *Antioche,* 485.

94. Libanius, *Oratio* 33.11 (III.171), in Norman, *Libanius 2,* 204.

95. Augustine, *Ep.* 10*.4.3, ed. Divjak, p. 48; *Lettres 1*–29*,* 174; Eno, *Saint Augustine: Letters VI,* 78.

96. Libanius, *Oratio* 52.16 (IV.33); Ammianus Marcellinus, *Res gestae* 29.2.20; cf. Libanius, *Ep.* 1414.5 (XI.456); Augustine, *Ep.* 104.1.1.

the claims of friendship and esteem, that linked one "servant of the Muses" to another, to take effect.[97] Either form of anger was held to constitute a serious breach of decorum. It carried a stigma. Given the uncertain situation that many governors faced in the provinces, the stigma of indecorous behavior might at any moment be translated into political isolation, into loss of office and eventual exposure to revenge.

By treating anger as a failure in decorum, those who commented on the politics of their time discreetly emphasized a principle of reversibility in an otherwise relentless system. For anger was a passion of the soul that the upright man could regret.[98] Anger might be cooled. A governor, or an emperor, could cancel out an act of official violence by treating it as a momentary, all-too-human lapse: he could reverse his decision by demonstrating *praotés* and *hémerotés,* the "gentle courtesy" that figured, with such ominous insistence, on the inscriptions and in the petitions of the later empire.[99] In this way, emphasis on anger formed part of the late Roman language of amnesty. The counterpart of anger was clemency. A governor who allowed his "boiling passion" to subside as the result of pleas for mercy might leave the city with "a fair name for having conquered anger."[100]

The studied generality of appeals to the linked notions of anger and decorum is their most striking feature. They ignored the protection offered by the existing Roman laws. Yet despite the ominous exceptions that we have mentioned, the persons of town councillors were legally exempted from flogging by a series of imperial edicts.[101] Libanius was eager to report any cases when notables had availed themselves of the protection offered by these laws.[102] But the effect of an appeal to the imperial laws could never be predicted. Attempts to impeach governors for having flouted the laws were known to have failed.[103]

In this respect, the notables of the Greek East suffered from the constrictions imposed upon them by their own codes of formalized speech. Only by such speech were they certain of holding the moral and cultural high ground in their relations with officials. It was through Greek rhetoric that they demonstrated their claim to exercise unchallenged authority as the

97.   Ammianus Marcellinus, *Res gestae* 29.2.18; see R. S. Rogers, "The Emperor's Displeasure," *Transactions of the American Philological Association* 90 (1959): 224–37, on the long prehistory of this notion.

98.   Libanius, *Oratio* 51.25 (IV.17).

99.   L. Robert, *Hellenica* 4 (1948): 15, n. 7; idem, *Hellenica* 13 (1965): 224.

100.   Libanius, *Oratio* 11.155–56 (I.488), trans. Downey, p. 669.

101.   *Codex Theodosianus* 12.1.75 (A.D. 371), 12.1.80 (A.D. 380), and 12.1.82 (A.D. 382).

102.   Libanius, *Oratio* 50.12 (III.476), in Norman, *Libanius 2,* 68; Libanius, *Oratio* 28.4–5 (III.49).

103.   Libanius, *Oratio* 42.18 (III.316).

"natural" leaders of society. To appeal to Roman law was not only to become enmeshed in a body of conflicting edicts, not all of which were available locally or relevant to a particular case.[104] It was also to step down from a secure position onto the less-firm terrain of the Latin language. Many, of course, did so, by learning Latin and Roman law, much to the disgust of Libanius.[105] But as native Greek speakers, they could never move in that alien territory with the same aplomb as did Libanius in his appeals to *paideia*. They no longer enjoyed the considerable advantage in a traditional society of being able to invoke an unquestioning consensus crystallized in centuries-old moral notions of correct behavior.

One development in the public life of the later empire actively encouraged such appeals to decorum. It was an age of ceremony. Those who wielded power tended to make their presence felt by means of "an array of ceremonial relationships, expressed in the stylized 'instant language' of gesture, decor, pose."[106] Such a heavy emphasis on ceremonial could have been as intimidating to the local elites as was the insistence on *civilité* maintained by the agents of Louis XIII and Louis XIV.[107] Yet this was not what happened in the later empire. The huge ceremoniousness of late Roman life proved a two-edged weapon in the hands of those who wielded power. Ceremonious behavior was not only imposed from the imperial court down, but it also depended for its effectiveness on appealing to precisely the ideals of harmony and self-control associated with *paideia*. As a result, ceremony did not simply exalt the powerful; it controlled them, by ritualizing their responses and by bridling their raw nature through measured gestures. By so doing, ceremony insensibly worked the ideals of *paideia* into the texture of government. Only power wielded in a self-controlled and dignified manner carried full authority. Like neglect of procedure in a modern law case, neglect of the decorum silently and insistently imposed upon governors by the ceremonial that upheld their authority might at any moment invalidate their actions. *Aschémoneis hégemôn*, "Governor, you forget yourself": the phrase (placed in the mouth of a Christian martyr) was a rebuke that touched on the "symbolic Achilles' heel" of the powerful.[108]

104. Augustine, *Ep.* 10*.4.1, ed. Divjak, p. 48; *Lettres 1*–*29*, 172; Eno, *Saint Augustine: Letters VI*, 78.

105. Libanius, *Oratio* 49.29 (III.466), in Norman, *Libanius 2*, 484.

106. Matthews, *Roman Empire of Ammianus*, 255.

107. Orest Ranum, "Courtesy, Absolutism and the Rise of the State," *Journal of Modern History* 52 (1980): 426–51.

108. *Martyrdom of Conon* 5.6, in *The Acts of the Christian Martyrs*, ed. H. Musurillo, (Oxford: Clarendon Press, 1972), 190. I have taken the term from James Scott, *Domination and the Arts of Resistance* (New Haven: Yale University Press, 1990), 105.

To act in this manner was to risk being caught off balance. It was always possible to be angry with the wrong persons. In that case, an eventual fall from power and exposure to vengeance carried with it the taint of dishonor. When alienated on such issues, the notables showed that they had long and merciless memories. The moment that Florentius, governor of Syria, fell from power in 392, Libanius wrote a pamphlet against him.[109] It took the form of an indictment of a man who had progressively isolated himself by his arrogance and cruelty. Florentius, Libanius wrote, had brought to Antioch the art of inflicting death by flogging.[110] His brother, Lucianus, count of the East, was even worse. He had imposed such corporal punishments on Antiochene notables that their own slaves pitied them: they had suffered injuries that none of their servants had ever borne.[111]

This was a cautionary tale. For what Libanius did not need to tell his readers was that Lucianus himself had ended his life by being flogged to death at Antioch and that the new praetorian prefect, Rufinus, had made a special journey to the city, carefully combined with gestures of conciliation to the town council—conversations with the right people, a display (by this ruthless Westerner) of newly acquired skills in speaking Greek, even the building of a new portico—in order to preside, in person, over his enemy's execution.[112] Lucianus got what he deserved, and his victims in Antioch, through Libanius, made sure that his shameful death would not be forgotten.

Against this background, we can understand why our sources are so preoccupied with the deportment of the great and why they describe in such vivid terms their occasional, chilling outbursts of rage and cruelty. These were the points on which some leverage could be brought to bear. Modern historians have found the "overemphasis upon moralizing and character" a peculiarly unsatisfactory feature of the historians of the age, such as Ammianus Marcellinus and Eunapius of Sardis.[113] Yet by writing history in this way, the educated classes concentrated on one of the few aspects of the imperial system which they thought might change for the better. A historiography in which "character became the central preoccu-

---

109. Otto Seeck, "Libanius gegen Lucianus," *Rheinisches Museum*, Neue Folge 73 (1920–24): 84–101.

110. Libanius, *Oratio* 46.8–10 (III.382–83); A. H. M. Jones, J. R. Martindale, and J. Morris, *The Prosopography of the Later Roman Empire*, vol. 1 (Cambridge: Cambridge University Press, 1971), 364–65, Florentius 9.

111. Libanius, *Oratio* 56.7 (IV.135).

112. Libanius, *Epp.* 1106.2, 1111.3 (XI.213, 218); Jones, Martindale, and Morris, *Prosopography* 1:516–17, Lucianus 6.

113. R. C. Blockley, *The Fragmentary Classicising Historians of the Later Roman Empire*, ARCA 6 (Liverpool: Francis Cairns, 1981), 25.

pation"[114] reflected a politics of decorum, through which members of the elite hoped to restrain the powerful and even, on occasion, to persuade them to change their minds.

Imperial Deportment

The achievements of *paideia* were most widely publicized in the person of the emperor himself. As in the early empire, the emperor was both the guarantor of all power in the empire and the model for its exercise.[115] In Libanius' speeches, for instance, "the imperial personality permeates the whole of society."[116] It was in terms of an image of supreme, unquestioned power, agreeably saturated with their own values, that notables exercised authority in their own society and judged, controlled, and colluded with the local representatives of the power of the emperor.

The emperors accepted this view of themselves. Aware of acting before an alert and tenacious audience scattered throughout the cities of the empire, they were careful to show their power in the approved manner. Throughout these centuries, emperors drawn from a wide variety of social backgrounds maintained a high level of decorum. To become an emperor was to assume, in public, a mask of upper-class dignity and self-restraint.[117]

Adjustment to so decorous a role was often sudden and was a strain for many. In the early third century the newly elevated emperor Macrinus made a fool of himself in Antioch by growing a beard and by "speaking to people at audiences very slowly and laboriously, so that frequently he could not be heard because of his low voice."[118] It was a painful attempt by a brusque military man to tune himself, as emperor, to a style of philosophical serenity associated with Marcus Aurelius. In the mid–fourth century, Julian the Apostate did better, in the opinion of his pagan admirers. He was, after all, acclaimed on public inscriptions as a "master-practitioner

114. Ibid., 15.
115. See A. Wallace-Hadrill, "Civilis Princeps: Between Citizen and King," *Journal of Roman Studies* 72 (1982): 32–48, esp. 47; and Richard Gordon, "The Veil of Power: Emperors, Sacrificers and Benefactors," in *Pagan Priests,* ed. Mary Beard and John North (Ithaca, N.Y.: Cornell University Press, 1990), 209.
116. A. F. Norman, "Libanius: The Teacher in an Age of Violence," in *Libanios,* ed. G. Fatouros and T. Krischer, Wege der Forschung 621 (Darmstadt: Wissenschaftliche Buchgesellschaft, 1983), 153.
117. Ammianus Marcellinus, *Res gestae* 25.10.15. Had the newly elected emperor Jovian lived a little longer, he would have corrected his easy habits "out of regard for the imperial dignity."
118. Herodian, *History* 5.2.3, in *Herodian,* ed. and trans. C. R. Whittaker, Loeb Classical Library (Cambridge, Mass.: Harvard University Press, 1970), 2:13.

of philosophy."[119] He was careful to take the advice of his doctor, Oribasius, "that even if he felt anger, he should not show it in his eyes or his voice."[120] Faced by opposition, he knew how to "disperse the imperial rage" by literary play.[121] Hence he wrote a remarkable festive satire on the city of Antioch, the *Misopôgon*. This pamphlet was posted for all to read. Far from revealing the tortured psyche of Julian, it should be read as testimony to the skill with which late Roman rulers displayed, on occasion, the civilized good humor that contemporaries liked to associate with a gentle, because secure, style of rule.[122] In a situation that merited a memorable outburst of imperial rage, the *Misopôgon* was Julian's quirky way of showing that he could be "redoubtable, but without cruelty."[123] In the next century, the Christian historian Socrates of Constantinople praised the emperor Theodosius II: no one had ever seen him angry, while Julian, the pagan, "although he professed himself to be a philosopher," had lost his temper when at Antioch.[124]

It is the *longue durée* of these anecdotes that is impressive. Those who looked on the public bearing of Macrinus, Julian, and Theodosius II knew that they looked on the only effective constitution that the Roman empire possessed. They scanned the faces and gestures of each ruler, anxiously concerned to gauge the extent to which the man who wielded such awesome power would allow himself to be held in check by the silken web of a code of deportment that was supposed to bind him to his upper-class subjects.

When the young Julian arrived at Milan to be declared Caesar, the courtiers gathered around this total stranger, unexpectedly summoned from Asia Minor: "Gazing long and earnestly on his eyes . . . and on his face . . . they divined what manner of man he would be, as if they were perusing those ancient books, the reading of which discloses from bodily signs the inward qualities of the mind."[125]

Physiognomics were a serious business in the later empire. They were

119. H. Dessau, *Inscriptiones Latinae Selectae,* no. 751 (Berlin: Weidmann, 1892), 1: 167–68.

120. Eunapius, *Fragment 28.2,* in *The Fragmentary Classicising Historians of the Later Roman Empire,* ed. and trans. R. C. Blockley, ARCA 10 (Liverpool: Francis Cairns, 1983), 43.

121. Eunapius, *Fragment,* 25.3, ed. Blockley, p. 37.

122. Maud W. Gleason, "Festive Satire: Julian's *Misopôgon* and the New Year at Antioch," *Journal of Roman Studies* 76 (1986): 106–19.

123. Ammianus Marcellinus, *Res gestae* 25.4.8.

124. Socrates, *Ecclesiastical History* 7:22, in *Library of the Nicene and Post-Nicene Fathers,* vol. 2, trans. A. C. Zenos (Grand Rapids, Mich.: Eerdmans, 1979). Cf. Gregory Nazianzen, *Carmina* 1.2.25, lines 290–303: *Patrologia Graeca* 37:833–34, on the good temper ascribed, by Christians, to Constantius II.

125. Ammianus Marcellinus, *Res gestae* 15.8.16.

the form of "Kremlin-watching" most appropriate to an age of personal power. Gregory Nazianzen, a Christian, had met the young Julian at Athens and had drawn his own conclusions. Those restless eyes, that heavy breathing through the nose, the shuffling gait, and the uncontrolled bursts of laughter were ominous signs. Here was a young man on whom the benign immunization of *paideia* would not take.[126] Christians should beware of such a man as emperor.

Reading the pages of the historian Ammianus Marcellinus, who wrote his Latin history of the empire in Rome in the 390s, we find ourselves scanning the faces of the great with frightened eyes. He offers us a sinister physiognomics of power. What Arnaldo Momigliano once characterized as the "acute, almost demonic perception" betrayed in his works is disturbing because it is so grippingly visual.[127] The fatal tendency to anger in Valentinian I, for instance, was increasingly shown in the details of his "voice, expression and style of walk."[128] For Ammianus judged the actions of contemporaries against the tranquil, almost iconic image of the public man associated with the proper exercise of power. In his history, anger was "recorded almost always when displayed by supposedly civilized men"; "burning, seething, swelling" were his favored terms.[129] The figures in his account were grotesquely contorted by the qualities that flouted Ammianus' ideals. Extravagant sweeps of the arm, prancing steps, eyebrows raised like horns, head swung back like a tossing bull, eyes that flashed with lethal rage, and the smile fixed on the face of the chief interrogator, "like the snarl of a wild beast": Ammianus wrote of these, and in this graphic manner, to remind his cultivated readers of the nightmare into which persons like themselves had fallen in recent years.[130]

It is a dramatic shadow play from whose pages modern readers have derived an unforgettable impression of the cruelty, venality, and panic-fear that could surround the late Roman autocracy.[131] Yet we must remember that, as in a shadow play, these horrific incidents loom in such extravagant shapes because they were thrown onto the screen by the bright and carefully tilted

126. Gregory Nazianzen, *Orationes* 4.56, 5.21–23, 34: *Patrologia Graeca* 35:560B, 689B–692B, 717A.

127. A. D. Momigliano, "The Lonely Historian Ammianus Marcellinus," *Annali della Scuola Normale superiore di Pisa*, ser. 3, 4 (1974): 1404, now in *Essays in Ancient and Modern Historiography* (Oxford: Blackwell, 1977), 136; Matthews, *Roman Empire of Ammianus,* 258–62, 459–60.

128. Ammianus Marcellinus, *Res gestae* 29.3.2.

129. Robin Seager, *Ammianus Marcellinus: Seven Studies in His Thought and Language* (Columbia: University of Missouri Press, 1986), 49, 34.

130. Ammianus Marcellinus, *Res gestae* 14.7.1, 28.1.3, 20.1.2, 28.4.10, 20.9.2, 28.1.12.

131. Matthews, *Roman Empire of Ammianus,* 460.

light of educated opinion. Ammianus may have been a compatriot of Libanius': he certainly shared in the same culture as did Libanius. A widely traveled soldier, he knew better than did Libanius that, in the high politics of the empire, *paideia* went so far and no further. But like Libanius, he ensured that it would be he and his readers who would live to tell the tale in their own, savagely precise terms. The "nostalgia" that has rightly been seen to pervade Ammianus' account of his own times was based on a fierce refusal to relinquish the last prerogative of his class—the ability to record events that he wished had never happened.[132]

Parrhésia: The Philosopher

The elites, therefore, faced those who wielded power with many advantages. They possessed a singularly tenacious common code. They could show an unforgiving memory against those who flouted their ideals of public behavior. They were capable of quiet obstinacy in withholding collaboration from unpopular officials. What they lacked was courage. Their freedom of speech, the *parrhésia* that was the true legacy of the city-state, was strictly curtailed. They might still hope to persuade, but they could not challenge, those who exercised power.

The reason for this was simple enough. To remain effective, the notables depended on remaining within the patronage networks that linked the cities to the imperial administration and, hence, to the court. *Parrhésia,* for them, was the outcome of *philia.* It could only be exercised by those who felt that they could count on the friendship of the great. Libanius, for instance, was sufficiently sure of his friendship with the emperor Julian to stand up for the town council of Antioch in his presence in 362. Even that required some nerve. As he spoke, courtiers were overheard remarking, in loud voices, that the Orontes flowed beneath the windows of the palace: it might be a good idea to toss the tiresome professor into the river.[133]

Libanius knew that he could go so far and no further. When he delivered the funeral oration on his uncle, Phasganius, the last third of his speech had to be delivered behind closed doors, for it spoke of Phasganius' *parrhésia* in standing up to the Caesar Gallus, Julian's brother. Julian might be touchy on the subject. So Libanius withdrew to a room, "requesting

---

132. T. D. Barnes, "Literary Convention, Nostalgia and Reality in Ammianus Marcellinus," in *Reading the Past in Late Antiquity,* ed. Graeme Clarke (Rushcutters Bay, New South Wales: Australian National University Press, 1990), 83. On the home country of Ammianus, see G. W. Bowersock, *Journal of Roman Studies* 80 (1990): 247–48, suggesting Alexandria, not Antioch.

133. Libanius, *Oratio* 1.126 (I.143–48), in Norman, *Libanius' Autobiography,* 74.

the hearers . . . not to draw the attention of a crowd by loud applause. And so far—may Nemesis remain kind—no frightening consequence has resulted."[134]

The fact that Libanius' most telling attacks on officials took place after they had fallen from power and their replacements had indicated that a character assassination would be welcome remains a peculiarly disagreeable aspect of his career.[135] The kindest thing that can be said about Libanius' behavior is that his dilemma was widespread. As under the Ottoman Empire, the "politics of notables" was subject to very strict limits of the possible: their "modes of action must in normal circumstances be cautious and ambiguous . . . the use of influence in private; the cautious expression of discontent, by absenting themselves from the ruler's presence; the discreet encouragement of opposition—but not up to the point when it may call down the fatal blow of the ruler's anger."[136]

Parrhésia, therefore, was devolved to another, notoriously eccentric, figure—the philosopher. He was a well-chosen spokesman. He almost always belonged to the notable class and shared in their *paideia* to a high degree. The philosopher-heroes of Eunapius of Sardis, for instance, moved in a world whose solid backdrop, rarely glimpsed behind accounts of their more memorable eccentricities, remained the life of well-to-do provincial notables. They represented a "typical blend of philosophy, rhetoric and divine learning."[137] But the philosopher's way of life was pointedly different. He was held to owe nothing to ties of patronage and friendship. He was a man who, by a heroic effort of the mind, had found freedom from society. For that reason, he carried his right to *parrhésia* in his own person. He could address the great directly, in terms of a code of decorum and self-restraint that he himself exemplified to the highest degree, because he was uncompromised by political attachments.

In the earlier centuries of the empire, the tranquil, bearded figure of the philosopher, with bare chest and simple cloak, carrying a leather satchel and a staff, had been the focus of clearly defined and stable expectations: owing nothing to any man, the philosopher acted as the privileged counterpoint to those who exercised power.[138] In late antiquity, this image of the philosopher had remained alive; it survived the "gradual drift to the pe-

134. Libanius, *Ep.* 283.2 (X.268); Liebeschuetz, *Antioch,* 26.

135. Paul Petit, "Recherches sur la publication et la diffusion des discours de Libanius," *Historia* 5 (1956): 479–509.

136. A. Hourani, "Ottoman Reform and the Politics of Notables," in *Beginnings of Modernization in the Middle East in the Nineteenth Century,* ed. W. R. Polk and R. L. Chambers (Chicago: University of Chicago Press, 1968), 46.

137. Penella, *Greek Philosophers and Sophists,* 75.

138. Now excellently studied in Johannes Hahn, *Der Philosoph und die Gesellschaft:*

riphery of society" that characterized the leaders of the pagan philosophical schools in Athens and elsewhere.[139]

It was, of course, mainly an image. Fourth-century views of the philosopher were frequently as far removed from the reality of the intense and profoundly apolitical study circles of a Plotinus or a Iamblichus as the modern image of Einstein is distant from the real work of a scientist. Yet it should not be dismissed for that reason. As has been shown in the case of the image of Einstein, such images "reinforce specific prejudices."[140] And the "specific prejudices" reinforced by the image of the philosopher concentrated, above all, on the control of power. A man who had mastered his passions had gained the right to speak with authority to those who struggled to master theirs as a spiritual guide and, if need be, even as a critic.[141] When Sopater the philosopher made his way from Apamea to the new city of Constantinople, his admirers were convinced that he had done so in order to "control and reform through reason the impulsiveness that was the basis of Constantine's character."[142] History would have been very different, Eunapius thought, if he had succeeded.

Hence the fourth-century image of the philosopher was double-sided. The philosopher was a man free from society. He owed nothing to his peers and positively avoided those who exercised power. If he enjoyed wealth, culture, and social status (as many did), he did not allow these material advantages to compromise his freedom. He was often by temperament a recluse and was frequently committed to traditions of philosophy, most notably to an extreme Platonism, that prized contemplation above all other human activities.

But it was precisely in a self-created solitude that the philosopher developed the intelligence and strength of character which enabled him to in-

---

Selbstverständis, öffentliches Auftreten und populäre Erwartungen in der höhen Kaiserzeit (Stuttgart: Franz Steiner, 1989), esp. 12–29.

139.   Garth Fowden, "The Pagan Holy Man in Late Antique Society," *Journal of Hellenic Studies* 102 (1982): 33, 51–59; see R. R. R. Smith, "Late Roman Philosopher Portraits from Aphrodisias," *Journal of Roman Studies* 80 (1990): 144–46, 148–50, for striking new visual evidence.

140.   A. J. Friedman and C. C. Douley, *Einstein as Myth and Muse* (Cambridge: Cambridge University Press, 1985), 193–94.

141.   I. Hadot, "The Spiritual Guide," in *Classical Mediterranean Spirituality,* ed. A. H., Armstrong (New York: Crossroad, 1986), 436–59; Hahn, *Der Philosoph und die Gesellschaft,* 61–65.

142.   Eunapius, *Lives of the Philosophers* 462, in Wright, *Philostratus and Eunapius,* 380; I have preferred the translation in Penella, *Greek Philosophers and Sophists,* 51. Constantine, of course, had other reasons for patronizing philosophers than his own self-improvement; see Garth Fowden, "Nicagoras of Athens and the Lateran Obelisk," *Journal of Hellenic Studies* 107 (1987): 51–57.

tervene in the world around him. The fact that many philosophers were quite content with solitude did not mean that others did not feel obliged, even tempted, to undertake the occasional venture into public life. It is a tribute to the pressure that could still be brought upon them by their social peers and, above all, to the loyalty that they were expected to show to their hometown that a few philosophers, at least, agreed to play their allotted parts in the drama of persuasion in the course of the fourth century. On those occasions, the other, less-reclusive side of the image of the philosopher gave them a firm platform from which to act. Only the philosopher, a man who had overcome anger and fear in himself, could stand in the way of the anger of others. He could brave the menacing power of the great and ensure that his voice was heard in their councils. He was expected to bring amnesty for those caught in the toils of a political system in which, as we have seen, anger was ever-present. For this reason, we find philosophers continually admired for their ability to mingle with the *celsae potestates,* the emperor and his entourage, as few notables would have dared to have done.

The philosopher brought to his task certain carefully nurtured virtues. The first was *karteria,* "endurance," the ability to tough it out in confrontations with the powerful. In a society where cruelty was so pervasive, we should never underestimate the political weight of physical courage. A primal awe surrounded those who were known to have withstood torture. So many could not. During the treason trials instigated by the emperor Valens at Antioch in 376, a leading figure summoned Libanius. This man "regarded friendship as something sacred, but could not steel himself against torture. Thus he begged us to pray Fortune for his death. . . . He bathed, dined and welcomed sleep, and with it, came death; and next day, at dawn, we were attending his funeral, when people arrived from the palace to arrest him."[143] What Libanius presented as a merciful heart attack may in fact have been suicide, which Libanius himself had advised.[144]

In the pages of Ammianus, philosophers, by contrast, show no such fear. They stand out in high relief against the terrible glow of the torture chamber. During the treason trials of 356, only one, Epigonus, revealed himself to be "a philosopher in garb alone": he broke under interrogation.[145] The rest held firm. Such was Pasiphilus, "who, though cruelly tortured to bring about the ruin [of a colleague] through a false charge, could not be shaken from the firmness of a steadfast mind."[146]

---

143. Libanius, *Oratio* 1.173–74 (I.164), in Norman, *Libanius' Autobiography,* 99.
144. Eunapius, *Fragment* 39.2, ed. Blockley, p. 55.
145. Ammianus Marcellinus, *Res gestae* 14.9.5.
146. Ibid., 29.1.36; cf. 14.9.5, 19.12.12, 29.1.37, 29.2.25.

An acute sense of the need for physical courage led Ammianus, though loyal to the old gods, to speak with respect of the Christian cult of the martyrs. No better than executed criminals and objects of charnel horror to many others,[147] true Christian martyrs impressed Ammianus because, like philosophers, they had put their bodies "on the line" by facing suffering and death: "When forced to deviate from their observance, they endured the pains of torture, going so far as to meet a glorious death with inviolated faith."[148]

In situations where courage, obstinacy, and intelligence were needed, fourth-century communities still turned, at times, to their local philosophers. Ruined by the exactions of the praetorian prefect, Petronius Probus, the gentry of Epirus were "further compelled to send envoys to the emperor to offer him thanks." They forced a philosopher called Iphicles, "a man renowned for his strength of soul," to perform the duty. His courage and skill enabled him to confront the studiously ferocious Valentinian I and to turn what had been planned as a routine display of celebratory rhetoric into an occasion for plain-speaking.[149]

Furthermore, the philosopher, precisely because he was known to be fearless, brought to bear the decisive quality of *parrhésia*, candid speech and good counsel offered without fear or favor. In the world we have described, this was an infinitely precious social elixir. Galen had been convinced that no civic notable, no *politeuomenos*, could be trusted to tell the truth; notables were incapable of receiving confidences and giving disinterested advice.[150] By contrast, the philosopher, as the purveyor of candor, was thought to have brought to public life a virtue that was of immediate political relevance. In a system of personal autocracy, the notion of "good counsel" summed up late Roman hopes for a remedy for public ills in a manner as resonant as does the word *democracy* today.[151]

147.   Eunapius, *Lives of the Sophists* 472, in Wright, *Philostratus and Eunapius,* 424; Isidore of Pelusium, *Epp.* 1.55, 4.27: *Patrologia Graeca* 78:217BC, 1080c; Theodoret of Cyrrhus, *Graecarum Affectionum Curatio* 8.11: *Patrologia Graeca* 83:1012C; P. Canivet, *Théodoret de Cyr: Thérapeutique des Maladies Helléniques* 2, Sources chrétiennes 57 (Paris: Le Cerf, 1958), 314; Severus of Antioch, *Homeliae cathedrales* 72: *Patrologia Orientalis* 12:84–87.

148.   Ammianus Marcellinus, *Res gestae* 22.11.10; see E. D. Hunt, "Christians and Christianity in Ammianus Marcellinus," *Classical Quarterly* 35 (1985): 192–99.

149.   Ammianus Marcellinus, *Res gestae* 30.5.9–10.

150.   Galen, *De cognoscendis animi morbis* 1.3, ed. Kühn, 5:8–9, trans. Harkins, pp. 32–33.

151.   Paul Veyne, *Le Pain et le Cirque* (Paris: Le Seuil, 1976), 711, trans. *Bread and Circuses* (London: Allen Lane Penguin Press, 1990), 404; Fergus Millar, *The Emperor in the Roman World* (London: Duckworth, 1977), 83–122; Karlheinz Dietz, *Senatus contra principem, Untersuchungen zur senatorischen Opposition gegen Kaiser Maximinus Thrax* (Munich: C. H. Beck, 1980), 313–14. See Ammianus Marcellinus, *Res gestae* 27.7.9, on Valentinian I;

The philosopher, of course, was not alone in this. Despite the grim impression left by many contemporary accounts, good counsel was never lacking in the higher reaches of the government. Ammianus blamed only those *celsae potestates,* those heads of government departments and advisers of the emperor, who failed in their duty. It was they who should have controlled the emperor's anger and modified his vindictiveness. His strictures assume that many still did so.[152] Forthright speech in the *consistorium,* by professional experts on warfare and taxation, remained a possibility. The Gothic general Fravitta was no philosopher, yet he "spoke loudly and openly to the emperor . . . grimacing as he spoke." Despite the annoyance of the eunuchs at such a breach of the ceremonious hush that usually reigned in the emperor's presence, he was invited to continue.[153] On hearing of an edict that would force an unwelcome theological formula on the bishops of Cilicia in 432–433 the praetorian prefect, Taurus, "moved by a divine force [and, perhaps, by discreet gifts from the patriarch of Alexandria] would not allow it to be published. Entering into the imperial presence, he swore that the cities would be ruined, and stated, quite plainly, that what Thrace [a province ruined by barbarian raids] is now, Cilicia would be, where hardly a city remains to pay its taxes."[154]

Yet these incidents from real life did not receive the same degree of attention from upper-class contemporaries as did the notion of intervention by the philosopher. For the philosopher's activity condensed an acceptably stylized traditional image of the workings of power. He was not a mere public servant, as men such as Fravitta and Taurus had been. In an age of personal rule, he spoke directly to the all-important personal qualities of the ruler. For Ammianus, anger was the ulcer that festered beneath the surface of the autocracy.[155] And anger had always been the specialty of the philosopher. It was a philosopher who had taught the emperor Augustus to recite all the letters of the Greek alphabet, in order to give himself time to take possession of himself, whenever he felt anger rise within him.[156]

For this reason, the scenario of the philosopher who tamed the heart of the emperor remained important in the political imagination of the later

Aurelius Victor, *De Caesaribus* 4.1, on Claudius; for the ideal, *Scriptores Historiae Augustae: Severus Alexander* 16.3; and the dangers of lack of counsel, *Scriptores: Aurelian* 43.3.

152. Ammianus Marcellinus, *Res gestae* 14.1.10, 28.1.25, 29.3.2.

153. Eunapius, *Fragment* 48.8, ed. Blockley, pp. 111–13.

154. *Collectio Casinensis* 211, ed. E. Schwartz, in *Acta Conciliorum Oecumenicorum* 1.4 (Berlin: de Gruyter, 1932–33), 155.

155. Ammianus Marcellinus, *Res gestae* 27.7.4.

156. *Epitome de Caesaribus* 48.14–15.

empire. It explained why the worst did not always happen. To take one example: faced by the embarrassing fact that, for all his assumed fury against the church and for all the imagined heroism of the Christians of his age, the reign of Julian the Apostate produced so few martyrs, the author of the later Syriac *Romance of Julian the Apostate* (who probably wrote in the late fifth century) fell back on the image of the court philosopher.[157] In the *Romance* the rage of Julian, the pagan tyrant, is invariably brought to a standstill by a succession of discreet advisers. The first such figure is the philosopher Aplatus,

> a man expert in knowledge, and renowned among the philosophers; and although he was much of a pagan, he gave good counsel and just. . . . "The power of your kingdom [he said] is to destroy or have mercy. . . . There is no person above you to reprove your will. . . . Since I have received liberty from your power and have the assurance not to gloss over what is a duty, I reply that you have the power as king, . . . [but] God have mercy on your kingdom when it overrides the laws of justice, seeing that all the regulations of duty come from you alone."[158]

Shop-soiled though it might be through constant use, the image of the philosopher continued to condense an ideal of integrity and plain-speaking not usually current in governing circles. For bureaucrats, to adopt the persona of a philosopher was to cast a cloak of old-world integrity over risky business. Hermogenes had acted as personal secretary to the fierce Caesar Gallus.[159] He was praised for having retired from that difficult post with a clean record. According to his panegyrist, the rhetor Himerius, Hermogenes "spoke out in conversations [with Gallus] to such effect that he made the ruler's rule milder, by narrating ancient myths and stories from poetry and history."[160]

In reality, of course, not all interventions involved the imperial wrath. The normal business of the court concerned the workings of a vast patronage system. As in the Duke of Milan's court in Shakespeare's *Tempest,* the art of government depended on grace and favor:

157. M. van Esbroeck, "Le soi-disant Roman de Julien l'Apostat," in *IV Symposium Syriacum 1984,* Orientalia Christiana Analecta 229 (Rome: Pontificium Institutum Studiorum Orientalium, 1987), 191–202.

158. H. Gollancz, trans., *Julian the Apostate* (Oxford: Oxford University Press, 1929), 39–49.

159. T. D. Barnes, "Himerius and the Fourth Century," *Classical Philology* 82 (1987): 219.

160. Himerius, *Oratio* 48.19, ed. A. Colonna (Rome: Istituto Poligrafico, 1951), 205.

how to grant suits,
How to deny them, who t'advance and who
To trash for over-topping.[161]

To be considered capable of telling the truth about the personal worth of individuals and the rights and wrongs of a case made the philosopher, the man of *parrhésia,* the perfect patronage secretary. His reputation further refurbished by a spell of philosophical retirement, Hermogenes went on to serve in the petitions office under Julian: "What laws by him were not generous? What man in peril did not escape danger through him? What men deserving of office failed to obtain it through him?"[162]

In the fourth century the ancient image of the philosopher as a privileged adviser of emperors could still guide the actions of real persons on the fringes of government. This was the case for one memorably successful philosopher, Themistius of Constantinople. Under emperors as different from each other as Constantius II, Valens, and Theodosius I, Themistius condensed for contemporaries expectations of a style of rule that still found room for the figure of the philosopher at court.[163]

Accident and the tenacious bonds of family tradition and regional loyalty ensured that Themistius happened to be a philosopher at Constantinople at a time when the city was on its way to becoming the pivot of the eastern empire. He exploited this situation with remarkable effectiveness. He lived out an ancient role. When he dined and traveled with the emperor Constantius II, he was always careful to be seen wearing the sober *tribônion* of the philosopher; he made plain his indifference to wealth by foregoing the usual grain allowance of a proconsul of Constantinople.[164] A man with a solid reputation for *parrhésia,* Themistius could make direct suggestions to even the morose and ill-educated emperor Valens, "who was always on the alert to detect personal advantage behind every seemingly

---

161. *The Tempest* 1.2.79–81. Quoted from Stanley Wells and Gary Taylor, eds., *William Shakespeare: The Complete Works* (Oxford: Clarendon Press, 1986), 1318.

162. Himerius, *Oratio* 48.30, ed. Colonna, p. 209.

163. G. Dagron, "L'Empire romain d'Orient au ive. siècle et les traditions politiques de l'Hellénisme: Le témoignage de Thémistius," *Travaux et Mémoires* 3 (1968): 1–242; Jones, Martindale, and Morris, *Prosopography* 1:889–94; L. J. Daly, "In a Borderland: Themistius' Ambivalence toward Julian," *Byzantinische Zeitschrift* 73 (1980): 1–11; idem, "Themistius' Refusal of a Magistracy," *Jahrbuch der österreichischen Byzantinistik* 32 (1982): 177–86; Scott Bradbury, "The Date of Julian's Letter to Themistius," *Greek, Roman and Byzantine Studies* 28 (1987): 235–51. See B. Colpi, *Die paideia des Themistius* (Bern: Peter Lang, 1987), on Themistius' sources.

164. Themistius, *Oratio* 34.14, 23.291c–292b, in *Themistii Orationes* ed. G. Downey and A. F. Norman (Leipzig: Teubner, 1971), 2:222, 85–86.

public-spirited request."[165] The correspondence of Libanius shows Themistius at the head of a tentacular network of patronage. As nominal head of the Senate of Constantinople, he had a hand in expanding its membership from three hundred to two thousand and so was in a position to extend his favors to a wide constituency of provincial notables anxious to secure the privileges of senatorial rank and posts at court.[166]

The related themes of amnesty and anger play a large role in Themistius' public utterances. He acted as the spokesman of the imperial benevolence. He even cited "an Assyrian maxim" (in fact, the Old Testament) to the effect that "the heart of the king is in the hand of God."[167] As the source of all amnesty, the emperor was the "living law," the embodiment of God's mercy on earth.[168]

For over thirty years the presence of Themistius near the emperors gave flesh and blood to the maxims of the imaginary Aplatus. At Antioch he even pacified the emperor Valens, by giving a speech in favor of religious toleration. He was believed by Christians to have succeeded in persuading the emperor to commute into exile the death penalty that had threatened obdurate supporters of the creed of Nicaea.[169] It was because of a man such as Themistius that the figures of philosophers in medieval Byzantine legends retained, for all the fantastic accretions of a later age, the firm outline of their role in late antiquity. Philosophers were supposed to be men of the court, "at one and the same time close to power and independent of it."[170]

Thus, the image of the philosopher still stood at the top of an imaginative pyramid that linked a discreet but persistent network of upper-class persuasion to the imperial court. Cautious and fundamentally unheroic

165.   Themistius, *Oratio* 34.14, ed. Downey and Norman, 2.222; see Daly, "Themistius' Refusal of a Magistracy," 163.

166.   Themistius, *Oratio* 34.13, ed. Downey and Norman, 2:221; G. Dagron, *La naissance d'une capitale: Constantinople et ses institutions de 330 à 451* (Paris: Presses universitaires de France, 1974), 129–32.

167.   Themistius, *Oratio* 7.89d, 11.147c, 19.229a, ed. Downey and Norman, 1:135, 2:22, 333, citing Proverbs 21:1; Lellia Cracco Ruggini, *Simboli di battaglia ideologica nel tardo ellenismo* (Pisa: Pacini, 1972): 17, n. 35.

168.   Themistius, *Oratio* 5.64bc, ed. Downey and Norman, 1:93–94. On the aftermath of the death of Julian and combined with a plea for religious tolerance, see 5.67b, ed. Downey and Norman, 1:98–99; cf. 11.154a and 16.212d, ed. Downey and Norman, 1:230, 303–4; Dagron, "L'Empire romain de l'Orient," 127–34.

169.   Sozomen, *Ecclesiastical History* 6.36; R. Snee, "Valens' Recall of the Nicene Exiles and Anti-Arian Propaganda," *Greek, Roman and Byzantine Studies* 26 (1985): 413–17.

170.   G. Dagron, *Constantinople imaginaire* (Paris: Presses universitaires de France, 1984), 123.

though those who operated within this network might be, they enjoyed an almost total monopoly of access to the imperial government for most of the fourth century. The conversion of Constantine to Christianity in 312 had little effect on a style of rule still based on collaboration with the local elites. When in 388 the emperor Theodosius I left Constantinople to conquer Italy from the Gallic usurper Maximus, he acted in the traditional manner. The venerable Themistius, now approaching seventy, was among those left in charge of the education of Theodosius' son, the young prince Arcadius. Yet soon after, another tutor of the prince, Arsenius, would flee the palace and disappear for a generation into the deserts of Egypt: among the illiterate monks he claimed to have found a fascinating new alphabet of the heart that owed nothing to his knowledge of the Greek and Latin classics.[171] And when it came to the all-absorbing topic of the emperor's wrath, Theodosius would soon have to deal with a former provincial governor now entering his fifties, Ambrose, Catholic bishop of Milan: the encounter was to prove more drastic than any he had experienced in his dealings with the urbane Themistius. A new type of "philosopher" had emerged. It is to this development that we must turn in our next chapter.

171. *Apophthegmata Patrum: Arsenius 5: Patrologia Graeca* 65:89A.

CHAPTER THREE

Poverty and Power

Universalis via

In the early fourth century two philosophers came to visit Saint Anthony. He recognized them instantly "from their appearance" as they trudged up the mountain path to his hermitage.[1] On another occasion a visiting philosopher was surprised to learn that Anthony had brought no books with him into the desert. Turning to the awesome stillness outside his cell, Anthony said: "My book, o philosopher, is the nature of God's creation; it is present whenever I wish to read His words."[2]

The incident is related in a series of anecdotes about the monks of Egypt put into circulation in fifth-century Constantinople by upper-class Christians. The monks, in reality, came from a wide variety of social backgrounds and were far from averse to reading and producing books.[3] But Christian writers consistently presented them as men untouched by *paideia*. The monk was the antithesis of the philosopher, the representative of the educated upper classes. Anthony had been a farmer's son, ignorant of Greek and

1. Athanasius, *Life of Anthony* 72.
2. Socrates, *Ecclesiastical History* 4.23, in *Library of the Nicene and Post-Nicene Fathers,* trans. A. C. Zenos, (Grand Rapids, Mich.: Eerdmans, 1979), 2:107.
3. Peter Brown, *The Body and Society: Men, Women and Sexual Renunciation in Early Christianity* (New York: Columbia University Press, 1988), 252; Clemens Scholten, "Die Nag-Hammadi-Texte als Buchbesitz der Pachomianer," *Jahrbuch für Antike und Christentum* 31 (1988): 144–72.

taught by God alone.[4] This was the message which a document such as the *Life of Anthony,* soon associated with none other than Athanasius, patriarch of Alexandria, and rapidly translated into Latin, was intended to convey to the elites of the empire.[5] The reaction of Augustine, at that time a teacher of rhetoric in Milan—the Latin equivalent of his older contemporary, Libanius of Antioch—was not unique. On being told the story of Saint Anthony by a visiting official in 386, he drew a single, drastic conclusion. It was his culture that stood condemned; "the uneducated rise up and take heaven by storm, and we, with all our learning, here we are, still wallowing in flesh and blood."[6]

The hatred of the monks expressed by non-Christians all over the empire is a further measure of their instantaneous impact on the imagination of contemporaries. Writing at the very end of the fourth century, the pagan Eunapius of Sardis found it not surprising that the barbarous Visigoths should claim to have Christian monks. This was only to be expected, given the lamentable state of the empire: for "it was sufficient to trail along grey cloaks and tunics, to be a ne'er do well and to have the reputation of being one. The barbarians used these devices to deceive the Romans, since they shrewdly observed that these things were respected amongst them."[7]

The rise to prominence of Christian monks was a warning signal. It announced wider changes in late Roman culture and society. The notables had based their authority on a monopoly of highly formalized codes of speech. Their ability to persuade the powerful depended on a grudging recognition that, in large areas of the day-to-day administration of the provinces, their collaboration was essential, just as their culture—based as it was on centuries of unbroken tradition—seemed irreplaceable. The two aspects went together. The traditional culture, with its distinctive forms of speech and behavior, was appropriate to persons who were called upon, as town councillors, to control their cities and to collect taxes according to traditional, well-tried methods. The notables' monopoly of formalized speech was mirrored in their monopoly of an equally formalized "theatrical style" of local politics.[8]

Hence the sharpness of the challenge was summed up in the persons

4. Athanasius, *Life of Anthony* 1, 73, 93.
5. See T. D. Barnes, "Angel of Light or Mystic Initiate? The Problem of the *Life of Anthony," Journal of Theological Studies,* n.s., 37 (1986): 353–68. Many arguments still support the traditional ascription of the *Life of Anthony* to Athanasius.
6. Augustine, *Confessions* 8.8.19.
7. Eunapius, *Fragment* 48.2, in *The Fragmentary Classicising Historians of the Later Roman Empire,* ed. and trans. R. C. Blockley, ARCA 10 (Liverpool: Francis Cairns, 1983), 77.
8. E. P. Thompson, "Patrician Society, Plebeian Culture," *Journal of Social History* 7 (1974): 389.

of the monks. They were presented as the spearhead of a drive to subvert a cultural and political monopoly: "Because the old power-holders work within a code of formalization, they cannot be challenged gradually but only altogether, by an almost deliberate, sacrilegious disregard for a traditional culture."[9]

The monks could utter the *gros mots* that broke the spell of *paideia*. As tutor to the sons of Theodosius I, Arsenius would have known the aging philosopher Themistius, his colleague at the court. He fled from the palace of Constantinople to Egypt, to save his soul. Over a decade later he emerged from the hermitages of the Wadi Natrun to settle for a time at Canopus, near Alexandria, on the site of a temple complex that had been frequented, only a generation previously, by a philosopher-hero of Eunapius of Sardis.[10] Arsenius was a changed man. He had once represented the prestige of *paideia* at the imperial court. Now he hung on the words of his spiritual guide, an elderly Egyptian: "I knew Greek and Latin learning. But I have not yet learned the ABC with this peasant."[11]

Anecdotes from the desert carried weight because they confirmed attitudes that had been prepared in the cities. Following a long tradition that reached back to the apologists of the second and third centuries, Christian writers insisted that the miraculous character of their religion was proved by the manner in which it had been spread throughout the Roman world by humble men, without *paideia*.[12] The "God-taught" wisdom of the monks of Egypt was so important to Christian contemporaries because it was held to be an avatar of the first, Spirit-filled preaching of "fishermen, publicans and the tentmaker"—the apostles and Saint Paul—for "God hath chosen the foolish things of this world to confound the wise."[13]

It was a commonplace of Christian polemic that the church had brought to the Roman world a wisdom and a moral code that had previously been the fragile acquisition of, at best, a few great minds. In the words of Augustine, in his *City of God,* any old woman, as a baptized Christian, now knew more about the true nature of the invisible world of angels and de-

---

9. M. Bloch, "Why Oratory?" in *Political Language and Oratory in Traditional Society,* ed. M. Bloch (London: Academic Press, 1975), 25.

10. Eunapius, *Lives of the Philosophers* 470, in *Philostratus and Eunapius,* ed. and trans. W. C. Wright, Loeb Classical Library (Cambridge, Mass.: Harvard University Press, 1952), 416.

11. *Apophthegmata Patrum: Arsenius* 6: *Patrologia Graeca* 65:89A; B. Ward, trans., *Sayings of the Desert Fathers,* Cistercian Studies 59 (Kalamazoo, Mich.: Cistercian Publications, 1975), 8.

12. Origen, *Contra Celsum* 7.60; cf. 6.2.

13. 1 Corinthians 1:27. Theodoret of Cyrrhus, *Graecarum affectionum curatio* 5.6: *Patrologia Graeca* 83:945B; P. Canivet, ed., *Théodoret de Cyr: Thérapeutique des maladies helléniques,* Sources chrétiennes 57 (Paris: Le Cerf, 1957), 246.

mons than did Porphyry, the most learned of near-contemporary philosophers.[14] Christ had brought to the world an *universalis via,* a "universal way" of salvation which only proud worshipers of the gods continued to ignore.[15] The Catholic church had gathered all nations and all classes into its bosom, *populari sinu.*[16] The Bible itself, with its seemingly endless layers of meaning, was a microcosm of the social and intellectual diversity to be found in the Christian churches. "Its plain language and simple style make it accessible to all. . . . this book stands out alone on so high a peak of authority and yet can draw the crowds to the embrace of its inspired simplicity."[17] The Roman empire, in Augustine's opinion, had never been so fortunate as when Christian teaching spread throughout its populations: "From the raised benches of the clergy, the precept *Render to no man evil for evil* is read out as given by divine authority, and wholesome counsel is proclaimed in the midst of our congregations, as if it were in schoolrooms open, now, to both sexes, to all ages and to all ranks of society."[18]

We are dealing with what might be called a Christian populism, that flouted the culture of the governing classes and claimed to have brought, instead, simple words, endowed with divine authority, to the masses of the empire.

To have presented Christianity in this manner was a masterstroke of writers who were, themselves, highly educated men. Christian writers of the fourth and fifth centuries wielded with dazzling effect the rhetoric of paradox.[19] It was a rhetoric that owed its effect to the close juxtaposition of the high with the low, of traditional marks of status, wealth, and culture with their charged absence. Such language discreetly emphasized the high social position of those who used it: we look with them over the edge of a precipice, on which they themselves stood, viewing the world from a great height. Master practitioners of Greek and Latin style, men such as Ambrose, Jerome, and Augustine and their innumerable colleagues in the Greek world backed into the limelight that they had brought to bear on the illiterate monks, apostles, and martyrs. Their very insistence

14.   Augustine, *City of God* 10.11.37; John Chrysostom, *Baptismal Catechism* 8.6, in *Jean Chrysostome: Huit catéchèses baptismales,* ed. A. Wenger, Sources chrétiennes 50bis (Paris: Le Cerf, 1970), 250.

15.   Augustine, *City of God* 10.32.

16.   Augustine, *Confessions* 6.5.8; see J. H. W. G. Liebeschuetz, *Barbarians and Bishops: Army, Church and State in the Age of Arcadius and Chrysostom* (Oxford: Clarendon Press, 1990), 173–74, for similar sentiments in John Chrysostom.

17.   Augustine, *Confessions* 6.5.8.

18.   Augustine, *Letter* 138.2.10.

19.   Averil Cameron, *Christianity and the Rhetoric of Empire: The Development of Christian Discourse* (Berkeley: University of California Press, 1991), 178–88.

on the extent to which their own conversion and subsequent duties in the Christian church had led them to sacrifice the advantages attached to wealth and refined diction drew attention to just those qualities. Like the great Indian leaders of political mass movements in our own century, they could not escape (and often they did not wish to escape) the tenacious web of markers of high status that supported their authority in Roman society. Men of great possessions, in culture if not always in material wealth, they lived as best they could with the ambiguities of a "*babu*-coolie relationship": "An appeal to the idea of sacrifice was really an appeal to the power that flowed from inequality. In order to be able to make sacrifices, one needed to possess. . . . To talk of sacrifice was then to talk of possessions, and hence of power."[20]

It was an open secret that many Christian bishops owed their prestige in society at large to the fact that they had once been rhetors. A recently discovered letter of Augustine's shows him as an old man who had just completed the *City of God*. He was approached by Firmus, a notable of Carthage. Firmus was not yet a baptized Christian. He had made little headway in reading the *City of God*. But he thought nothing of asking the bishop of Hippo, an old, sick man, for his expert opinion, as a former rhetor, on the style of model declamations composed at school by his son![21] Theodoret, bishop of Cyrrhus, Augustine's younger contemporary in the Greek East, a zealous biographer of monks and the proponent of views similar to those of Augustine on the spread of Christianity in his *Remedy for the Malady of Hellenic Beliefs*, maintained warm relations with a leading sophist and known non-Christian, Isocasius.[22]

Yet the pronounced populist streak in late Roman Christian literature should not be dismissed as mere rhetoric. We are dealing with a tenacious "representation" of the entire social and cultural evolution of the later empire.[23] It was in these terms that articulate Christians chose to make sense, to themselves quite as much as to others, of the success of the church.

20.   Dipesh Chakrabarty, *Rethinking Working Class History: Bengal, 1890–1940* (Princeton: Princeton University Press, 1989), 144, 152.

21.   Augustine, *Ep.* 2*.12–13, ed. J. Divjak, in *Corpus Scriptorum Ecclesiasticorum Latinorum* 88 (Vienna: W. Tempsky, 1981), 19–21; *Bibliothèque augustinienne: Oeuvres de Saint Augustin 46B: Lettres 1*–29** (Paris: Etudes augustiniennes, 1987), 88–93; R. B. Eno, trans., *Saint Augustine: Letters VI (1*–29*)*, Fathers of the Church (Washington, D.C.: Catholic University of America Press, 1989), 28–29.

22.   R. A. Kaster, *Guardians of Language: The Grammarian and Society in Late Antiquity* (Berkeley: University of California Press, 1988), 89.

23.   This helpful term of art has been exploited in Françoise Thélamon, *Païens et chrétiens au ivème siècle: L'apport de l'"Histoire ecclésiastique" de Rufin d'Aquilée* (Paris: Etudes augustiniennes, 1981), 86, 96.

Carefully selected fragments of late Roman experience—the undoubted social diversity of the Christian congregations,[24] the simplicity of the Christian Scriptures, the lack of culture of many Christian heroes, and, as we
shall see, the extent of the Christian care of the poor—were fastened on
by contemporaries. They were given exceptional prominence, in Christian
preaching and in Christian narratives of their own times. For these vivid
traits lent a sense of concreteness to the grandiose outlines of the Christian
image of a church empowered, by God's providence, to absorb all levels
of Roman society.

Fourth-century Christianity, in fact, was far from being a "popular" movement. It is not certain that it had become the majority religion of any
one region before the conversion of Constantine in 312, still less that it
appealed to any broad stratum of the population.[25] By the end of the fourth
century, the church, far from being a church of the lower classes, reflected
the sharp divisions in Roman society: its upper echelons were occupied
by highly cultivated persons, drawn from the class of urban notables. Their
preaching tended to address the wealthier and more educated members of
the congregation.[26] In a partially Christianized region such as northern
Italy, the effectiveness of Christian teaching depended on an alliance between the clergy and those families of notables who had become Christians.[27] Yet it is just at this time that the more aggressively populist components of the Christian representation of the triumph of the church reached
their peak.

This is hardly surprising. We are dealing with the dramatic self-image
of a group poised to take over the high ground of Roman society. It was
essential to invoke such themes in order to challenge, in as dramatic a
manner as possible, the monopoly of culture associated with traditional
non-Christian leaders. For many town councillors, loyalty to the city still
demanded loyalty to its gods. There were many who feared the worst
for their city under a Christian dispensation: "All the temples that are
in it will fall, the religion of the town will cease, our enemies will rise
against us, our town will perish and all this great honor which you see
will pass away."[28] But despite Christian claims to have triumphed over the
gods of the city and despite the tenacious, if muffled, resentment of well-

24.   R. Lane Fox, *Pagans and Christians* (New York: A. Knopf, 1987), 293–312.
25.   Fox, *Pagans and Christians,* 265–93; but see T. D. Barnes, *Constantine and Eusebius*
(Cambridge: Mass.: Harvard University Press, 1981), 191.
26.   Ramsay MacMullen, "The Preacher and His Audience," *Journal of Theological Studies,*
n.s., 40 (1989): 503–11.
27.   Rita Lizzi, *Vescovi e strutture ecclesiastiche nella città tardoantica* (Como: New Press,
1989), 15–57; idem, "Ambrose's Contemporaries and the Christianization of Northern
Italy," *Journal of Roman Studies* 80 (1990): 157–61, 164–68.
28.   A. Mingana, ed. and trans., *The Vision of Theophilus,* Woodbrooke Studies 3 (Cam-

placed non-Christians throughout this period, the issue was not a straightforward conflict of religions. It was only presented as such by Christian sources. We are dealing, rather, with a struggle for a new style of urban leadership.

Already severely fissured by the processes that we have described, the civic elites of the fourth century were faced by a relatively new, but determined, faction, very largely drawn from their own ranks. The Christian bishop and his clergy claimed an ever-increasing share in the exercise of authority in the city. In doing so, they offered new ways to mobilize and also to control the city's inhabitants. These, in turn, gave new weight to strategies of persuasion that had already been deployed by the men of *paideia* in their dealings with governors and with the imperial court. Under the cover of a Christian language shot through with paradox, which seemed to threaten brutal discontinuity between the old and the new, a regrouping took place among the dominant factions in the late Roman cities. The tacit acceptance by the civic notables of a new partner, in the never-ending task of exercising control within the city and of representing its needs to the outside world was hastened by clear signals from a Christian court. The Christian bishop became a *vir venerabilis,* a person deemed "worthy of reverence" by the powerful.[29] With the bishop, the voice of a newly formed urban grouping, the local Christian congregation, came to be heard in the politics of the empire.

The sharpness and dramatic tones of the Christian self-image sprang from the very closeness of the conflicting parties. Its assertive clarity was designed to counter considerable blurring in day-to-day practice. Notables who agreed to collaborate, as Christians, with bishops such as Ambrose of Milan, Augustine of Hippo, and Theodoret of Cyrrhus found that their culture and the wealth and political influence that went with it were by no means dismissed out of hand.[30]

Nowhere was the Christian representation of the church's novel role in society more aggressively maintained than in the claim of Christian bish-

---

bridge: W. Heffer, 1931), trans. p. 25, Syriac p. 65. See esp. Claude Lepelley, *Les cités de l'Afrique romaine au Bas-Empire* (Paris: Etudes augustiniennes, 1979), 1:351–69; M. Salzman, "Aristocratic Women: Conductors of Christianity in the Fourth Century," *Helios* 16 (1989): 207–20. Salzman effectively criticizes the trend to exaggerate the success of Christian women in spreading Christianity among the Roman aristocracy. Pierre Chuvin, *A Chronicle of the Last Pagans* (Cambridge, Mass.: Harvard University Press, 1990), 55–56; E. Wipozycka, La christianisation de l'Egypte au ive.–ve. siècles. Aspects sociaux et ethniques." *Aegyptus* 68 (1988), 117–64; Z. Borkowski, "Local Cults and Resistance to Christianity," *Journal of Juristic Papyrology* 20 (1990): 25–30.

29. Ernst Jerg, *Vir venerabilis: Untersuchungen zur Titulatur der Bischöfe in den ausserkirchlichen Texten der Spätantike,* Wiener Beiträge zur Theologie 26 (Vienna: Herder, 1970), 94–128.

30. Kaster, *Guardians of Language,* 76–81.

ops to act as "lovers of the poor." The theme of "love of the poor" exercised a gravitational pull quite disproportionate to the actual workings of Christian charity in the fourth century. It drew into its orbit the two closely related issues of who, in fact, were the most effective protectors and pacifiers of the lower classes of the cities and of how wealth was best spent by the rich within the city. Both themes went far beyond the narrow limits of the church's traditional, somewhat inward-looking concern for the poor. This had amounted to little more than care for destitute believers, the support of newly arrived coreligionists from other cities, and the protection of the widows and orphans of Christian families.[31] In fourth-century conditions, however, "love of the poor" took on a new resonance. It was an activity that came to affect the city as a whole. In the apposite words of Arnaldo Momigliano, the Christian bishops and the educated admirers of the monks brought about the equivalent of the patrician's *transitio ad plebem* in the early days of Rome. In the name of a religion that claimed to challenge the values of the elite, upper-class Christians gained control of the lower classes of the cities.[32] By the end of the fourth century their authority rested on a newly created constituency. Acting, frequently, in alliance with monks, bishops could display a form of *parrhésia* that was better calculated to sway the will of the emperor and of his servants than was the discreet lobbying of the men of *paideia*. For they claimed to speak for the populations of troubled cities at a time of mounting crisis.

Nourisher of the City

It is important to realize the potential perils of the situation in which this development occurred. The notables were held hostage by their cities. In the eyes of the emperor, the value of the town councils was not limited to their collaboration with the imperial representatives for the annual collection of taxes. Tax collecting took them into the very different world of the countryside. The urban *plebs* was not subject to the land tax. It has been estimated that the cities contributed only one-twentieth of the tax budget of the empire.[33] From the fiscal point of view, the later empire was an agrarian society. But the inhabitants of the cities—most especially

31. Fox, *Pagans and Christians,* 322–25; A. Harnack, *Die Mission und Ausbreitung des Christentums* (Leipzig: J. C. Hinrichs, 1924), 127–61; H. L. Strack and P. Billerbeck, *Kommentar zum Neuen Testament aus Talmud und Midrasch* (Munich: C. H. Beck, 1975), 4:536–610. These remain the most comprehensive collections of evidence for early Christianity and Judaism.

32. A. D. Momigliano, "After Gibbon's *Decline and Fall,*" *Annali della Scuola Normale Superiore di Pisa,* ser. 3, 8 (1978): 435–54, now in *Sesto Contributo alla storia degli Studi Classici e del mondo antico* (Rome: Edizioni Storia e Letteratura, 1980), 282–83.

33. A. H. M. Jones, *The Later Roman Empire* (Oxford: Blackwell, 1964), 1:464–65.

those of the major centers of the eastern Mediterranean, whose populations ran to hundreds of thousands—had to be kept quiet. As an outstanding recent study of urban autonomy in North Africa and Italy in the second and third centuries has made plain, the self-government of the cities
had relieved the imperial administration of the need to police the lower
orders. The civic notables were responsible for the good behavior of the
populace. It was for the notables to instill feelings of deference and a respect for law that would ensure a *quietissimus populus,* an *innocens ordo.*[34]

This had remained the case in the fourth century. The maintenance of
deference was a constant preoccupation of the urban upper classes.[35] It was
important, for Libanius, that he should be greeted by the shopkeepers as
he passed through Antioch: "'Decent and polite, isn't he? He replies in
kind to the greetings even of the penniless.' . . . they like the sight and
sound of me."[36] His students were prepared for civic life by learning to
show a well-bred civility to their inferiors: "May an artisan never be roughly
handled by a boy dedicated to *paideia.* He must learn to live at peace with
such people and never be considered unworthy of the praises of those who
earn their bread with the work of their hands."[37]

Above all, the resident notable was expected to act as a spokesman and
patron for members of the lower classes. Libanius was proud of his record
in this respect. He protected artisans and, especially, the members of the
bakers' guild. At a time of rising prices in 382–383, the governor decided to
placate the populace by ordering the public flogging of a group of bakers:

> He sat there in his carriage and inquired at every stroke how much had gone
> in bribes and to whom, for them to charge prices like this for bread. . . . I
> approached in all ignorance, following my usual path. I heard the sound of
> the lash, so dear to the common folk who were all agog at the sight of the
> bleeding backs. . . . Straightway I parted the crowd with my hands, and ad-
> vanced to the wheel, silent and reproachful. There I spoke out loud and long
> . . . that if he did not abate his wrath, he would see a morrow such as he would
> not wish to see.[38]

34.   François Jacques, *Le Privilège de la Liberté,* Collection de l'école française de Rome
76 (Rome: Palais Farnèse, 1984), 801, 379–404.
35.   Peter Brown, "Dalla 'plebs romana' alla 'plebs Dei': Aspetti della cristianizzazione
di Roma," in *Passatopresente 2* (Turin: Giapichelli, 1982), 126–27.
36.   Libanius, *Oratio* 2.6 (I.240–241), in *Libanius: Selected Works 2,* ed. and trans. A. F.
Norman, Loeb Classical Library (Cambridge, Mass.: Harvard University Press, 1977), 12;
cf. Eunapius, *Lives of the Philosophers* 481, in Wright, *Philostratus and Eunapius,* 462.
37.   Libanius, *Oratio* 58.4 (IV.468), trans. A. J. Festugière, *Antioche paienne et chrétienne,* Bibliothèque des écoles françaises d'Athènes et de Rome 194 (Paris: E. de Boccard,
1959), 468.
38.   Libanius, *Oratio* 1.208 (I.176), in *Libanius' Autobiography,* ed. and trans. A. F. Norman, (London: Oxford University Press, 1965), 113, 207–8.

One of the most vehemently expressed concerns of Libanius in his old age was that, if young notables were unwilling or incompetent to speak out before governors, they would lose the respect of their lower-class clients. A manual laborer would not look up to a notable who was unable to defend himself, let alone others.[39] Disrespect for town councillors on the part of a governor was a serious matter. It meant the erosion of the subtle ties of deference and patronage that guaranteed the safety of the city.[40]

The situation in the fourth century was truly dangerous. The deference exacted by the upper classes was based, in part, on their involvement in the economic life of the city. From the greatest cities of the empire to the smallest, a proportion of the foodstuffs consumed by the urban populace came from the estates of the notables. Much of the income of the urban upper classes was realized from the sale of food, especially of grain and wine, to an urban market.[41] Those who expected deference, in the well-bred manner that Libanius advocated, were precisely those who could be accused of oppressing the populace through engineering food shortages and taking advantage of the consequent steep rise in prices, or through failing to sell at sufficiently low prices the foodstuffs provided by the emperor for the city. Both the Caesar Gallus in 354 and the emperor Julian in 362–363 held the town council of Antioch responsible for the high price of food during their residences in the city.[42] In Rome, the beautiful townhouse in Trastevere owned by L. Aurelius Avianius Symmachus (the father of Quintus Aurelius Symmachus, the orator and upholder of the old religion) was set on fire by a mob in 375, "spurred on by the fact that a common fellow among the plebeians had alleged . . . that [Symmachus] had said that he would rather use his wine for quenching lime-kilns than sell it at the price which the people had hoped for."[43] If the web of patronage and deference that was supposed to guarantee the good behavior of the

---

39.   Libanius, *Oratio* 35.7 (III.213), in Festugière, *Antioche,* 485.

40.   Libanius, *Oratio* 33.11 (III.171), in Norman, *Libanius 2,* 204.

41.   Lellia Cracco Ruggini, *Economia e società nell'Italia Annonaria* (Milan: A. Giuffre, 1961), 112–52; Peter Garnsey, *Famine and Food Shortage in the Graeco-Roman World* (Cambridge: Cambridge University Press, 1988), 257–68; M. Wörrle, *Stadt und Fest im kaiserzeitlichen Kleinasien,* Vestigia 39 (Munich: C. H. Beck, 1988), 66–68. See J. Durliat, *De la ville antique à la ville byzantine,* Collection de l'école française de Rome 136 (Rome: Palais Farnèse 1990), 514–39 and 564–602. This important study presents the imperial administration as the exclusive provider of basic foodstuffs for all major cities. If valid, this view would modify the model, of extensive private commerce, assumed by all other authors.

42.   J. H. W. G. Liebeschuetz, *Antioch: City and Imperial Administration in the Later Roman Empire* (Oxford: Clarendon Press, 1972), 129–31; John Matthews, *The Roman Empire of Ammianus* (London: Duckworth, 1989), 406–14. Durliat, *De la ville antique à la ville byzantine,* 360–65, sees the town council as no more than administrators of imperial food supplies. This is too trenchant a conclusion in this case.

43.   Ammianus Marcellinus, *Res gestae* 27.3.4; Symmachus, *Epp.* 1.44, 2.38.

lower classes could be unravelled so swiftly by such incidents, then it is not surprising that men such as Libanius felt that they had to work so hard to maintain it.

The town councils faced the people of their cities with virtually no coercive force. The armies were usually stationed at a considerable distance from the major urban centers of the Mediterranean. Only in quite exceptional circumstances were units of regular troops sent in to impose order.[44] In the normal course of affairs, the governor had only a small retinue; this group, however, might include archers to deal with an emergency.[45] The normal maintenance of law and order in a late Roman city devolved on the heads of artisan guilds and on the headmen of neighborhoods. They, at least, could be held responsible for any disorder, after the event.[46]

In Rome, a gigantic conglomeration of almost half a million inhabitants in the fourth century, the three urban cohorts and the seven units of urban *vigiles* set up by Augustus had been allowed to melt away. The prefects of Rome found themselves with no armed force whatsoever at their disposal.[47] When the mob attempted to torch his house in 365, the prefect Lampadius beat a hasty retreat to the far side of the Milvian Bridge, "as though to wait there for the cessation of the tumult," leaving his neighbors, with their household servants, to drive off the attackers by pelting them with stones and tiles from the housetops.[48] The very next year his successor, Viventius, was faced by riots caused by a disputed election to the bishopric of Rome. On one day, 137 corpses of the slain were found after a clash in the large basilica of Sicinnius, the future Santa Maria Maggiore.[49] Viventius "was able neither to end nor to diminish this strife, . . . was compelled to yield to its great violence, and retired to the suburbs."[50] Alexandria, a notoriously riot-prone city, was equally devoid of regular police: governors entered the city "in fear and trembling."[51]

Rome, Antioch, and Alexandria were exceptionally large and disintegrated cities by ancient standards. But they were the most brilliant representatives of urban life in the Roman world. What happened in their streets set the tone for smaller cities and was watched anxiously by the imperial court. Throughout the Mediterranean, therefore, town councillors were responsible for the good behavior of urban populations, whom they had

44. Liebeschuetz, *Antioch,* 126.
45. Libanius, *Oratio* 19.35–36 (II.401–2), in Norman, *Libanius 2,* 290.
46. Liebeschuetz, *Antioch,* 122–24; *Codex Theodosianus* 16.4.5 (A.D. 404).
47. Jones, *Later Roman Empire* 2:693.
48. Ammianus Marcellinus, *Res gestae* 27.3.8–9.
49. Ibid., 27.3.13.
50. Ibid., 27.3.12.
51. *Expositio Totius Mundi et Gentium* 37, ed. J. Rougé, Sources chrétiennes 124 (Paris: Le Cerf, 1966), 174.

no means to control other than traditional, frail skills of urban leadership, inherited from earlier centuries.

Hence a "representation" of the notable's relation to his city continued to have relevance throughout the fourth century. It goes without saying that this representation was as stylized, and as deliberately blind to many aspects of late Roman reality, as was the very different representation propounded by many Christians. But it still made sense of much of late Roman civic life. It summed up centuries of experience of urban politics. Instilled as part of the educational process associated with *paideia* and consequently expressed in highly traditional terms, an image of their role in the city formed part of the collective mentality of the urban upper classes all over the Greek world (as it did, also, in a slightly different manner, but with the same tenacity, among the resident members of the Senate of Rome). Phrases from late antique inscriptions from many cities and the frequent occurrence of images taken from the language of urban generosity in the sermons of contemporary Christian preachers show that, far from being the product of an archaizing rhetoric, a traditional representation of the ancient city remained an enduring and weighty presence in the minds of contemporaries.[52]

What was at stake was the use of wealth in the city. As predominant landowners, often controlling extensive networks of transport and the means of trade, the urban upper classes controlled much of the wealth of their locality.[53] This economic predominance was supposed to be transmuted, through a traditional image of the urban community, into a gracious and paternal relationship. The town councillors were "fathers" of the *démos,* the *plebs.*[54] The good notable was a "nourisher," a *tropheus,* to his city.[55] He repaid the "nurture" which his city had bestowed upon him in his youth by means of a continuous stream of gifts.[56] These gifts were directed to the city as a whole—in the form of buildings—or to a clearly defined group of beneficiaries, to the *démos,* that is, to the citizen body of the city as distinct from the town council—in the form of distributions of money and food.

52.   See the classic exploration of Christian preaching to illustrate an epigraphic theme in L. Robert, *Hellenica* 13 (1965): 226–27.

53.   C. R. Whittaker, "Later Roman Trade and Traders," in *Trade in the Ancient Economy,* ed. P. Garnsey, K. Hopkins, and C. R. Whittaker (Berkeley: University of California Press, 1983), 169–80.

54.   Libanius, *Oratio* 11.51 (I.486–87), in "Libanius' Oration in Praise of Antioch," trans. G. Downey, *Proceedings of the American Philosophical Society* 103 (1959): 669; Paul Veyne, *Le Pain et le Cirque* (Paris: Le Seuil, 1976), 271–327, trans. *Bread and Circuses* (London: Allen Lane Penguin Press, 1990), 131–56; Evelyne Patlagean, *Pauvreté économique et pauvreté sociale à Byzance* (Paris: Mouton, 1977), 181–88. See M. Sartre, *L'Orient romain. Provinces et sociétès provinciales* (Paris: Le Seuil, 1991), 163–66.

55.   Robert, *Hellenica* 13 (1965): 226–27.

56.   Charlotte Roueché, *Aphrodisias in Late Antiquity,* Journal of Roman Studies Monographs 5 (London: Society for the Promotion of Roman Studies, 1989), 46.

Just as the innate superiority of a wellborn man was brought to its finest polish through *paideia,* so *eunoia,* unfailing goodwill to one's hometown; *euergesia,* the urge to do good things for the city; and *megalopsychia,* a high-minded zest for open-handed gestures of largesse, were held to run in the blood of a notable. A fifth-century mosaic from a great villa at Daphne, in the suburbs of Antioch, shows *megalopsychia* personified, with gold coins streaming from her outstretched hand.[57] Already on his wedding night, the young notable was sent to join his bride with the stirring admonition: "Go fight in a manner worthy of your fathers . . . so that you can provide children for the city, who will flourish in letters, in generosity, in charitable benefactions."[58] Lavish spending was supposed to be a family tradition: notables "had their forebears as teachers of good-will towards the city. . . . For these men inherited their ancestral property by good fortune, and spend it freely by their generosity."[59]

Their wealth, then, was not a matter of good luck; still less could it be said to rest on exploitation. It was wealth held "for the common benefit."[60] It provided the opportunity to display the most desirable of personal qualities, an "innate high-mindedness" that would let no notable rest content until he had spent more on his city than had any of his peers and had ensured, by so doing, that his city was the envy of all others.[61]

Preaching against vainglory in Antioch, the priest John Chrysostom (himself a pupil of Libanius') conjured up the scene that was still regarded as the high moment of the career of an Antiochene notable:

> The theater is filling up, and all the people are sitting aloft presenting a splendid sight and composed of numberless faces. . . . You can see neither tiles nor stones but all is men's bodies and faces. Then, as the benefactor who has brought them together enters in the sight of all, they stand up and as from a single mouth cry out. All with one voice call him protector and ruler of the city that they share in common, and stretch out their hands in salutation . . . they liken him to the greatest of rivers . . . they call him the Nile of gifts . . . and say that he in his lavish gifts is what the Ocean is among waters. . . . What next? The great man bows to the crowd and in this way shows his regard for them. Then he sits down amid the congratulations of his admiring peers, each of whom prays that he himself may attain to the same eminence.[62]

57.   Patlagean, *Pauvreté,* 183.

58.   Menander, *Epideictica* 2.406, 408, in *Menander,* ed. and trans. D. A. Russell and N. G. Wilson (Oxford: Clarendon Press, 1981), 149, 151.

59.   Libanius, *Oratio* 11.133–34 (I.480–81), trans. Downey, p. 667.

60.   Libanius, *Oratio* 11.133 (I.480), trans. Downey, p. 667.

61.   Libanius, *Oratio* 11.138 (I.482), trans. Downey, pp. 667–68.

62.   John Chrysostom, *De inani gloria* 4–5, in *Christianity and Pagan Culture in the Later Roman Empire,* trans. M. L. W. Laistner, (Ithaca, N.Y.: Cornell University Press, 1951), 87–88; A. M. Malingrey, ed., *Jean Chrysostome: Sur la vaine gloire et l'éducation des enfants,* Sources chrétiennes 188 (Paris: Le Cerf, 1972), 74–79.

What the notable was expected to give and to whom were clearly laid down by tradition. It was the city as a whole that received most benefactions. Public giving was intended to make the city a place of dazzling amenities, an oasis of *apolausis,* of civic "good cheer" and "delight," sharply distinguished from the deprived conditions of the surrounding countryside.[63] Hence there was persistent emphasis on maintaining the facades of public buildings, on the sheer sensuous delight of elaborate pools and fountains that brought clear water to the heart of sweltering Levantine cities, on the high ceremonies associated with the public games, and on the embellishment of the theaters and hippodromes in which such ceremonials took place. These were deliberately grandiose, distant, if impressive, gestures. They were designed to confirm the impression of an innate *eunoia,* of an ungrudging goodwill, on the part of the individual notables towards their city.

The principal recipients of such giving were the *démos,* the citizen body in a strict, ancient sense. The *démos* did not cover all inhabitants in the city. A notable was obliged only to his "fellow citizens." For only they had been "nurtured" by the same city as himself. Though far less wealthy than their benefactors, the members of the *démos* of Antioch were solid, married householders and the descendants of citizens.[64] They were, indeed, just the sort of artisans and laborers whose deference Libanius had elicited by civility and patronage. The more prosperous of them, as headmen and members of guilds, were responsible for keeping order in the city's neighborhoods.

It was crucial for the self-image of the traditional city that the *démos* should not consist only of the poor. Indeed, the exact opposite was the case. The homeless and destitute were excluded. The "Nile of gifts" fell on every class that had an active stake in the city, from the highest downwards, like water cascading over the cataracts of a mighty river. For the care for all classes in their city exercised by urban benefactors mirrored, and so validated, the vast care of the emperor himself for all classes within his empire.[65]

The citizen body was no abstraction in late antiquity. It became a reality by assembling on frequent occasions in the great theaters and hippodromes that remained an enduring feature of late Roman urban life. The hippodrome of Antioch had room for 80,000 persons,[66] the theater of Ephesus,

---

63. Patlagean, *Pauvreté,* 183; *Expositio Totius Mundi,* ed. Rougé, pp. 245–46.

64. Libanius, *Oratio* 11.151 (I.486), trans. Downey, p. 669.

65. This is clearly seen in Richard Gordon, "The Veil of Power: Emperors, Sacrificers and Benefactors," in *Pagan Priests,* ed. Mary Beard and John North (Ithaca, N.Y.: Cornell University Press, 1990), 220–30; see also Wörrle, *Stadt und Fest,* 254.

66. John H. Humphrey, *Roman Circuses* (Berkeley: University of California Press, 1986), 444–61.

for 24,000.[67] The theater of Aphrodisias in Caria held 8,000, the smaller odeon, 1,700, and the stadium beside the walls of the city, 30,000.[68] These gigantic meeting places would not always have been full. Those at major provincial capitals had room for visitors from neighboring cities and, even, for the villagers of the region. Yet seated row upon row in this manner, the theater crowd *was* the city. It was at the theater that the Antiochenes made their wishes known to the governors by means of carefully orchestrated acclamations. Their occasional stony silence was enough to cause an unpopular governor to turn pale with anger and anxiety.[69]

Thus assembled, the *démos* was a diverse body. The inscriptions scratched on the benches in the theater and in the stadium of Aphrodisias make this plain. We find seats marked for "younger men," for "Jews," for "the elders of the Jews," for the supporters of the Blue and Green racing factions, for the butchers, the tanners, the gardeners, and the goldsmiths.[70] But it was always a community of those who belonged. To be a member of the *démos* one had to come from a citizen family and, as the case of Aphrodisias now shows, one had to be a member of a recognized civic group. Urban amenities, even theaters, were likely to be open to all comers; but entitlement to other forms of gifts — most particularly entitlement to free or cheap food — required proof of identity.[71] Those entitled could be trusted to police the distributions of food: the Roman *plebs* was notorious for "crying out" against outsiders of whatever class or region in times of shortage.[72]

The traditional representation of the city, therefore, was made up of rigidly defined components. Only a certain group, the core of the traditional community, considered themselves entitled to the gifts of the notables. Even in small cities, not all inhabitants were members of this group: much of the lower-class population was left unaccounted for. The gifts themselves were highly formalized and rather distant. In late Roman conditions, their quantity and frequency were seriously diminished. Higher taxation, and the large sums now required for the pursuit of office and status within the imperial system, meant that surplus wealth was no longer available

67. Clive Foss, *Ephesus after Antiquity* (Cambridge: Cambridge University Press, 1979), 61.

68. Kenan T. Erim, *Aphrodisias* (New York: Facts on File, 1986), 79, 62, 68.

69. Libanius, *Oratio* 41.3, 5 (III.296), 301–2); idem, *Ep.* 811.4 (X.734); Liebeschuetz, *Antioch,* 211–19.

70. Roueché, *Aphrodisias in Late Antiquity,* 218–26. See C. Roueché, *Performers and Partisans at Aphrodisias,* Journal of Roman Studies Monographs 6 (London: Society for the Promotion of Roman Studies 1992).

71. R. J. Rowland, "The 'Very Poor' and the Grain Dole at Rome and Oxyrhynchus," *Zeitschrift für Papyrologie und Epigraphik* 21 (1976): 69–72.

72. Ammianus Marcellinus, *Res gestae* 14.6.19, 28.4.32; Ambrose, *De officiis* 3.45.

for potential "nourishers" to spend on their city. Far from betraying an innate urge to show goodwill to their fellow citizens, the gestures required of civic notables, such as the upkeep of the public baths and the regular provision of games in the theater or hippodrome, were imposed upon them by the imperial government. Never, perhaps, as wholehearted as they claimed to be, acts of *euergesia* were now extorted from the wealthy like any other tax—and were as frequently evaded.[73]

Nor did the notables have control over the impact of *euergesia* on the populace. The actual staging of the games ceased to be a purely local matter. It required constant imperial intervention. The cost of mobilizing wild animals and pedigreed racehorses from all over the empire had increased dramatically. It was only through collaboration with the imperial administration that games offered by members of the town council could take place at all.[74] They took place less often, and in fewer towns. The great hunting shows offered by one of the leading families of Antioch had to be postponed for as many as seven years.[75] When such shows did happen, they were presented in such a way as to foster loyalty to the emperor and his representatives, and only indirectly to heighten the prestige of the resident upper classes of the city. Altogether, in the conditions of the fourth century, the economic power of the leading town councillors, and their consequent responsibility for the well-being of the city, was as blatant as ever previously. But now they were more often seen as scapegoats rather than as "nourishers."

Everyone sensed the dangers which the notables faced in their cities. The relations of the great Roman families with a potentially riotous *plebs* formed a major theme in the life of a fourth-century senator such as Symmachus: it is one of the few issues on which he spoke with feeling in his letters.[76] The account of fourth-century Rome left by Ammianus Marcellinus contains memorable scenes of successful confrontation, in which the urban prefect, frequently (though not invariably) a senator and a long-established resident of the city, faced down potential disorder. Leontius drove slowly in his official coach through an ominous mob: "Seated in his carriage, with every appearance of confidence he scanned with keen eyes the faces of the crowd in their tiers."[77] The very sound of the rumble of the wheels of the prefect's coach was supposed to inspire respect.[78]

73.   A. Marcone, "L'allestimento dei giochi a Roma nel iv secolo d.C.," *Annali della Scuola Normale Superiore di Pisa*, ser. 3, 11 (1981): 105–22.

74.   Brown, "Dalla 'plebs romana' alla 'plebs Dei,'" 137.

75.   Paul Petit, *Libanius et la vie municipale à Antioche au ive. siècle après J.C.* (Paris: P. Geuthner, 1955), 129.

76.   J. F. Matthews, "The Letters of Symmachus," in *Latin Literature of the Fourth Century*, ed. J. W. Binns (London: Routledge and Kegan Paul, 1975), 70–73.

77.   Ammianus Marcellinus, *Res gestae* 15.7.4.

78.   Cassiodorus, *Institutiones* 1.5, ed. R. A. B. Mynors (Oxford: Clarendon Press, 1937),

Others were forced to plead with the *plebs*. At a time of famine, the prefect Tertullus "held out his little sons to the wildly riotous populace . . . and said with tears: 'Behold your fellow-citizens, who with you will endure the same fate.'"[79]

These stories were told because they had a happy ending. They showed that some notables, at least, could still count on reserves of traditional deference in their dealings with the lower classes. But neither Ammianus nor Libanius was confident that the traditional relation with the *démos* would inevitably prove effective. A notable from Beirut, known to Libanius, refused to become prefect of Rome: he knew too much of the habitual tension between Senate and *plebs* to welcome such a post.[80] A few incidents of violence were all that was needed to create an atmosphere of chilling anxiety. Of the lynching of one governor in Antioch at a time of famine in 354, Ammianus wrote, "After his wretched death each man saw in the end of one person an image of his own peril."[81] Libanius recalled the grisly incident some forty years later, as a warning to the town council.[82]

Yet as in eighteenth-century England, the "license of the crowd" was the price that the civic notables were prepared to pay for the relative autonomy of their cities.[83] Even when rioting, the crowd was still *their* crowd. Its worst violence had taken the form of lynching, which in the famine of 354 at Antioch would not have happened if the Caesar Gallus had not virtually handed over the victim to the Antiochene mob.[84] The riots had not, within living memory, escalated into full-scale uprisings.

Rioting took the form of "swift, evanescent direct action" against individual unpopular figures.[85] It usually reached its climax in attempts to torch the palaces of powerful residents.[86] On one such occasion, Libanius remembered looking out to see smoke rising from an unpopular town councillor's mansion, as the man and his family withdrew, precipitately, to the hills.[87] At times, popular violence even merged with the festive life of the city. In the heady nights of the Kalends of January, the "ranks of the city are overturned and renewed" (to use the words of a fifth-century Syriac poet).[88]

---

81. This referred to the monk's fear of the dread approach of Christ at the Last Judgment. I owe this reference to the kindness of Dr. S. J. B. Barnish.

79.   Ammianus Marcellinus, *Res gestae* 19.10.2–3.

80.   Libanius, *Ep.* 391.14 (X.387).

81.   Ammianus Marcellinus, *Res gestae* 14.7.6.

82.   Libanius, *Oratio* 46.29 (III.393).

83.   E. P. Thompson, "Eighteenth-Century English Society," *Social History* 3 (1978): 145.

84.   Ammianus Marcellinus, *Res gestae* 14.7.6.

85.   Thompson, "Patrician Society, Plebeian Culture," 402; Ammianus Marcellinus, *Res gestae* 27.3.4; see Symmachus, *Epp.* 1.44, 2.38, and *Oratio* 5.1, for the case of Symmachus.

86.   Ammianus Marcellinus, *Res gestae* 14.7.6, 27.3.8; Ambrose, *Ep.* 40.15.

87.   Libanius, *Oratio* 1.103 (I.133), in Norman, *Libanius' Autobiography*, 62.

88.   Isaac of Antioch, *Homily on the Night Vigil*, line 17, in *Homiliae S. Isaaci Syri An-*

Even the emperor could be mocked, as Julian had been, by wicked ditties sung in the streets during the festival.[89] It was an occasion for the populace to assert its right to riot. In 384 the Kalends proved a dangerous time for Candidus, a notable held responsible for the food shortages of the preceding summer: "He sat at home and covered his face . . . all fear and trembling for his own palace, as a torrent of lads bore down upon it, torch in hand, calling upon him to disgorge what he had unjustly consumed."[90]

It was, indeed, the tolerance with which such license was treated in the cities, and the relative ease with which outbursts of violence were defused, that is the most striking feature of the urban life of the empire in the generations preceding the reign of Theodosius I.[91] Civic notables and imperial administration alike accepted a looseness of authority in the cities that they would never have tolerated in the countryside. Urban food riots, clashes between competing religious groups, and, later, fights between rival circus factions were regarded with relative insouciance. They seemed to be part and parcel of the dazzling *ambitio,* the boisterous pride of life, associated with big-city living.[92] They were treated as very different phenomena from the unremitting, grim war on brigandage waged throughout the countryside of the eastern empire and the obscure but tenacious menace of the Bagaudae in rural Gaul and northern Spain.[93]

Yet it was a strictly conditional tolerance. The notables might weather the occasional riot, but a more serious uprising, even if it did not lead to great loss of life or destruction of property, was a "governmental catastrophe" for them.[94] They were held accountable for the disorder. After a riot against the Christians in Alexandria in 366, "many town-councillors were reduced to the last extreme of affliction" in the investigation that fol-

---

tiocheni, ed. P. Bedjan, (Leipzig: O. Harassowitz, 1903); S. Landersdorfer, trans., *Ausgewählte Schriften der syrischen Dichter,* Bibliothek der Kirchenväter (Munich: J. Kosel, 1913), 212.

89.   Maud W. Gleason, "Festive Satire: Julian's *Misopôgon* and the New Year at Antioch," *Journal of Roman Studies* 76 (1986): 108–14.

90.   Libanius, *Oratio* 1.230 (I.184), in Norman, *Libanius' Autobiography,* 121.

91.   H. P. Kohns, *Versorgungskrisen und Hungerrevolten in spätantiken Rom,* Antiquitas 1.6 (Bonn: R. Habelt, 1961), 104–8; Lellia Cracco Ruggini, "Felix Temporum Reparatio," in *L'Eglise et l'empire au ive. siècle,* ed. A. Dihle, Entretiens de la Fondation Hardt 34 (Vandoeuvres: Fondation Hardt, 1989), 229.

92.   Ammianus Marcellinus, *Res gestae* 27.3.14.

93.   Brent Shaw, "Bandits in the Roman Empire," *Past and Present* 105 (1984): 3–52; K. Hopwood, "Bandits, Elites and Rural Order," in *Patronage in Ancient Society,* ed. A. Wallace-Hadrill (New York: Routledge and Kegan Paul, 1990), 171–87; J. Drinkwater, "Patronage in Roman Gaul and the Problem of the Bagaudae," in *Patronage in Ancient Society,* 189–204.

94.   W. Beik, *Absolutism and Society in Seventeenth-Century France* (Cambridge: Cambridge University Press, 1985), 191.

lowed.[95] This was not all: a riot called into question the town council's ability to control the city. Once the civic notables could no longer vouch for the peace of the cities, their credibility with the imperial government was severely weakened.

Lovers of the Poor

The peace of the cities, therefore, proved to be the Achilles' heel of the traditional civic elites. By the end of the fourth century they were faced by a rival. The "universal way" of a religion that claimed to dispense with the advantages of *paideia* was not simply a cultural challenge. It took social form: in the city itself, the organization of the Christian church touched more people and was shown to generate a more effective level of deference than did the impressive, but relatively infrequent and somewhat distant, public appearances of the notables.

Why this should have happened is a complex story that admits no simple answer. The privileges lavished on the Christian church by Constantine and Constantius II constituted a grandiose overture to the later position of the churches.[96] The use of force against temples of the gods in the reign of Constantius II shows that some bishops already felt that they could act with impunity. Their violence, in itself, constituted a claim to stand for the majority of the population of their cities.[97] Paradoxically, the frequent divisions of the Christians throughout the fourth century may have contributed more to the assertiveness of the churches in local society than did imperial favor and imperial connivance at isolated acts of violence.

Late Roman cities were characterized by massive underemployment.[98] The many phases of the Arian controversy in the East and the Donatist schism in North Africa provided the inhabitants of these cities with endless occasions for argument and for confrontation. Educated Christians spoke, though not always with enthusiasm, of the involvement of all classes in their quarrels: "If you ask about your change, the shopkeeper talks theology to you, on the Begotten and the Unbegotten; if you inquire the price of a loaf, the reply is: 'The Father is greater and the Son is inferior'; and if you

95.   Annick Martin and Micheline Albert, *"Histoire Acéphale" et Index Syriaque des lettres festales d'Athanase d'Alexandrie,* Sources chrétiennes 319 (Paris: Le Cerf, 1985), 268.

96.   C. Pietri, *Roma christiana,* Bibliothèque des écoles françaises d'Athènes et de Rome 224 (Rome: Palais Farnèse, 1976), 1:77–96; idem, "La politique de Constance II: Un premier "césaropapisme" ou *imitatio Constantini?*" in Dihle, *L'Eglise et l'empire,* 140.

97.   T. D. Barnes, "Christians and Pagans under Constantius," in Dihle, *L'Eglise et l'empire,* 324–27.

98.   Patlagean, Pauvreté, 170.

say, 'Is the bath ready?' the attendant affirms that the Son is of nothing."[99]

Christian controversies mobilized individual congregations of believers within each city, provoking, on occasions, major riots,[100] and frequent processions and counterprocessions.[101] All over the empire, Christian factionalism led to a perceptible increase in the climate of violence.[102] Whether violence was widespread or not, accusations of violence were a standard feature of Christian polemics against rival Christian groups. Ammianus Marcellinus understandably concluded that Christian groups behaved to each other "like wild beasts."[103]

Such sporadic violence, in itself, would hardly have commended the Christian churches to the authorities as guarantors of law and order in the cities. But the violence betrayed the growth of local organizations able to mobilize and control large congregations. Rival churches competed by replicating the social services provided by their opponents. The bishop's control of almsgiving, for instance, became a hotly contested issue. Almsgiving was used to secure support. Already in the third century Cyprian of Carthage had distributed funds for the poor in such a way as to reward only those who remained loyal to him.[104] In the fourth century both Donatus, bishop of Carthage, and Athanasius of Alexandria complained that the authorities had taken away, or substituted, alms traditionally distributed by themselves to the loyal poor of their congregations.[105] From services to the poor to new basilicas, the Christian presence was heightened by men in a hurry.[106] Each Christian group was anxious to leave a permanent mark on the city. In the same way, the most poignant statements on the unity and potential comprehensiveness of the Christian church were made by preachers whose congregations were, in fact, in a minority among competing Christian factions. This was true both of Augustine, in an Africa where every city was divided between Donatists and Catholics, and of John Chrysostom, as priest of the beleaguered "orthodox" community in Antioch.[107]

99.   Gregory of Nyssa, De deitate Filii et Spiritus Sancti: Patrologia Graeca 46:557.

100.   Socrates, Ecclesiastical History 2.13.

101.   Socrates, Ecclesiastical History 6.8; Sozomen, Ecclesiastical History 8.8.

102.   Ramsay MacMullen, "The Historical Role of the Masses in Late Antiquity," in Changes in the Roman Empire (Princeton: Princeton University Press, 1990), 267–76.

103.   Ammianus Marcellinus, Res gestae 22.5.4.

104.   Cyprian, Ep. 5.1.2, 12.2.2; see esp. G. W. Clarke, trans., The Letters of Saint Cyprian, Ancient Christian Writers (New York: Newman Press, 1984), 1:163.

105.   Optatus of Milevis, De schismate Donatistarum 3.3; see G. A. Cecconi, "Elemosina e propaganda: Un'analisi della 'Macariana persecutio' nel III libro di Ottato di Milevi," Revue des études augustiniennes 36 (1990): 42–66; Athanasius, Historia Arianorum 61.2.

106.   R. Krautheimer, Three Christian Capitals: Topography and Politics (Berkeley: University of California Press, 1983), 88–92.

107.   Peter Brown, Augustine of Hippo (Berkeley: University of California Press, 1967),

Imperial support and vigorous infighting go some way to account for the impact of Christian congregations on the cities of the fourth century. What is significant, however, is the manner in which the Christian bishops and clergy consistently presented their claims to prominence. This was based on the singling out for particular concern of a category of persons that had no place in the traditional model of the urban community. The bishop was a "lover of the poor," and the wealth of the church was the "wealth of the poor": "A bishop that loveth the poor, the same is rich, and the city and its district shall honor him."[108]

Urban notables had presented themselves as standing at the head of an entire social hierarchy, made up of all active participants in the life of the city. The Christian bishop, by contrast, erected his claim to authority over a social void. The poor were defined as those who belonged to no urban grouping. The butchers and tanners of Aphrodisias in Caria might be humble persons, even impoverished by modern criteria; but by inscribing their names on the benches of the stadium and by sitting there as a clearly recognizable group through the long ceremonies that celebrated the prosperity and loyalty of their city, they staked out a claim to be considered members of the *démos,* of the traditional urban community.[109] By contrast, in the opinion of Libanius, the poor had no place in the theater: outcasts without home or city could never be considered members of a citizen body.[110] If the poor had figured at all on civic occasions, it had been as actors in paradoxical gestures by the great that consciously mocked the traditional claim of citizens to be the exclusive recipients of gifts from civic benefactors. This happened in Rome around 335–340: Lampadius was

a man who took it very ill if even his manner of spitting was not praised, on the ground that he did that also with greater skill than anyone else. . . . When this man, in his praetorship [that is, at the beginning of his career] gave magnificent games and made very rich largesses, being unable to endure the blustering of the *plebs,* who often urged that many things should be given [to the performers] . . . in order to show his generosity and his contempt for the mob, he summoned some beggars from the Vatican hill [a graveyard area occupied by beggars long before it became the site of the shrine of Saint Peter] and presented them with valuable gifts.[111]

225; R. L. Wilken, *John Chrysostom and the Jews: Rhetoric and Reality in the Late Fourth Century* (Berkeley: University of California Press, 1983), 16, 159.

108. Ps.-Athanasius, *Canon 14,* in *The Canons of Athanasius,* ed. and trans. W. Reidel and W. E. Crum (Amsterdam: Philo Press, 1973), 25–26.

109. Roueché, *Aphrodisias in Late Antiquity,* 225.

110. Libanius, *Oratio* 41.11 (III.300).

111. Ammianus Marcellinus, *Res gestae* 27.3.5.

Nor were the poor "nourished" by anyone. By not belonging to any social group, the poor remained untouched by the care lavished by the great on the city as a whole. Nothing makes this more plain than the crucial issue of entitlement to food, in the form either of free doles or foodstuffs at reduced prices. As the supreme benefactors, the emperors made every effort to maintain the *annona,* the privileged food supply, of Rome, "their" city, of Constantinople, and, apparently, of other late Roman cities.[112] In the later third and fourth centuries imperial measures continued to take the ancient, civic model of the urban community for granted. Whenever emperors gave gifts of food to individual cities, these were made to the citizen body as a whole, irrespective of whether they were rich or poor. Citizen status, not need, gave access to such grants. In late third-century Oxyrhynchus, for instance, Aurelius Melas could not even sign his name in Greek. Like two-thirds of his fellow citizens, Melas was illiterate.[113] He was evidently a humble person. But he did not receive his grain because he was poor; he did so because he was the son and the grandson of citizens of the "most glorious city of Oxyrhynchus . . . and now necessarily pro-ducing . . . the proof of my descent . . . I request that I too may share the gift of grain . . . in like manner with my equals."[114] Only later, Chris-tian sources show us the true poor of Oxyrhynchus, sleeping out on the porch of the main church through the cold desert night, so as not to miss their places in the Sunday distribution of food.[115] This huddling mass of the destitute was not the world of Aurelius Melas. Many were countryfolk and "strangers," refugees from the war-torn South. A rich Christian at Oxyrhynchus could provide as much as one thousand *solidi* per year for the care of the poor—enough to support 250 families. But he provided these sums to monks, to beggars, and to refugees.[116] He was not "nourish-ing" his city.

Altogether, the poor had remained a blank on the notables' map of the city. We should not exaggerate the hardheartedness of pagan attitudes to-wards the poor. It is misleading to speak of the "harsh climate" that char-acterized attitudes to the poor in a world where only the citizen counted.[117]

---

112.   J. M. Carrié, "Les distributions alimentaires dans les cités de l'empire romain tardif," *Mélanges de l'école française de Rome: Antiquité* 87 (1975): 995–1101; P. Herz, *Studien zur römischen Wirtschaftsgesetzgebung,* Historia Einzelschrift 55 (Stuttgart: F. Steiner, 1988), 208–337; Durliat, *De la ville antique à la ville byzantine,* 3–163 (Rome); 185–317 (Constan-tinople); 326–34 (Alexandria); 351–81 (Antioch).

113.   Kaster, *Guardians of Language,* 38.

114.   *Oxyrhynchus Papyri* 40, no. 2898 (London: British Academy, 1972), 46–47.

115.   F. Nau, "Histoire des solitaires d'Egypte," *Revue de l'Orient chrétien* 13 (1908): 282.

116.   Richard Raabe, *Petrus der Iberer* (Leipzig: J. C. Hinrichs, 1895), 61; Syriac text p. 60.

117.   Veyne, *Le Pain et le Cirque,* 58–59; idem, *Bread and Circuses,* 30–31.

We simply do not know in sufficient detail how the destitute were cared for in the small, cohesive towns that were the norm in the Roman Mediterranean. It is possible, for instance, that as many destitute found shelter around the great temples in cities such as Antioch, and in more rural areas, as would later gather in the courtyards of the Christian basilicas.[118] In small Italian towns in the second and early third centuries, many lower-class residents may have been saved from destitution by the banqueting and distributions of largesse offered by the civic notables: in such cities, the poor existed, but they were held above the survival line by a network of institutions that still called them "citizens" and not "the poor."[119]

In the fourth century, however, the numbers of the poor seem to have increased perceptibly in many East Roman cities. Population appears to have risen in the surrounding countryside.[120] Immigration was increased by a tendency for the metropolitan cities to absorb the wealth and the population of lesser provincial centers.[121] Not all such immigrants would have been destitute. But they were "poor" in the sense that they were strangers to the city. As in the "Home Towns" of nineteenth-century Germany, the larger cities, such as Antioch, Alexandria, and Rome, were better able than were small towns to absorb immigrants without having to face immediate conflicts over entitlement.[122] Outsiders faced expulsion only at times of major food shortages. Yet the presence of so many newcomers eroded the sharp distinction between members of the *démos,* many of whom happened to be poor, and other members of the lower classes who, if not "poor" in the strict sense of being destitute, were vulnerable because, as strangers, they were not full members of the *démos.* Such persons were anxious to find a group to which to belong. They might look to other leaders and be grateful for other forms of gifts. Their presence in the city was a dis-

118. Libanius, *Oratio* 2.30, 30.20 (I.248, III.98), in Norman, *Libanius 2,* 26, 118; F. Nau, "Résumé de monographies syriaques," *Revue de l'Orient chrétien* 18 (1913): 385. Barsauma and his monks mingle with the crowd of beggars outside a large temple in Moab. G. W. Bowersock, "The Mechanisms of Subversion in the Roman Provinces," in *Opposition et résistance à l'empire d'Auguste à Trajan,* Entretiens de la Fondation Hardt 33 (Vandoeuvres: Fondation Hardt, 1987), 304–10.

119. S. Mrozek, *Les distributions d'argent et de nourriture dans les villes italiennes du Haut Empire romain,* Collection Latomus 198 (Brussels: Latomus, 1987), 103–6. P. Garnsey, in the *Journal of Roman Studies* 79 (1989): 232, is less optimistic.

120. Patlagean, *Pauvreté,* 231–35; G. Tate, "La Syrie a l'époque byzantine," in *Archéologie et histoire de la Syrie II,* ed. J. M. Dentzer and W. Orthmann (Saarbrücken: Saarbrücker Drückerei, 1989), 107–9.

121. Santo Mazzarino, *Aspetti sociali del quarto secolo* (Roma: Bretschneider, 1951), 251–55.

122. W. Walker, *German Home Towns* (Ithaca, N.Y.: Cornell University Press, 1971), 391–98.

quieting reminder of a larger, less manageable urban community than was the neat, traditional image presented by a man such as Libanius.

Preaching in Antioch, John Chrysostom spoke of the poor as making up one-tenth of the city's population.[123] It is a convincing statistic, similar to the level of destitution current in late medieval Paris.[124] For Chrysostom, these poor belonged as if "to another city."[125] It was by stressing their relationship with the "other city" of the poor that the bishops projected a form of authority within the city that outflanked the traditional leadership of the notables quite as effectively as Christian admiration of the monks, the illiterate heroes of the desert, outflanked their claim to esteem based upon a monopoly of *paideia*.

For the poor stood for the width of the bishop's range of concern. On the social map of the city, they marked the outermost boundary of the "universal way" associated with the Christian church, just as the bookless wisdom of the monks indicated a cultural desert that stretched far beyond the narrow confines of Greek *paideia*. A mystical link was held to bind the bishop to the poor of his city. This link passed through every rank of society, "bracketing," as it were, the whole urban community from the very top to the very bottom, as an all-embracing "people of God." Rich man and beggar alike went down into the baptismal pool and crowded around the altar to receive the Eucharist.[126] Even if it were still a minority, in the face of polytheists and Jews, a church that was seen to reach out to the distant fringe of society, as dramatically represented by the poor, had already established a prospective moral right to stand for the community as a whole.

Love of the poor also provided an acceptable *raison d'être* for the growing wealth of the church. Here, the heightened symbolic role of the bishop as "lover of the poor" resolved a tension that had long existed within the Christian community itself, about who was the authorized giver of gifts within the community. Ideally, Christian almsgiving was not the exclusive province of the rich. For Jews and Christians alike, it was a pious action that redeemed the sins of each believer, irrespective of his or her wealth. Small sums of money would do. Like late Roman cavalry armor, made up of overlapping round scales, the "breastplate of righteousness" put on

123. John Chrysostom, *Homiliae in Matthaeum* 66.3: *Patrologia Graeca* 58:630.
124. B. Geremek, *The Margins of Society in Late Medieval Paris* (Cambridge: Cambridge University Press, 1987), 193–94.
125. John Chrysostom, *De elemosyna* 1: *Patrologia Graeca* 51:261.
126. John Chrysostom, *Baptismal catechism* 2.13, ed. Wenger, p. 140; idem, *Homiliae in I Cor. 10.1: Patrologia Graeca* 51:247AB; Liebeschuetz, *Barbarians and Bishops,* 175–76, 187.

by the believer through almsgiving was made up of innumerable small coins, given frequently to the poor.[127]

In reality, each Christian household tended to provide for its own poor, and the wealthiest families provided most. The house of a rich Christian could be imagined as a center of wealth and protection: "All the poor called Marcellus their patron, and his house was called the house of pilgrims and of the poor."[128] Care of the poor, therefore, was a potential centrifugal force within the Christian community. It favored wealthy families and could bypass the bishop and clergy. It was by a massive gift of alms to the poor that the wealthy widow Lucilla secured the election of one of her servants, Majorinus, as bishop of Carthage in 311.[129] Tracts that describe the ideal order of a church enable us to measure the strength of the current towards a "privatization" of almsgiving, as this was perceived by bishops and clergy in the fourth century: "If any man should do something apart from the bishop, he does it in vain; for it shall not be accounted a good work. . . . For the bishop is well acquainted with those who are in affliction."[130]

Yet the taint of private wealth remained. One had only to enter a church in fourth-century northern Italy and elsewhere to see the manner in which private persons displayed their wealth within the Christian community. The shimmering mosaic floors of the new basilicas were divided up into sections, each one of which bore the name of a donor, of his family, or even portraits of donors.[131] The civic ideal of *euergesia*, the ancient search for personal fame through well-publicized giving, had entered the church in a peculiarly blatant form.

It was essential that the increased wealth of the Christian church, made up as it was of innumerable private benefactions, should be presented as

---

127.   *Baba Bathra* 9a, in *Babylonian Talmud*, trans. M. Simon (London: Soncino Press, 1935), 45. The scales on the horse armor discovered at Dura Europos, now in the National Archaeological Museum at Damascus, are exactly the size of coins.

128.   Acts of Peter 4, in *New Testament Apocrypha,* ed. E. Hennecke and W. Schneemelcher (Philadelphia: Westminster Press, 1965), 2:289.

129.   Augustine, *Ad Catholicos Epistula* 25.73; W. H. C. Frend, *The Donatist Church* (Oxford: Clarendon Press, 1952), 21.

130.   *Didascalia Apostolorum* 9, ed. A. Vööbus, *Corpus Scriptorum Christianorum Orientalium* 402: *Scriptores Syri* 176 (Louvain: C.S.C.O., 1979), 100.

131.   Lizzi, "Ambrose's Contemporaries," 164–65; idem, *Vescovi e strutture ecclesiastiche,* 141–45. I have seen similar panels, for instance, in the garden of the National Archaeological Museum at Damascus. See M. Piccirillo, *I Mosaici di Giordania* (Rome: Quasar, 1986), 68–69, 71, 82–83, 85, 204–5; idem, *Madaba* (Milan: Edizioni Paoline, 1989), 288–89, for further donor portraits. I owe this information to the kindness of Priscilla Henderson of the Australian National University.

the wealth of the Christian community as a whole. And this wealth could not be more effectively disjoined from its family-oriented connotations than when distributed to the nonpersons who huddled on the edge of the community. By melting down the church plate of Milan in order to ransom prisoners of war in the distant Balkans, Ambrose of Milan, in fact, destroyed the memory of those Christian families (supporters of his Arian predecessor) whose names would certainly have been engraved on the edges of the great silver patens and along the rims of the Eucharistic chalices.[132] By being taken into the hands of the bishop, as the "wealth of the poor," the wealth of the church became public wealth. It would be displayed by the bishop in a manner calculated to put all other groups to shame. "The property of the church consists of the support of the destitute. Let pagans enumerate how many captives the temples have ransomed, what doles they have given to the poor, to how many refugees they have provided living allowances."[133]

We do not know, region by region, what the Christian church actually did for the poor in the cities of the later empire.[134] What we do know, from our evidence, is how the care of the poor became a dramatic component of the Christian representation of the bishop's authority in the community.

The activities of the bishop and clergy heightened the visibility of the poor.[135] The buildings of the church replaced temples as spacious new gathering points for the needy. In Ancyra, for instance, "what is wont to happen in great cities occurred here too: for on the portico of the church there

132.   Ambrose, *De officiis* 2.28.136–41; cf. Socrates, *Ecclesiastical History* 4.25. The bishop of Jerusalem was almost deposed on the accusation of a layman, whose gift to the altar, in the form of a silk cloth, was sold by the bishop and later used as the robe of a famous actress. A generation later, Rabbula, bishop of Edessa, was dissuaded from such a sale by those who had donated church plate for the souls of their relatives: *Panegyric on Rabbula,* in *S. Ephraemi Syri, Rabbulae episcopi Edessensis, Balaei et aliorum opera selecta,* ed. J. J. Overbeck, (Oxford: Clarendon Press, 1865), 173.5–7. On such plate, see Marlia Mundell, *Silver from Early Byzantium: The Kaper Karaon and Related Treasures* (Baltimore: Walters Art Gallery, 1986), 68–85.

133.   Ambrose, *Ep.* 18.17.

134.   C. Pietri, "Les pauvres et la pauvreté dans l'Italie de l'Empire chrétien," in *Miscellanea Historiae Ecclesiasticae* 6, Bibliothèque de la Revue d'Histoire ecclésiastique 67 (Brussels: Nieuwelaarts, 1983), 267–300; K. Mentzou-Meimari, "Eparkhiaka evagé idrymata mekhri tou telous tés eikonomakhias," *Byzantina* 11 (1982): 243–308; Judith Herrin, "Ideals of Charity, Realities of Welfare: The Philanthropic Activity of the Byzantine Church," in *Church and People in Byzantium,* ed. R. Morris (Birmingham: Centre for Byzantine, Ottoman and Modern Greek Studies, 1990), 151–64.

135.   John Iliffe, *The African Poor* (Cambridge: Cambridge University Press, 1987), 29, 42.

was gathered a crowd of people, some married, some unmarried, lying there for their daily food."[136]

Attracted to such centers, the poor rapidly came to be mobilized as part of the "symbolic retinue" of the bishop. Their presence in the bishop's following, along with that of monks and of consecrated virgins, symbolized the unique texture of the bishop's power. He was the protector to those persons who owed least to the traditional city, the unmarried and the homeless.[137] On the great feasts of the year, the poor were put on view, through processions and solemn banquets: "This word have we spoken concerning the poor: God hath established the bishop because of the feasts, that he may refresh them at the feasts."[138]

These occasions may not, in fact, have significantly alleviated the state of the poor, but they carried a clear ceremonial message that was closely watched by contemporaries. Ambrose was accused by his enemies of having scattered gold pieces to the poor.[139] His gesture of almsgiving was presented by his enemies as the usurpation of an imperial prerogative. Only the emperor, a man raised by fortune above all concern for wealth, could shower gold, the most precious of all metals, on the populace.[140]

It is significant that ceremonial rivalry of this kind came to be tolerated in the fourth century. By being made visible, the poor were also made amenable to control. A potentially disruptive element on the margins of the great cities, the poor were enlisted to acclaim the bishop and the Christian rich with the same deferential fervor as that with which the *démos* acclaimed the civic notables. Their hands upraised in thanks in the courtyards of great churches now echoed in miniature the solemn scenes in the theater that bound the city to its benefactors.[141]

Compared with the "Nile of gifts" expected of a civic notable, the sums involved on such occasions were minute. The elementary necessities of life—food, clothing, shelter, small coins, and, eventually, a decent burial—not buildings and great games, were the gifts appropriate to the care of the poor.[142] But these outlays happened on a regular basis, and in a more frankly face-to-face manner than was the case with the high ceremonials of a no-

136.   Palladius, *Lausiac History,* trans. R. T. Meyer, Ancient Christian Writers 34 (New York: Newman Press, 1964), 149.

137.   Brown, *Body and Society,* 259–60.

138.   Ps.-Athanasius, *Canon* 16, ed. Reidel and Crum, p. 27.

139.   Ambrose, *Sermo contra Auxentium* 33.

140.   Justinian, *Novella* 105.2.1; Wörrle, *Stadt und Fest,* 129, n. 296.

141.   Paulinus of Nola, *Ep.* 13.11, 13–15.

142.   Palladius, *Dialogus de Vita Johannis Chrysostomi: Patrologia Graeca* 47:22; Durliat, *De la ville antique à la ville byzantine,* 552–58, 176.

table's *euergesia*. They offered a means of fostering goodwill, broken down into smaller units and displayed more frequently, for a trifle of the cost of civic munificence.

Such care was considered necessary. The mobility of the lower classes preoccupied the emperors. In 382 the emperor Valentinian II legislated against vagrancy in Rome. The traditional solution, favored by the upperclass residents, was that all able-bodied beggars should become the slaves or the serfs (depending on their previous status) of those who denounced them to the authorities.[143] The Christian church offered a less-drastic way of stabilizing the population. It bore the cost of keeping the poor in one place. They were enrolled on the *matricula*, on poor rolls kept by the bishop and clergy. These rolls are referred to in cities as far apart as Hippo in North Africa and Edessa in eastern Syria.[144] In becoming the "poor of the church," the poor were stabilized: they could not move to other cities. Begging itself came to require a permit that bore the bishop's signature.[145] It was perhaps for that reason (and not only to increase the appeal of Christianity) that Constantine ostentatiously fostered the expansion of poor relief in major cities. He assigned supplies of food and clothing to the poor of the churches, to be administered by the bishop alone.[146]

Once set in place, such a system could be dismantled only with dangerous results. In Armenia, an alarming rise in vagrancy was said to have resulted from the destruction, by his enemies, of the poorhouses set up by the patriarch Narseh in the 350s.[147] The great hospital founded outside Caesarea by

143. *Codex Theodosianus* 14.18.1; cf. Raabe, *Petrus der Iberer,* 30–31, Syriac text 25.3–5.

144. M. Rouche, "La matricule des pauvres," *Etudes sur l'histoire de la pauvreté,* ed. M. Mollat (Paris: Publications de la Sorbonne, 1974), 1:83–110; M. de Waha, "Quelques réflexions sur la matricule des pauvres," *Byzantion* 46 (1976): 336–54. For Edessa, see *Panegyric on Rabbula,* ed. Overbeck, p. 190.7–8; G. G. Blum, *Rabbula von Edessa, Corpus Scriptorum Christianorum Orientalium* 300: *Subsidia* 34 (Louvain: C.S.C.O., 1969), 71–73. For Hippo, see Augustine, *Ep.* 20*.2, ed. Divjak, p. 95; *Lettres 1*–29*,* 294; Eno, *Saint Augustine: Letters VI,* 134. For Egypt, see Ps.-Athanasius, *Canons,* Coptic fragment, ed. Reidel and Crum, pp. 98, 127.

145. *Council of Chalcedon: Canon 11,* ed. J. J. Mansi, *Sacrorum Conciliorum Nova et Amplissima collectio* (Florence, 1762), 7:364AB; J. Flemming, ed., *Akten der ephesinischen Synode vom Jahre 449,* in *Abhandlungen der königlichen Gesellschaft der Wissenschaften zu Göttingen,* Phil.-hist. Klasse 15.1 (1917): 82.17, trans. 83.25.

146. Athanasius, *Apologia contra Arianos* 18.30; cf. Eusebius, *Life of Constantine* 3.58. The heretic Eunomius was accused of joining the church at that time simply in order to be fed. See R. P. Vaggione, "Some Neglected Fragments of Theodore of Mopsuestia's *Contra Eunomium,*" *Journal of Theological Studies,* n.s., 31 (1980): 413.

147. Faustus of Byzantium, *History of Armenia* 5.31, trans. N. Garsoian, *The Epic Histories Attributed to P'awstos Buzand* (Cambridge, Mass.: Harvard University Press, 1989), 212; N. Garsoian, "Sur le titre du *Protecteur des Pauvres,*" *Revue des études arméniennes,* n.s., 15 (1981): 21–32.

Basil, around 370, avoided the same dangers. It gathered the lepers of the surrounding countryside into a single, carefully controlled sanctuary.[148]

Schemes for the sick, the destitute, and vagrants would never, in themselves, have offered the lower classes of the city a convincing substitute for the ancient ideal of membership in the *démos*. Humble householders would have felt themselves demeaned by being equated with mere beggars. But in the fourth century, the notion of the "poor" itself insensibly widened its scope. Membership of a citizen body still counted in the cities of the Greek East, as, also, in fourth-century Rome. Yet it was an intensely local perception of one's identity. It did not reflect legal practice. Ever since the second century, the universal penal code of the Roman empire had made a single, brutal distinction between *honestiores* and *humiliores,* between the well-to-do and the humble.[149]

The dramatic devaluation of the legal protection associated with citizenship gathered momentum in the fourth century with the increasing adoption of an alternative language of social relations, long current in Jewish and Christian circles. This language looked through the fine distinctions associated with the classical Greco-Roman city. The language of the Psalms echoed a Near Eastern social order, more ancient and more starkly divided. It emphasized the clear disjunction between the "rich," who had the power and, hence, the responsibility to help their fellows, and the "poor," who possessed no means of helping themselves. On this model of society, the "poor" were not simply the destitute. They were *all* persons—beggars, artisans, small householders, clients—who found themselves dependent on the mercy and good graces of the powerful.[150]

It was a representation of society that spoke only too truthfully to large areas of late Roman social life, as experienced by the lower classes in the cities. Nor was it exclusively Christian. The fierce "popular legalism" of cursing tablets—such as those, from the fourth century, discovered in the healing spring of Minerva Sulis at Bath and perspicaciously analyzed by Roger Tomlin—shows that the average late Roman provincial expected his gods to show their power as judges, through punishing theft, perjury, and sorcery.[151] In Egypt, worshipers still approached the gods in ancient terms

148.   Gregory Nazianzen, *Oratio* 43.63: *Patrologia Graeca* 35:577; Sozomen, *Ecclesiastical History* 6.34; Patlagean, *Pauvreté*, 195; T. S. Miller, *The Birth of the Hospital in the Byzantine Empire* (Baltimore: Johns Hopkins University Press, 1985), 50–88; M. Avi-Yonah, "The Bath of the Lepers at Scythopolis," *Israel Exploration Journal* 13 (1963): 325–26.

149.   Patlagean, *Pauvreté*, 11–17. See D. Grodzynski, "Pauvres et indigents, vils et plebéiens," *Studia et Documenta Historiae et Iuris* 53 (1987), 140–218.

150.   G. J. Botterweck and H. Ringgren, eds., *Theologisches Wörterbuch zum alten Testament* (Stuttgart: W. Kohlhammer, 1973), 1:28–43, s.v. *'ebyon*.

151.   R. S. O. Tomlin, "The Curse Tablets," in *The Temple of Sulis Minerva at Bath:*

that paralleled the language of the Hebrew Psalms. They were the outraged "poor," unable to find redress other than through the justice of their
god.[152]

For this reason, the recognition by Constantine of the bishop's court
of arbitration, his *episcopalis audientia,* proved decisive for the elaboration
of a Christian representation of society. For this court gave reality to the
subtle shift by which the bishop, as "lover of the poor," became also the
protector of the lower classes.

The *episcopalis audientia* was not, by any means, a court open only to
the humble. By the end of the fourth century it depended for its jurisdic-
tion on the agreement of both parties to abide by the bishop's judgment.[153]
These parties could be rich landowners. Some even became Christians in
order to avail themselves of the services of the bishop, as a cheap and ex-
peditious arbitrator.[154] Bishops were frequently accused of siding with the
wealthy in their courts.[155] Nor was there anything exotic or particularly
religious about the procedure of the bishop's court. Roman law, based on
careful consultation with experts, determined the bishop's judgment.[156]
But the bishop's *audientia* was a constant presence in the city. Augustine
would sit in judgment all morning and even into the time of the *siesta.*[157]
In this day-to-day, intimate contact with their bishop or his clergy, the
lower classes of the late Roman cities insensibly took on an Old Testament
coloring. It was more convenient to think of themselves no longer as fellow citizens, but as members of the "poor" of ancient Israel — as disadvan-
taged persons, entitled to justice at the hands of a new, patriarchal leader,
the Christian bishop.

It was as the "poor of the church" that the lower classes, in general,
also gained a voice in an exciting new form of local politics. When a bishop

---

The Finds from the Sacred Spring, ed. B. Cunliffe et al. (Oxford: Oxford University Com-
mittee for Archaeology Monographs, 1988), 71.

152.   C. L. Gallazzi, "Supplica ad Atena su un ostraka di Esna," *Zeitschrift für Papyrologie und Epigraphik* 61 (1985): 107.

153.   *Codex Theodosianus* 1.27.2 (A.D. 408); A. Steinwenter, s.v. *Audientia episcopalis,*
in *Reallexikon für Antike und Christentum* (Stuttgart: A. Hiersemann, 1950), 1:916–17.

154.   Augustine, *Enarratio in Psalmos* 46.5.

155.   Augustine, *Enarratio in Psalmos* 25, *Sermo* 2.13; *Life of Epiphanius of Salamis* 55:
Patrologia Graeca 41:93A. This colorful text was brought to my attention by the kindness
of Claudia Rapp. J. G. Keegan, "A Christian Letter from the Michigan Collection," *Zeitschrift für Papyrologie und Epigraphik* 75 (1988): 267–71, may be a bishop's judgment in
an arbitration. The case concerns burial rights in family tombs — hardly the preoccupation
of a poor person.

156.   Augustine, *Ep.* 24*, ed. Divjak, pp. 126–27; *Lettres 1*–29*,* 382–86, with commentary on pp. 547–53; Eno, *Saint Augustine: Letters VI,* 172–74.

157.   Possidius, *Life of Augustine* 19.

was elected, the "poor" of the city were able to make themselves heard as a special group. The bishop was "their" bishop. It was, for instance, the "poor of the church" who pelted the unfortunate Gregory Nazianzen with stones when he was made bishop of Constantinople.[158]

In Mauretanian Caesarea in 419, the poor of the church supported the election of Honorius, a formerly married man, who was already the bishop of a smaller see (in which he promptly placed his son as successor!). The choice distressed Augustine and other "religious minded persons." But Honorius was known to be an able patron. He was already active at the imperial court, as other bishops of the city had been before him.[159] It was the lower classes of Mauretanian Caesarea as a whole, not simply the destitute inscribed on the church's poor rolls, who supported the election as bishop of a man known to be effective in dealing with the authorities.

The care of the poor, therefore, facilitated a less-publicized but decisive process by which the bishop became a major urban patron. To take the case of Basil: just before he became bishop of Caesarea, Basil had played a major role in organizing relief for the victims of the famine of 368.[160] On becoming bishop, he founded a large leper hospital on the outskirts of Caesarea. These were spectacular ventures that could be spoken of in old-fashioned terms. His hospital was a new city outside the city. It soon came to bear his name, called the Basileias.[161] Writing to an official, he claimed to have done no more than any well-intentioned governor was expected to do: he had restored the city to its ancient glory by new building.[162] Yet as his friend Gregory Nazianzen was careful to point out, all this activity was directed to the care of persons who counted for nothing in the political life of Caesarea: the fact that Basil could be seen serving at the tables of the poor and nursing the lepers proved that the bishop harbored none of the urges of a worldly patron.[163]

Based on the poor, Basil's power in the city was a power innocent of ambition. In fact, we know from his correspondence that Basil sought to

158. Gregory Nazianzen, *Ep.* 77.3, in *Saint Grégoire de Nazianze: Lettres,* ed. P. Gallay (Paris: Belles Lettres, 1964), 1:95.

159. Augustine, *Ep.* 22*.7–10, ed. Divjak, pp. 116–19; *Lettres 1*– 29*,* 354–63; Eno, *Saint Augustine: Letters VI,* 158–60.

160. Gregory Nazianzen, *Oratio* 43.63: *Patrologia Graeca* 36:577; P. Maraval, "La date de la mort de Basile de Césarée," *Revue des études augustiniennes* 24 (1988): 31.

161. Sozomen, *Ecclesiastical History* 6.34; Firmus of Caesarea, *Letter* 43, ed. M.-A. Calvet-Sébasti and P.-L. Gatier, *Firmus de Césarée: Lettres,* Sources chrétiennes 350 (Paris: Le Cerf, 1989), 167.

162. Basil, *Ep.* 94, in *Saint Basil: The Letters,* ed. and trans. R. Deferrari, Loeb Classical Library (Cambridge, Mass.: Harvard University Press, 1962), 2:150–53; L. Robert, "Epigrammes du Bas-Empire," *Hellenica* 4 (1948): 60–64.

163. Gregory Nazianzen, *Oratio* 43.64: *Patrologia Graeca* 36:577.

extend his influence throughout the governing classes as far afield as Constantinople. Even his monastic experiments depended on his skills as a patron. Basil exploited to the full his prestige as a local notable and man of *paideia* in order to gain tax exemptions and personal immunities for prospective monks and founders of poorhouses.[164] Basil's patronage also reached deep into the urban populace of Caesarea itself.[165] On one occasion, the guilds of the city rallied behind him during a memorable confrontation with a governor: "Each man was armed with the tool he was using, or with whatever came to hand at the moment. Torch in hand, amid showers of stones, with cudgels ready, all ran and shouted together with united zeal."[166]

It is in Alexandria that we can see most clearly the stages of the bishop's fateful conquest of the bazaar. The great patriarchs had gained a foothold among the guilds of the city in the reign of Constantine. In a strange gesture of subcivic generosity, Constantine had not only granted the patriarch levies of linen, to be distributed as clothing to the poor, but he had also instituted free burial services, to be administered by the clergy.[167] The personnel for these services, however, were provided by the artisan guilds of the city, in exchange for exemptions so considerable that rich shop owners were anxious to join in the scheme.[168] The patriarch had the right to decide on all applications: in 395 he was given the right to insist that no non-Christian might act as the head of a guild.[169] By 418 the "most reverend bishop" commanded, in effect, a hand-picked force of some five hundred men with strong arms and backs, the *parabalani,* who were nominally entrusted with the "care of the bodies of the weak" as stretcher-bearers and hospital orderlies.[170] The massed presence of the *parabalani* made itself felt in the theater, in the law courts, and in front of the town hall of Alexandria. The town council was forced to complain to the emperor of such intimidation.[171]

164.   Basil, *Epp.* 3, 36, 104, 117, 142, in Deferrari, *Saint Basil* 1:28, 191; 2:197, 237, 345.

165.   Lellia Cracco Ruggini, "Le associazioni professionali nel mondo romano-bizantino," in *Settimane di Studio sull'Alto Medio Evo* 18 (Spoleto: Centro italiano di Studio sull'Alto Medio Evo, 1971), 171.

166.   Gregory Nazianzen, *Oratio* 43.57: *Patrologia Graeca* 36:568–69, trans. in *Library of the Nicene and Post-Nicene Fathers* (Grand Rapids, Mich.: Eerdmans, 1974), 7:413.

167.   Justinian, *Novella* 59, Praef. (A.D. 537); cf. *Novella* 43.1 (536) and *Codex Justinianus* 1.2.4 (409); Epiphanius, *Panarion* 3.1.76; *Patrologia Graeca* 42:516D–517A.

168.   *Codex Theodosianus* 16.2.43.1.

169.   *Codex Theodosianus* 1.4.5.

170.   *Codex Theodosianus* 16.2.43.

171.   *Codex Theodosianus* 16.2.42; J. Rougé, "Les débuts de l'épiscopat de Cyrille d'Alexandrie et le *Code Théodosien,*" in *Alexandrina: Mélanges offerts au P. Claude Mondésert* (Paris: Le Cerf, 1987), 346–49.

While the patriarch of Alexandria became notorious for his use of such groups, he was by no means alone. The patriarch of Antioch also commanded a threatening body of *lecticarii,* pallbearers for the burial of the urban poor.[172] The extensive development of the underground cemeteries of the Christian community in Rome, the famous catacombs, from the early third century onwards, placed at the disposal of the bishop a team of *fossores,* grave diggers skilled in excavating the tufa rock, as strong and as pugnacious as were the legendary Durham coal miners who intervened in the rowdy elections of the nineteenth century.[173] During the disputed election in which Damasus became bishop of Rome in 366, the *fossores* played a prominent role in a series of murderous assaults on the supporters of his rival.[174] Throughout the empire, the personnel associated with the bishop's care of the poor had become a virtual urban militia.

Controllers of Crowds

As protector of the poor, the Christian bishop had achieved an unexpected measure of public prominence by the last decade of the fourth century. Reviewing a catalog of unpunished riots in the cities of the empire —public acclamations against emperors and the repeated burnings of the palaces of high officials—Ambrose of Milan drew his own conclusion in 388: "The bishops are the controllers of the crowds, the keen upholders of peace, unless, of course [he added ominously], they are moved by insults to God and to His church."[175]

Political and fiscal developments gave weight to Ambrose's words. After the battle of Adrianople in 378, we enter a more dangerous age. The eastern empire bore the main cost of the reestablishment of the Balkan frontier.[176] Theodosius I was proclaimed emperor of the East in January 379. After campaigning in the Balkans against the Visigoths, he fell dangerously

172. Flemming, *Akten der ephesinischen Synode,* 118, 133; *Life of John of Tella,* ed. E. W. Brooks, in *Vitae Virorum apud Monophysitas celeberrimorum, Corpus Scriptorum Christianorum Orientalium, Scriptores Syri,* ser. 3:25 (Leipzig: O. Harrassowitz, 1907), 55.33, Syriac text p. 88.24.

173. H. Brandenburg, "Überlegungen zum Ursprung und Entwicklung der Katakomben Roms," in *Vivarium: Festschrift für T. Klauser,* Jahrbuch für Antike und Christentum: Ergänzungsband 11 (Münster im Westfalen: Aschendorff, 1984), 11–49; Marc Griesheimer, "Génèse et développement de la catacombe S. Jean à Syracuse," *Mélanges de l'école française de Rome: Antiquité* (1989): 751–82.

174. *Collectio Avellana* 1.7, *Corpus Scriptorum Ecclesiasticorum Latinorum* 35 (Vienna: Tempsky, 1895), 3; Ammianus Marcellinus, *Res gestae* 27.3.12.

175. Ambrose, *Ep.* 40.6.

176. John Matthews, *Western Aristocracies and Imperial Court* (Oxford: Clarendon Press, 1975), 101–45; Liebeschuetz, *Antioch,* 164.

ill at Thessalonica and was baptized in the autumn of 380. He entered Constantinople in November 380, "not only as a victorious general, but also as a baptized Catholic Christian. It proved to be a potent combination."[177]

Baptized or not, Theodosius, as eastern emperor, was the direct heir of Constantine's revolution. He ruled those regions where it had seemed most possible, to Constantine and his Christian successors, to replace the old religion by an unambiguously Christian empire.[178] But he was a man who inherited a dream without inheriting the means to implement it. He could never feel as secure as Constantine had been. From 383 to 388 his authority was challenged in the West by Maximus, a relative, who claimed to be as zealous a Catholic as himself. By entering Italy in 387, Maximus drew Theodosius into a campaign to reestablish the young emperor Valentinian II in the West. The outcome of the civil war was so uncertain that riots broke out in Constantinople, on the rumor that Theodosius had died on campaign; the patriarch of Alexandria took the precaution of sending his representative to Rome with two letters, one for Maximus and one for Theodosius, to be delivered to whichever emperor proved victorious![179]

In the same years, the economy of the empire as a whole was affected by a final hardening of the currency in favor of gold coinage.[180] A situation which one contemporary traced back to the reign of Constantine now became irreversible. The rich, who enjoyed access to gold through their collaboration with the imperial administration, were further isolated from the rest of the population, who were forced to make use of money of little value and yet had to pay taxes which were increasingly demanded in gold *solidi:* "The houses of the powerful were crammed full and their splendor enhanced to the destruction of the poor. . . . But the poor were driven by their afflictions into various criminal enterprises, . . . losing sight of all respect for law, all feelings of loyalty."[181]

177. Matthews, *Western Aristocracies,* 122.

178. T. D. Barnes, "Religion and Society in the Age of Theodosius," in *Grace, Politics and Desire: Essays on Augustine,* ed. H. A. Meynell (Calgary, Alberta: University of Calgary Press, 1990), 157–60, is judicious and important.

179. Socrates, *Ecclesiastical History* 6.2.

180. J. P. Callu, "Le 'centénaire' et l'enrichissement monétaire au Bas Empire," *Ktema* 3 (1978): 311.

181. *Anonymus de rebus bellicis* 2.2, ed. and trans. E. A. Thompson, in *A Roman Inventor and Reformer* (Oxford: Clarendon Press, 1952), 94, 110. In dating this text to the age of Theodosius I have been influenced by the arguments in H. Brandt, *Zeitkritik in der Spätantike: Untersuchungen zu den Reformsvorschlagen des Anonymus de rebus bellicis,* Vestigia 40 (Munich: C. H. Beck, 1988), 83; but this particular dating is far from certain. Others would place the text twenty years earlier but would also see it as referring to eastern conditions, under Valens: Alan Cameron, "The Date of the *Anonymus de Rebus Bellicis,*" in *Aspects of the de Rebus Bellicis: Papers presented to Professor E. A. Thompson,* ed. M. W. C.

Theodosius was forced to tax the cities more heavily than ever before.[182] If he was to do this, he had to make plain, to the empire at large, with which group he preferred to negotiate in order to maintain the loyalty of the townsfolk in a time of increasing unpopularity. In the 380s, indeed, Theodosius had to adopt a new "theatrical style" in his relations with the cities. He did this with considerable skill. Opposition to his will, in the form of riots, elicited formidable demonstrations of his anger. But this anger was deployed according to long-established conventions. It was shown in order to be appeased. The issue was: Who would be allowed to do this? Theodosius used his displeasure prudently, to usher in, as the authorized appeasers of his rage, a new group of persons whom he considered, for a mixture of religious and political reasons, more useful to his purposes. It was to the bishops and the monks, rather than to the grave Themistius or the cautious Libanius, that Theodosius decided to turn.

This happened first in the spring of 387, after the Riot of the Statues in Antioch. For the civic notables, every detail of the riot was a "governmental catastrophe" of the first order. The uprising came after years marked by grain shortages, in which great efforts had been made to improve the food supply of the city.[183] News of yet another levy in gold on the townspeople proved the last straw.[184] Ignoring the town hall, the crowd flocked first to the bishop's palace.[185] Bishop Flavian was not to be found. In any case, it was already too late: the statues of the emperor and empress had been thrown from their pedestals and dragged through the streets.[186] A later Syrian writer caught the heinousness of the act in a simile: a Christian may sin, but only an apostate will deny his baptism; likewise, a city may riot, but only when it overturns the statues of the emperor in its midst has it committed high treason.[187] By such a gesture, Antioch had placed itself at the mercy of the emperor's wrath. This meant, in effect,

Hassall and R. I. Ireland, B.A.R. International Series 63 (Oxford: B.A.R., 1979), 1–10. For a full discussion of the problem, see A. Giardina, ed. and trans., *Anonimo: Le cose della guerra* (Milan: Mondadori, 1989), xxxvi–lii.

182. M. F. Hendy, *Studies in the Byzantine Monetary Economy* (Cambridge: Cambridge University Press, 1985), 189–90.

183. G. L. Kurbatov, "K voprosu o korporacii khlebopekov v Antiokhii," *Vestnik Drevnei Istorii* 109 (1965): 141–53; Franz Tinnefeld, *Die frühbyzantinische Gesellschaft* (Munich: W. Fink Verlag, 1977), 127; Libanius, *Oratio* 1.205–12 (I.175–77), in Norman, *Libanius' Autobiography,* 110–15.

184. Libanius, *Oratio* 19.25 (II.396–97), in Norman, *Libanius 2,* 285; R. Browning, "The Riot of 387 A.D. in Antioch," *Journal of Roman Studies* 42 (1952): 14.

185. Libanius, *Oratio* 19.28 (II.398), in Norman, *Libanius 2,* 287.

186. Libanius, *Oratio* 19.29–30 (II.398–99), in Norman, *Libanius 2,* 287.

187. A. Tanghe, "Memra de Philoxène de Mabboug sur l'inhabitation du Saint Esprit," *Le Mouséon* 73 (1960): 53, trans. 62–63.

that Theodosius found himself in the enviable position of being free to decide who would reap the credit for changing his heart to mercy. What followed was a fully public mobilization of the persuasive powers of both the bishop and the civic notables; and in this grand maneuver, the balance was allowed to tip, perceptibly, towards the Christian bishop and the monks.[188]

The imperial commissioners arrived at Antioch in March 387, entering the city in a deadly silence. The inhabitants feared a punitive massacre or, at best, the demotion of Antioch from its status as *métropolis* of Syria. But Bishop Flavian had already brought the monks of Syria, headed by the hermit Macedonius, into the city, to intercede with the commissioners before the public inquest on the riot began.[189] Macedonius was a Syrian of the hinterland. He knew so little Greek that Flavian had been able to ordain him as a priest without his understanding a word of the ceremony. On being told what had happened to him, Macedonius ran after the bishop to give him a thrashing with his walking stick![190]

Cultivated Christians relished such stories. They now needed intercessors of the caliber of Macedonius. While the urban clergy were forced to demean themselves, to kiss the knees and clasp the feet of the imperial commissioners, in order to secure the release of only a few persons,[191] Macedonius, as a holy man who owed nothing to Antioch, was able to speak for the city as a whole. He confronted the commissioners with a brusque courage so alien that it seemed to carry with it the awesome force of the Holy Spirit. "He charged them to tell the emperor that he was a man, with the same nature" as those who had rioted. By threatening full-scale executions, the emperor must know that "he had given rein to anger that was out of proportion." When what he said was translated to them, from Syriac into Greek, the commissioners "shuddered." For "the righteous has the confidence of a lion."[192] The wind of *parrhésia* had plainly come to blow from a different quarter. Cautious, as usual, when at a distance from

---

188.   Lellia Cracco Ruggini, "Poteri in gara per la salvezza di città rebelli: Il caso di Antiochia (387 d.C.)," in *Hestiasis: Studi di tarda antichita' offerti a Salvatore Calderone*. Studi tardoantichi 1 (Messina: Sicania, 1988), 265–90.

189.   John Chrysostom, *Homilies on the Statues* 17.6: *Patrologia Graeca* 49:174–75, trans. in *Library of the Fathers* (Oxford: J. Parker, 1842), 284.

190.   Theodoret, *Historia Religiosa* 9.4–5: *Patrologia Graeca* 82:1401C; R. M. Price, trans., *Theodoret: A History of the Monks of Syria*, Cistercian Studies 88 (Kalamazoo, Mich.: Cistercian Publications, 1985), 102.

191.   John Chrysostom, *Homilies on the Statues* 17.8: *Patrologia Graeca* 49:175, trans. *Library of the Fathers*, 285.

192.   Theodoret, *Historia Religiosa* 9.7–8: *Patrologia Graeca* 82:1404B–1405A, citing Proverbs 28:1.

their master, the commissioners decided to report back to Theodosius. Bishop Flavian set off, in a hurry, across Asia Minor, to throw himself on the emperor's mercy. He was later believed to have persuaded the choir-boys who sang at the emperor's table to chant the petitions of the Antiochenes in the form of a dirge. Theodosius "shed tears into the cup which he held in his hand."[193] It was a good sign.

But we must remember that the *parrhésia* of Bishop Flavian and the monks was so effective largely because Theodosius and his agents had made up their minds to listen to it. At Constantinople, Theodosius continued to patronize the aging pagan philosopher Themistius and had even attempted to woo conservative opinion by making him prefect of the city.[194] But he was also a devout Christian, anxious to close the temples of the East. In this task, Cynegius, his commissioner, had been aided by the monks of Syria. The monks took advantage of Cynegius' mission to fall on temples all over Syria, the Euphrates frontier, and Phoenicia.[195] These wild men could be convincingly presented by the notables of Antioch as lower-class fomenters of violence. As Libanius wrote at the time: "This black-robed tribe, who eat more than elephants . . . sweep across the country-side like a river in spate . . . and, by ravaging the temples, they ravage the estates."[196]

By this memorable characterization, Libanius implied that the activities of the monks cast a shadow of illegality over Cynegius' actions as a whole: their license was that of brigands, of men outside the law.[197] In deciding to allow himself to be swayed by Bishop Flavian and by a group of carefully chosen holy men, Theodosius legitimized the violence that had been committed by the monks in the previous year. As the prospect of war with Maximus, combined with the uncertainty usually associated with a change of ruler in Sassanian Persia, made it unadvisable to penalize

193. Sozomen, *Ecclesiastical History* 7.23, in *Library of the Nicene and Post-Nicene Fathers* (Grand Rapids, Mich.: Eerdmans, 1979), 2:393.

194. Themistius, *Orationes* 31, 34; Palladas, *Anthologia Graeca* 11.292; L. J. Daly, "Themistius' Refusal of a Magistracy," *Jahrbuch der österreichischen Byzantinistik* 32 (1982): 177–86.

195. Matthews, *Western Aristocracies,* 140–42; Garth Fowden, "Bishops and Temples in the Eastern Roman Empire, A.D. 320–425," *Journal of Theological Studies,* n.s., 29 (1978): 62–69.

196. Libanius, *Oratio* 30.9 (III.92), in Norman, *Libanius 2,* 109.

197. Libanius, *Oratio* 30.12, 48 (III.94, 114), in Norman, *Libanius 2,* 113, 145. Shenoute of Atripe was accused of "brigandage" in the same manner: Shenoute, *Letter* 24, ed. J. Leipoldt and W. E. Crum, *Corpus Scriptorum Christianorum Orientalium* 43: *Scriptores coptici* 3 (Leipzig: O. Harassowitz, 1898), 79.16, *mntléstés.* Cf. Eunapius, *Lives of the Sophists* 472, in Wright, *Philostratus and Eunapius,* 422, *tyranniké exousia.*

the leading city of the East, Theodosius could at least choose the party that would reap the credit for having assuaged his wrath. He chose the bishop and the monks.

Preaching in Antioch, John Chrysostom amplified the triumph of the church. In the monks, the city had found new bearers of *parrhésia:*

> Where now are those who are clad in tattered robes and display a long beard and carry staves in their right hand, the philosophers of this world? All these men forsook the city . . . the inhabitants of the city fled away to the mountains . . . but the citizens of the desert hastened into the city. . . . These things let us tell the pagans when they dare to dispute with us respecting the philosophers. Oh! how passing wonderful is the power of Christianity, that it restrains and bridles a man who has no equal on earth, a sovereign, powerful enough to destroy and devastate all things; and teaches him to practice such philosophy.[198]

Chrysostom later spoke of the conversion of whole families taking place at that time.[199] The fragment of a large mosaic pavement with many inscriptions (one of which is now preserved in the entrance hall of the Princeton University Museum) shows that an ambitious building program was undertaken at the shrine of Saint Babylas, in the well-to-do suburb of Daphne, by "the most reverend bishop" Flavian. This building took place in 387, at a time when the traditional centers of the city—the agora, the bathhouses, and the theater—lay silent, under the shadow of the emperor's wrath.[200]

By giving way in this manner, Theodosius further legitimized the local violence of Christians. The next year, in 388, at Callinicum, modern Raqqa in Syria, a major garrison town overlooking the wide confluence of the Euphrates and the Nahr al-Balikh, the Christian bishop and his monks set on a Jewish synagogue and burned it to the ground, having mopped up, in a similar brusque manner, a meeting place of Valentinian heretics.[201] The military authorities were furious. Even Theodosius agreed: "The monks commit many atrocities."[202] The bishop was ordered to pay for the rebuilding of the synagogue.

By that time Theodosius was in northern Italy, having defeated Maximus. In a tense interview in the cathedral basilica of Milan, Bishop Am-

---

198. John Chrysostom, *Homilies on the Statues* 17.5, 21.13: *Patrologia Graeca* 49:173, 217; trans. *Library of the Fathers,* 282–83, 357.

199. John Chrysostom, *De Anna* 1: *Patrologia Graeca* 54:634.

200. Sheila Campbell, *The Mosaics of Antioch* (Toronto: Center of Medieval Studies 1988), 43–44. John Chrysostom, *Homilies on the Statues* 15.1: *Patrologia Graeca* 49:153; trans. *Library of the Fathers,* 249.

201. Ambrose, *Ep.* 40.6, 16; Matthews, *Western Aristocracies,* 232–33.

202. Ambrose, *Ep.* 41.27.

brose refused, despite shouts of protest from the general Timasius, to begin the Eucharistic liturgy—with its solemn prayer for the emperor and his armies—until Theodosius countermanded the order.[203] If Theodosius could forgive the city of Antioch, Ambrose insisted, he could forgive the zealous bishop of Callinicum.[204] Theodosius was uncertain of himself in a newly pacified western province. He was anxious to please. He gave in to Ambrose. The repercussions of the manner in which he had pardoned Antioch, for the sake of the bishop and monks, were felt first on the Euphrates and now returned to embarrass him at Milan. He had been forced into the dangerous habit of giving way to bishops.

Only three years after the Riot of the Statues in Antioch, what everyone had dreaded came true. In early 390 seven thousand inhabitants of Thessalonica were killed on the emperor's orders. The cause had been a riot in which Butherich, the Gothic commander of the garrison, was lynched for having refused the petitions of the populace, chanted at a solemn gathering in the city's hippodrome, to free a charioteer whom he had arrested for sodomy. The riot threatened to jeopardize Theodosius' policy of using the Goths to defend the Balkans.[205] To make matters worse, Theodosius had recently celebrated the anniversary of his accession in the city: Thessalonica was *his* city, the center of his Balkan strategy, in a way that Antioch never was. It was an occasion when the imperial rage had to show itself in devastating form.

Theodosius was in Milan when the news of the riot arrived.[206] He left the city with his inner circle to deliberate what he should do. The debates in the *consistorium* took place among persons sworn to secrecy. Neither the bishop of Thessalonica nor Ambrose, the bishop's most effective ally in Italy, was allowed to learn anything of the emperor's decision.[207] The notion of the emperor's "wrath" masked a cold-blooded decision, taken after many weeks at the urging of military experts.[208]

203. Ambrose, *Ep.* 41.28–29.

204. Ambrose, *Ep.* 40.32.

205. Sozomen, *Ecclesiastical History* 7.25, trans. *Library of the Nicene and Post-Nicene Fathers,* 2:394.

206. Matthews, *Western Aristocracies,* 234–37, provides a clear summary of the events. On the relations of Ambrose with Theodosius, I have benefited from the dissertation abstract of and conversations with Dr. Neil McLynn of Oxford University, after the first draft of this chapter had been completed. His forthcoming book on the subject will, I suspect, dissipate many errors, including those that may well have been committed here.

207. Ambrose, *Ep.* 51.2.

208. This is made particularly plain in F. Kolb, "Der Bussakt von Mailand: Zum Verhältnis von Staat und Kirche in der Spätantike," in *Geschichte und Gegenwart: Festschrift für Karl Dietrich Erdmann,* ed. Hartmut Boockmann, Kurt Jurgensen, and Gerhard Stoltenberg (Neumünster: Wachholtz, 1980), 49.

As it was, what was probably planned as a selective killing of young men likely to have been involved in the demonstration at the hippodrome got out of hand. "The city was filled with the blood of many unjustly slain."[209] The news of a massacre of horrendous proportions reached Milan at a time when the bishops of Gaul were assembled for a synod in the city.[210] The Gallic delegation had only recently been subjects of the emperor Maximus, an upright Catholic, recently denounced by the rhetors of the victorious Theodosius as a "butcher in the purple."[211] Ambrose could not be seen by them to condone such bloodshed. He discreetly withdrew to the countryside, for reasons of health, lest he meet the emperor.[212] Both sides had to think of what to do next.

Fortunately, the summer heats closed in on Milan. The court left the city for the fresh air of the Alpine foothills. On August 18 Theodosius issued a law from Verona to the effect that "if, contrary to our custom," the emperor ordered a capital punishment, thirty days should elapse before the sentence was executed—presumably to allow the kind of intercession which Ambrose had been so pointedly denied earlier in the year.[213] Yet the law was addressed to the praetorian prefect, Flavianus, a known non-Christian. The law envisioned notables held in prison, not the innocent population of a whole city.[214] If anything, Theodosius wished to take the wind out of Ambrose's sails. The edict from Verona implied no more than that Theodosius would control his anger in his dealings with the largely non-Christian aristocracy of Italy, not that he regretted the penal massacre at Thessalonica.

What was remarkable was the skill with which Ambrose overcame his initial failure to influence Theodosius and his entourage. He did this by falling back on the time-honored role of the philosopher. Dealing with Theodosius at this time, Ambrose was no Hildebrand. In Theodosius, Ambrose faced the awe-inspiring incarnation of the Roman order. The crowds in Milan, who flocked to see the emperor in solemn procession, were led by the very "blaze of the purple" to see in his face "something more than human."[215] Confronting such awesome power, Ambrose the bishop gave way to Ambrose the heir of the philosophers. In 388 in the affair of Callinicum, Ambrose had outfaced Theodosius and his entourage on the relatively

209. Sozomen, *Ecclesiastical History* 7.25, trans. *Library of the Nicene and Post-Nicene Fathers*, 2:394.

210. Ambrose, *Ep.* 51.6.

211. Pacatus, *Panegyricus Theodosio dictus* 24.1, in *Panegyrici Latini*, ed. R. A. B. Mynors (Oxford: Clarendon Press, 1964), 101.

212. Ambrose, *Ep.* 51.5.

213. *Codex Theodosianus* 9.40.13.

214. Matthews, *Western Aristocracies*, 235, n. 2.

215. Ambrose, *Expositio in Psalmum cxviii* 8.19.

minor issue of pardon for a distant bishop. Now in the autumn of 390 he would play to the full the ancient role of the philosopher confronting a wrathful emperor.

We should not take Ambrose's success for granted. He had been bishop of Milan since 376. His early position had not been strong. Recently installed and the self-appointed spokesman of an intransigent pro-Nicene faction, the Ambrose of the late 370s and early 380s had no guaranteed lien on an emperor's conscience.[216] The courage of the philosopher, not the peremptory authority of a Catholic bishop, was what he wielded most effectively at that time. This saw him through his confrontation with the Arian entourage of Valentinian II in 386. When troops from the palace surrounded his basilica on that occasion, the series of remarkable sermons that he preached, the *De Isaac et beata vita,* showed a man who knew how to present himself to the world at large. In these sermons, the "philosophical" constancy of the Maccabaean martyrs merged with the ideal of the immobile and fearless sage, gathered from the works of Plotinus.[217] At that time, Ambrose posed as a Christian example of the ancient *karteria,* of the inspired obstinacy with which the philosopher faced the powerful. He had been fortunate in his choice of opponents. In 386 the boy-emperor Valentinian II had been in a peculiarly weak position. He was uncertain of the loyalty of his troops and was overshadowed by Maximus in Gaul and by Theodosius in the East. He was reluctant to restore order at the cost of a massacre of Catholics. He gave way.[218] The *karteria* of Ambrose was vindicated. Now, almost five years later, with Theodosius, the time for *parrhésia,* for plain-speaking, had come.

Ambrose knew the rules that governed the use of *parrhésia.* After the massacre of Thessalonica, no mitered prelate blocked Theodosius on the porch of the cathedral of Milan, as later ages liked to imagine. Instead, Ambrose deliberately approached the emperor as a spiritual guide. Theodosius received a long letter, "written with my own hand, for you alone to read."[219] The letter was supplemented, it seems, by the *Apologia David,* a disquisition on the penitential fiftieth psalm.[220] By writing in this way,

216. P. Nautin, "Les premières relations d'Ambroise avec l'empereur Gratien," in *Ambroise de Milan,* ed. G. Madec (Paris: Etudes augustiniennes, 1974), 229–44; Neil McLynn, "The 'Apology' of Palladius: Nature and Purpose," *Journal of Theological Studies,* n.s., 42 (1991): 70–73.

217. G. Nauroy, "La méthode de composition et la structure du *De Isaac et beata vita,"* in Madec, *Ambroise de Milan,* 115–53; idem., "Le fouet et le miel: Le combat d'Ambroise en 386 contre l'arianisme milanais," *Recherches augustiniennes* 23 (1988): 3–86.

218. Barnes, "Religion and Society in the Age of Theodosius," 162.

219. Ambrose, *Ep.* 51.14.

220. Ambrose, *Apologia David;* see esp. P. Hadot, *Ambroise de Milan: Apologie de David,* Sources chrétiennes 239 (Paris: Le Cerf, 1977), 38–43. It is Psalm 51 in the Authorized Version.

Ambrose deliberately styled himself as a philosopher. He addressed himself directly to the imperial rage. Anger, he wrote, was an illness of the soul, a sign of the endemic weakness of the human race, incurred by Adam's fall. But it was an illness that could be healed by Christian penance.[221]

Yet no philosopher had ever possessed a basilica that could house an audience of three thousand.[222] Theodosius knew that if he was to continue to hold court in Milan, the ceremonials of an imperial city demanded a procession from the palace to Ambrose's cathedral, the offering of imperial gifts at the sanctuary, and (for Theodosius, as a baptized Christian) the taking of the Eucharist. When the court resided in Milan, great purple veils were hung on the portals of the basilica that was to receive the imperial worshiper.[223] The emperors' need for a ritual space in the cities in which they resided had already led the less-tactful Arian emperor Valens into confrontations with bishops in the eastern empire: with Basil, when the imperial court passed through Caesarea, and with the bishop of Tomi, who simply removed his congregation from the basilica when the emperor arrived.[224]

The very majesty of the imperial ceremonial tied Theodosius to the Catholic church. To regain a central role in the solemn high mass at the cathedral of Milan was well worth a penance. Once reconciled with Ambrose, after a short penance that probably took the form of abandoning an imperial procession in full regalia, it is significant that Theodosius deliberately postponed his taking of the Eucharist until the high moment of the arrival in the city of his "sons"—his own son, Honorius, and his protégé, Valentinian II.[225] The "awesome spectacle" of an emperor without his regalia in church for a few Sundays may well have been blotted out in the minds of the citizens of Milan by the later splendor of a truly imperial celebration of the concord of the dynasty.[226]

Later Byzantine art shows King David as an emperor, in purple robe and diadem, bowing before the prophet Nathan, dressed, appropriately, as a philosopher, with long beard and classical dress.[227] This image, with its deep roots in the political imagination of the ancient world, not the dramatic Counter-Reformation bas-relief which Gibbon viewed with such

221. Ambrose, *Ep.* 51.4–5.
222. Krautheimer, *Three Christian Capitals,* 76.
223. Ambrose, *Sermo contra Auxentium* 20, 30; Nauroy, "Le fouet et le miel," 77–79.
224. Gregory Nazianzen, *Oratio* 43.52–53; Sozomen, *Ecclesiastical History* 6.21.
225. Ambrose, *De obitu Theodosii* 34.
226. G. W. Bowersock, "From Emperor to Bishop: The Self-Conscious Transformation of Political Power in the Fourth Century A.D.," *Classical Philology* 81 (1986): 299.
227. Zoltan Kadar, "Un rilievo frammentario del museo di Budapest," *Rivista di archeologia cristiana* 38 (1962): 149–50. It is uncertain whether the particular fragment discussed is authentic, or a copy based upon later Byzantine representations of Nathan and David. I owe this caution to the kindness of Professor A. Cutler.

distaste when he visited Milan,[228] was the rendering of Ambrose's confrontation with Theodosius that would have been most intelligible to a fourth-century person. In acting as he did after the massacre at Thessalonica, Ambrose could not have eclipsed more effectively, in the public eye, the dark-robed figure of his elder contemporary Themistius. The bishop had established himself as the critic of the imperial rage and, consequently, as the arbiter of imperial mercy.

Theodosius further refurbished his prestige as a pious emperor by a series of edicts against polytheism. In February 391 he forbade all forms of sacrifice. The old religion was to have no further place in public life. No governor—even a non-Christian—was to approach a temple to offer worship there.[229] This meant, in effect, that throughout the empire the governor's *adventus* now led only to one religious building—the basilica of the Christian bishop (much as the new basilica of San Lorenzo stood on the triumphal way leading into Milan, waiting to receive respectful official visitors).[230] The ceremony which, as we saw at the outset, made visible, in the form of a solemn arrival in state, the infrequent pulses of energy that linked local communities to a far-distant center now inevitably included a Christian bishop, the public display of symbols of the Christian religion in the procession of welcome—great copies of the Gospels and processional crosses—and gestures of respect, on the part of the new arrival, to Christian churches that now marked the threshold of the city.[231]

The law was applied to Egypt in June 391,[232] and it was repeated, in its most circumstantial form, when Theodosius returned to Constantinople in November 392.[233] But once again, Theodosius allowed local events to outstrip him. In 392 Theophilus, patriarch of Alexandria, took advantage of the mood created by the laws to stage a procession in which statues of gods taken from a deserted shrine were subjected to public ridicule.[234] The ensuing bloody riot enabled a Christian mob to drive their rivals into

228.   G. A. Bonnard, ed., *Gibbon's Journey from Geneva to Rome* (London: Nelson, 1961), 47.
229.   *Codex Theodosianus* 16.10.10.
230.   Krautheimer, *Three Christian Capitals,* 73, for map.
231.   For example, for the entry of the governor of Osrhoene into Edessa in 449, see Flemming, *Akten der ephesinischen Synode,* 14–15; for the imagined entry of Theodosius I into Alexandria, see *Vision of Theophilus,* ed. and trans. Mingana, pp. 14, 51.
232.   *Codex Theodosianus* 16.10.11.
233.   *Codex Theodosianus* 16.10.12.
234.   Rufinus, *Ecclesiastical History* 2.22: *Patrologia Latina* 21:528A; Socrates, *Ecclesiastical History* 5.16. See especially Thélamon, *Païens et chrétiens,* 160–394; Chuvin, *Chronicle of the Last Pagans,* 65–69. The date of the destruction of the Serapeum is uncertain: I have adopted 392. See A. Bauer and J. Strzygowski, *Eine alexandrinische Weltchronik, Denkschriften der kaiserlichen Akademie der Wissenschaften zu Wien,* Phil.-Hist. Klasse 51.2 (1905): 69.

the precinct of the Serapeum. The greatest shrine in the eastern Mediterranean, unique in its design and in the devotion that it inspired, was now within their grasp.

The patriarch Theophilus held back, careful to await the emperor's letter. Read out from the steps of the Serapeum itself, the letter began with an impassioned denunciation of the gods. That was enough. With a gasp of horror, the old believers scattered, to allow the Christians to commit the ultimate sacrilege.[235] Plainly the gods had abandoned the earth and retired, saddened by so much blasphemy, to heaven.[236] The great image of Serapis was destroyed. The temple was razed. The site once "polluted" by the gods was purified by monks and the bones of martyrs.[237] Yet in some corner of its mighty ruins, sorcery was practiced almost a century later.[238] On being told of the events in Alexandria, Theodosius was said to have praised Christ that "such ancient error has been snuffed out, without damage to that great city,"[239] Contemporaries, for whom the massacre of Thessalonica was an event of the recent past, knew that they had, indeed, been fortunate.

Encouraged by so spectacular a success, the tide of violence against temples, marked by occasional bloody clashes between Christians and polytheistic communities, continued all around the Mediterranean in the 390s.[240] Such events can be seen to have had a decisive effect on the attitudes of leading Christians to the cities in which they lived. The sudden fall of the temples made them yet more impatient of the continued existence of religious groups and of civic customs that still escaped their control.[241] Only on the eastern frontier did Theodosius consider it wise to listen, at last, to his

235.   Rufinus, *Ecclesiastical History* 2.22, 23: *Patrologia Latina* 21:529C, 531A.

236.   Eunapius, *Lives of the Philosophers* 470, in Wright, *Philostratus and Eunapius,* 416; Chuvin, *Chronicle of the Last Pagans,* 67–68.

237.   Rufinus, *Ecclesiastical History* 2:28: *Patrologia Latina* 21:536BC; Eunapius, *Lives of Philosophers* 472, in Wright, *Philostratus and Eunapius,* 422–24.

238.   Raabe, *Petrus der Iberer,* 71, Syriac text 72.5.

239.   Rufinus, *Ecclesiastical History* 2.30: *Patrologia Latina* 21:538A.

240.   For Phoenicia, see Sozomen, *Ecclesiastical History* 7.15, and Theodoret, *Eccesiastical History* 5.29. For Greece, see Eunapius, *Lives of the Philosophers* 476, in Wright, *Philostratus and Eunapius,* 438. For northern Italy, see Lizzi, *Vescovi e strutture ecclesiastiche,* 59–86. For North Africa, see R. A. Markus, *The End of Ancient Christianity* (Cambridge: Cambridge University Press, 1990), 107–23. For Gaul, see Aline Rousselle, *Croire et guérir: La foi en Gaule dans l'Antiquité tardive* (Paris: Fayard, 1990), 31–64.

241.   This is brilliantly portrayed in the case of Augustine in Markus, *End of Ancient Christianity,* 110–21; we can expect an edition of further, hitherto unknown sermons by Augustine relating to slightly later events, announced by their discoverer, F. Dolbeau, in "Sermons inédits de S. Augustin dans un manuscrit de Mayence (Stadtbibliothek I 9)," *Revue des études augustiniennes* 36 (1990): 355–59, and "Nouveaux sermons de Saint Augustin pour la conversion des païens et des donatistes," *Revue des études augustiniennes* 37 (1991): 37–78.

generals. Committed to yet another campaign against a western rival, he allowed the commander in chief of the eastern forces to receive a law in September 393: "Your Sublime Magnitude shall, upon receipt of this order, repress with due severity the excess of those who presume to commit illegal deeds under the name of the Christian religion and attempt to destroy and despoil synagogues."[242] It was a long-overdue ruling that made good the infirmity of purpose which he had shown on the incident of Callinicum.

But the end of the temples did not inevitably mean the end of a style of civic life in which the bishop remained accountable to the town council and to the city as a whole. Even the triumphant Theophilus could not feel entirely secure. When in 400 his attempt to depose his own overseer of the poor on a trumped-up charge of sodomy miscarried, the former worshipers of Serapis trooped into the square still associated with the temple of the Fortune of the city and joined with gusto in the clamor against the patriarch. Theophilus may well have been worsted at the public hearing that took place in the town hall.[243] For another twenty years the non-Christian elements in Alexandrian society stood firm. Then in 415 a further campaign of self-assertion by Theophilus' nephew and successor, Cyril, brought to a violent end the public role of the philosopher.

It is a testimony to the firmness of the role still allotted to philosophers that a woman could step into it. Hypatia of Alexandria was like Themistius, in that her father also had been a philosopher.[244] She practiced as a teacher in Alexandria and was acclaimed by contemporaries as "the stainless star of Wisdom's discipline."[245] An elderly woman by 415, she had been everything that a philosopher should be: "Of careful mind in performing the public duties affecting her city, [her] self-possession and freedom of speech derived from her culture."[246]

When the city was torn by riots in 415, the Augustal prefect, Orestes, held Cyril accountable for the disorders. The patriarch appeared before him, holding out the Gospels to him, as Flavian of Antioch had once done be-

242.   *Codex Theodosianus* 16.8.9.

243.   *Letter of Theophilus to the Bishops of Palestine,* in Jerome, *Ep.* 92.3: *Patrologia Latina* 22:765.

244.   J. R. Martindale, ed., *Prosopography of the Later Roman Empire,* vol. 2, *A.D. 395–527* (Cambridge: Cambridge University Press, 1980), 575–76: J. M. Rist, "Hypatia," *Phoenix* 19 (1965): 214–25. D. Shanzer, "Merely a Cynic Gesture?" *Rivista di filologia* 113 (1985): 61–66, posits influence by Plotinus. Chuvin, *Chronicle of the Last Pagans,* 85–90. The best account of the culture of Hypatia is now provided in Alan Cameron and Jacqueline Long, with Lee Sherry, *Barbarians and Politics at the Court of Arcadius* (Berkeley: University of California Press, forthcoming), chap. 2.

245.   Palladas, *Anthologia Graeca* 9.400.

246.   Socrates, *Ecclesiastical History* 7.15, trans. *Library of the Nicene and Post-Nicene Fathers* 2:160.

fore Theodosius, "believing that respect for religion would induce him to lay aside his anger."[247] But Orestes, though a baptized Christian, was convinced that Cyril needed to be curbed. Hypatia, the philosopher, not Cyril, was the person to whom he would grant the right of *parrhésia*. Only she must be seen to assuage his wrath.

The sight of so many official carriages drawn up outside the door of Hypatia's mansion was too much for the patriarch.[248] Cyril had been elected only a few years previously, in October 412. Riots had accompanied his hurried investiture and had left his authority tarnished. With the peculiar ruthlessness of the insecure, he set about establishing his position in the city. He closed the hitherto tolerated churches of the Novatians and appropriated their wealth. Taking advantage of clashes between Jews and Christians in the theater in 415, he set a mob to plunder the Jewish quarter. It was the end of a community that had lived in Alexandria for seven hundred years. Such actions made plain what he wanted. In the words of a hostile Christian writer, "from that time, the bishopric of Alexandria went beyond the limits of its sacerdotal functions, and assumed the administration of secular matters."[249]

It was essential to Cyril, as the newly installed patriarch, that he should have the monopoly of *parrhésia* in Alexandria. No unbeliever must be seen to carry weight with Orestes. After a series of demonstrations, organized by Cyril, had undermined Orestes' authority, the patriarch felt free to act. Hypatia was dragged from her coach as she drove through the city. A Christian mob, led by a lay reader and almost certainly reinforced by the dread *parabalani* of the patriarch, stoned her to death in the courtyard that opened up in front of a major church.[250] Her body was hacked to pieces with shards of pottery, and what was left was burned in a public square. It was a deliberate act of total annihilation, a "cleansing" of the land, similar to that achieved through the burning of the statues of the gods. To supporters of Cyril, Hypatia, the public-spirited philosopher, was the last of the idols.[251]

247. Socrates, *Ecclesiastical History* 7.13, trans. *Library of the Nicene and Post-Nicene Fathers* 2:159. Cf. John Chrysostom, *Homilies on the Statues* 21.17: *Patrologia Graeca* 49:219, trans. *Library of the Fathers,* 261; and John Lydus, *De Magistratibus populi romani* 3.59 (Leipzig: Teubner, 1967), 149.

248. Damascius, *Life of Isidore,* fragment 102, in *Damascii Vitae Isidori Reliquiae,* ed. C. Zintzen (Hildesheim: G. Olms, 1967), 79.

249. Socrates, *Ecclesiastical History* 7.7; Lionel R. Wickham, ed. and trans., *Cyril of Alexandria: Select Letters* (Oxford: Clarendon Press, 1983), xvi–xvii; J. Rougé, "La politique de Cyrille d'Alexandrie et le meurtre d'Hypatie," *Cristianesimo nella storia* 11 (1990): 487–92.

250. Wickham, *Cyril of Alexandria,* xvi.

251. Socrates, *Ecclesiastical History* 7.15; John of Nikiu, *Chronicle* 84, in *The Chronicle*

The major cities of the East had come to wear an alien face. The events of the late fourth century showed that such cities could no longer be controlled exclusively by men of *paideia*. Their new social texture and the increased weight of the imperial power that had come to rest upon them forced the notables to collaborate with the Christian bishop. For he appeared to enjoy ever-greater *parrhésia* at court and with local governors. Philosophers who sought to intervene in public affairs, as they had done in an earlier time, were easily cowed. Returning to Alexandria two generations later, the philosopher Isidore found that the fear generated by the murder of Hypatia still hung over the city.[252] Her style of outward-going philosophic life was dangerously out of date. It was safer and, of course, more elevating to the soul to remain a recluse. By the beginning of the sixth century no philosopher of the old religion could have any illusions about the world in which he now lived. Plato's meditations on the role of the philosopher in a "corrupt city" seemed to speak, only too well, of the non-Christian philosopher's role in his own times:

> The philosopher flees and yet does not flee. It is true that the philosopher who has arrived at the pitch of contemplative virtues flees without end, for he looks to the divine; but the philosopher, when practicing the political virtues, stays in the city, if he has fellow-citizens worthy of his discipline. But if his fellow-townsmen are unworthy, then he withdraws. . . . For those who stay among such men will meet with the same fate as those who rush in among wild animals and try to stroke them.[253]

Let us, therefore, conclude, in our next chapter, by looking at the emergence of new attitudes towards the exercise of imperial power in a political world that the philosopher had been forced to abandon and that the civic notables found themselves sharing with the bishops and the monks.

---

of John, Bishop of Nikiu, translated from Zotenberg's Ethiopic Text, trans. R. H. Charles (London: Williams and Norgate, 1916), 100–102; see Thélamon, *Paiens et chrétiens*, 232, for similar practices of annihilation in ancient Egypt.

252.   Damascius, *Life of Isidore*, fragment 276, ed. Zintzen, p. 219.

253.   Olympiodorus, *In Gorgiam* 485.d.5, in *Olympiodorus: In Platonis Gorgiam commentaria*, ed. L. G. Westerink (Leipzig: Teubner, 1970), 143; I. Hadot, *Le problème du néoplatonisme alexandrin: Hiéroclès et Simplicius* (Paris: Etudes augustiniennes, 1978), 38–39.

CHAPTER FOUR

Towards a Christian Empire

The Sublime Philosophy

Some time after his brother Basil's death in A.D. 377, Gregory of Nyssa heard, when traveling home from Sebaste (Sivas) to Cappadocia, that Helladius, Basil's successor as metropolitan-bishop of Caesarea, was celebrating the feast of a martyr in a nearby mountain village. Relations between Gregory and Helladius had been strained. A courtesy call to the metropolitan was worth the detour. Abandoning his mule cart, Gregory set off on horseback into the hills with a small retinue. After traveling from early dawn, partly on foot over rough tracks, the party finally descended into the village in the sultry heat of a late August day. Helladius made no move to greet them. They stood in the noonday sun outside the church, under the morose stares of the villagers. When, finally, Helladius condescended to invite Gregory into the cool of the sanctuary, the pair barely exchanged a word — no gesture to Gregory to take his seat on the priests' bench, no polite inquiry about his journey, no invitation to stay for the festival banquet. It was a resounding snub. Gregory was furious. He betrayed the ill-concealed anger of a local notable, a man of *paideia,* affronted by an upstart colleague who should have known better. He wrote immediately to the patriarch of Antioch: "But if you look at us, as ourselves, divested of our episcopal rank, which of us has more than the other? Birth? Education? Freedom of speech before great and esteemed persons? . . . What can justify that outrage of us, if the man enjoys neither superiority of birth, nor the swank of high office, nor outstanding power with words, nor preeminence in civic benefactions?"[1]

The bishops who had emerged, relatively suddenly, as new figures in local society tended, in the eastern empire, to come from backgrounds similar to that of Gregory. They were local notables, proud of their good birth and of their possession of *paideia*.[2] The victory of the church in their region had been accompanied by a heady rhetoric that stressed the paradoxical, because supernatural, novelty of the triumph of the faith. Acts of direct violence against ancient, holy buildings, even attacks on the persons and property of non-Christians, had occurred frequently. But after the death of Theodosius I in 395 and especially in the course of the preternaturally long, faceless reign of his grandson, Theodosius II, from 408 to 450, it was plain that a new equilibrium had been reached. Like stones shaken in a sieve, the upper classes of the cities took on a new complexion: the Christian bishop and his clergy were more prominent than before. But the same stones remained, if redistributed in a different pattern.

We do not know to what extent an emperor such as Theodosius I either foresaw or thought that he could control the outcome of his repeated decisions to grant *parrhésia* to Christian monks and bishops. But the reshuffling of local factions that resulted from this decision could not have been more consistent with the traditions of the Roman past, even if he had planned it. The eastern empire became a more markedly Christian state, as he had wished it to be, but little change had occurred in the profane structures that supported its civic life. When these structures changed, and changed profoundly, as they did in the coming centuries, this cannot be said to have happened as a result of the impact of Christianity. Rather, the Christian church, now irreversibly implicated in the life of the eastern cities, changed with them.

We can sense the tacit realignment of the governing class in innumerable small, but revealing, details. Even developments that could be presented, with good reason, as novel features of the rise of Christianity came to be expressed in a language that had not broken with the past. The passionate sermons of the Cappadocian Fathers and of John Chrysostom on the care

---

1.   Gregory of Nyssa, *Ep.* 1.32, 34, in *Grégoire de Nysse: Lettres,* ed. and trans. P. Maraval, Sources chrétiennes 363 (Paris: Le Cerf, 1990), 102–4; see pp. 54–55 on the ascription and circumstances of the letter. It is translated as *Letter* 18 in W. Moore and H. A. Wilson, eds., *Select Writings of Gregory, Bishop of Nyssa, Library of the Nicene and Post-Nicene Fathers* (Grand Rapids, Mich.: Eerdmans, 1976), 4:545–48.

2.   W. Eck, "Der Einfluss der konstantinischen Wende auf die Auswahl der Bischöfe im 4. and 5. Jahrhundert," *Chiron* 8 (1978): 561–85; Rita Lizzi, *Il potere episcopale nell'Oriente Romano* (Rome: Edizioni dell'Ateneo, 1987), 13–32.

of the poor presented the new Christian dispensation in the city in such a way that the wealthy Christian almsgiver took on the attributes of a *tropheus,* of a notable who "nourished" his hometown. The language of these sermons has enabled scholars to trace the abiding power of ancient notions of civic *euergesia,* now called upon to touch the consciences of the Christian rich.[3]

Nor were these merely rhetorical flourishes. In the small, relatively cohesive towns of Asia Minor, wealth could flow from the powerful only in a strictly delimited number of ways. Wealth released through symbolically charged gestures to new categories of the population — the poor — had a way of trickling towards more ancient watercourses, hollowed out by centuries of civic practice. The city benefited from the wealth of its church through buildings, through banquets, and through the support of distressed gentlewomen enrolled in the order of widows.[4] Many bishops, indeed, were thought to have fitted a little too readily into the role of *tropheus. Lithomania,* the itch to build, was regarded as the besetting sin of great bishops. Theophilus of Alexandria was accused of having spent money donated to him to buy shirts for the poor on the construction of grandiose new churches.[5] The complaint that the food of the poor was eaten up by stone, by the multicolored marbles and gold mosaic of new basilicas, ran all around the Mediterranean in this generation. Only a model bishop, such as Rabbula of Edessa, would boast of not having undertaken great building schemes out of concern for the poor.[6] Such bishops were not necessarily the most popular. Shocking though the phenomenon might be to sensitive souls, the conflict of priorities in the use of the church's wealth had come to stay.

Indeed, it was as a builder that the bishop made his clearest statement of good intent to the city. By the middle of the sixth century, for instance, the acts of wholesale destruction and the intercommunal violence that were believed to have led to the obliteration of the great temple of Marnas at

3.   L. Robert, *Hellenica* 11–12 (1960): 569–72; A. Natali, "Eglise et évergétisme à Antioche à la fin du ive siècle d'après Jean Chrysostome," in *Studia Patristica* 17.3 (Oxford: Pergamon Press, 1982), 1176–84.

4.   On enrollment of widows as a sinecure, see Palladius, *Dialogus de vita Johannis Chrysostomi* 5: *Patrologia Graeca* 47:20; as a bribe, see Theophilus, *Letter to the Bishops of Palestine,* in Jerome, *Ep.* 92.3: *Patrologia Latina* 22:766.

5.   Palladius, *Dialogus* 6:22. For the patriarchate of Theophilus as a turning point in ecclesiastical building, see A. Martin, "Les premiers siècles du christianisme à Alexandrie: Essai de topographie religieuse," *Revue des études augustiniennes* 30 (1984): 211–25.

6.   *Panegyric on Rabbula,* in *S. Ephraemi Syri, Rabbulae episcopi Edessensis, Balaei et aliorum opera selecta,* ed. J. J. Overbeck (Oxford: Clarendon Press, 1865): 190.13–23; A. Amiaud, *La légende syriaque de Saint Alexis l'homme de Dieu* (Paris: F. Vieweg, 1889), 9, Syriac text p. 13.2–20; cf. Jerome, *Epp.* 52.10, 58.7: *Patrologia Latina* 22:535, 584; Isidore of Pelusium, *Ep.* 3.246: *Patrologia Graeca* 78:648D–685C.

Gaza in the time of Bishop Porphyry, in the early fifth century, now lay in a semilegendary past.[7] The present bishop of Gaza, Marcianus, was a builder and the discreet instigator of building by the powerful, not a destroyer like his ferocious predecessor. Leading citizens could not miss the great octagonal church that stood on one side of the agora: its outer porch, supported by four tall columns of vivid Carystian marble, bore the sign of the Cross carved on the keystone of its arch. Their robes fluttering in the welcome breeze, the townspeople would cross the courtyard to enter the church, a great, cool space glimmering with silver and gold. This was money well spent: "Other benefactions contribute to the *décor* of a city, while outlays on a church combine beauty with a city's renown for godliness. . . . for wealth that flows out for holy purposes becomes an ever-running stream for its possessors."[8] A little to the north of the city, on a hillside fanned by the cool air rising from the Mediterranean, the colonnaded garden adjoining the shrine of Saint Stephen served Marcianus as a banqueting space. Here he would receive the notables of Gaza, "with guileless heart and smiling face, like Homer's Nestor, *whose speech ran sweeter than honey* (Iliad 1.249)." In a province that had recently been shaken by a savage Samaritan revolt, the benign Marcianus was a reassuringly solid presence.[9]

Placed in this way, against a *décor* of new buildings that continued, without a break, the highest, most "classical" standards of craftsmanship available at the time,[10] it is not surprising that most bishops maintained, also, the solid cultural *décor* associated with their status. Leadership in local society meant possession of *paideia*. Neither church nor empire, wrote Isidore of Pelusium to a newly ordained lay reader, could continue to function as humane institutions without *logoi*.[11]

We are dealing with a group of leading Christians who had "found their way around stark choices."[12] The current rhetorical antithesis between *pai-*

---

7.   The vivid *Life of Porphyry* by Mark the Deacon may be a later compilation. See H. Grégoire and M. A. Kugener, eds., *Marc le Diacre: Vie de Porphyre* (Paris: Belles Lettres, 1930), xxxiii–xiv, and P. Peeters, "La vie géorgienne de saint Porphyre de Gaza," *Analecta Bollandiana* 59 (1941): 65–201. The incident is analyzed in Raymond Van Dam, "From Paganism to Christianity at Late Antique Gaza," *Viator* 16 (1985): 1–20. See also Carol A. M. Glucker, *The City of Gaza in the Roman and Byzantine Period* (Oxford: B.A.R., 1987).

8.   Choricius, *Oratio* 1.18, 20, 30, 42, ed. R. Förster and E. Richtsteig (Leipzig: Teubner, 1929), 7, 8, 10, 13. See C. Mango, *The Art of the Byzantine Empire* (Englewood Cliffs, N.J.: Prentice Hall, 1972), 60–72, for further translations.

9.   Choricius, *Oratio* 2.23, 33, ed. Förster and Richtsteig, pp. 34, 36.

10.   This is well studied with a clear sense of its implications, for North Africa, in J. Christern, *Das frühchristliche Pilgerheiligtum von Tebessa* (Wiesbaden: F. Steiner, 1976), 257–60.

11.   Isidore of Pelusium, *Ep.* 1.322: *Patrologia Graeca* 78:369A.

12.   R. A. Kaster, *Guardians of Language: The Grammarian and Society in Late Antiquity*

deia and the artless wisdom of the Gospels; the somewhat strained attempts to lay down rules for a "proper use" of non-Christian literature: these were insubstantial afterthoughts compared with the solid weight of East Roman upper-class attitudes.[13] *Paideia* was there to stay. And this was because *paideia,* as we saw, was a weighty matter. It was not the trivial ornament of a leisure class. It was the exquisite condensation of hard-won skills of social living — the one, reliable code that governed the behavior of the powerful. *Paideia* offered ancient, almost proverbial guidance, drawn from the history and literature of Greece, on serious issues, issues which no notable — Christian or polytheist, bishop or layman — could afford to ignore: on courtesy, on the prudent administration of friendship, on the control of anger, on poise and persuasive skill when faced by official violence. To speak of the virtues instilled by Greek literature as "a shadow-outline," "a rough charcoal sketch" of true, Christian virtue, as Basil of Caesarea had once done, in his famous address *To Young Men, on how they might derive profit from pagan literature,* was to step back too far from late Roman reality.[14] For the average notable, they *were* virtue.

Paideia continued to provide the bishops of the fifth century with what they needed most — the means of living at peace with their neighbors. The newly edited letters of Firmus, bishop of Caesarea, Basil's former see (who died in 439), make this plain. Their interest lies in the fact that they are so uninteresting. They show how a bishop, whom we know to have been an active participant in the ecclesiastical maneuvering associated with the Council of Ephesus, maintained his alliances in the old manner. Firmus appealed to the natural friendship that should bind together those associated with Greek *paideia.* Later Byzantines, who copied these letters into anthologies, appreciated them for what they were: gems of old-world civility.[15] A neighboring bishop, Eugenios, received a hunting dog whose beauty rivaled that of Helen of Troy.[16] The two wines that Eugenios had sent to Firmus required a Homer to do justice to their bouquet.[17] Basil's poorhouse at Caesarea, the famous Basileias, is mentioned in only one letter, in which Firmus declared his determination that it should not serve

---

(Berkeley: University of California Press, 1988), 79; see esp. pp. 74–81, among the best pages in an indispensable book.

13. C. Gnilka, *Chrésis: Die Methode der Kirchenväter im Umgang mit der antiken Kultur* (Basel: Schwabe, 1984), 63–91, 103–32.

14. Basil, *To Young Men* 10.1, in *Saint Basil: The Letters,* vol. 4, ed. and trans. R. J. Deferrari and M. R. P. McGuire, Loeb Classical Library (Cambridge, Mass.: Harvard University Press, 1961), 430.

15. M.-A. Calvet-Sébasti and P.-L. Gatier, eds., *Firmus de Césarée: Lettres,* Sources chrétiennes 350 (Paris: Le Cerf, 1989), 35–51.

16. Firmus, *Ep.* 44, ed. Calvet-Sébasti and Gatier, p. 168.

17. Firmus, *Ep.* 45, ed. Calvet-Sébasti and Gatier, p. 174.

as a refuge for work-shy peasants fleeing from the estates of their owners.[18] Bishops such as Firmus cast the spell of *paideia* over what had remained a potentially faction-ridden community.

A subtle shift occurred by which the rhetorical antithesis between non-Christian *paideia* and "true" Christianity was defused. *Paideia* and Christianity were presented as two separate accomplishments, one of which led, inevitably, to the other. *Paideia* was no longer treated as the all-embracing and supreme ideal of a gentleman's life. It was seen, instead, as the necessary first stage in the life cycle of the Christian public man. A traditional ornament, *paideia* was also a preparatory school of Christian character.

Deeply rooted assumptions about culture and religion made this "two-stage" solution seem eminently sensible. Christianity, Gregory of Nyssa had insisted, was "the sublime philosophy."[19] Its theology and higher moral practices (increasingly identified, in effect, with the monastic life) were not for beginners, still less for the uninitiated. It was *paideia* for "those inside," not shared by "those outside."[20] But philosophy had always been seen in that light. Philosophy was a vocation to a higher level of intellectual and moral endeavor. The philosopher was called upon to adopt a distinctive and exacting way of life. In practice, the common culture of *paideia* provided the indispensable first stage in the formation of a philosopher. Groomed in the accustomed manner, a few serious young notables would rise, through becoming philosophers, to the forbidding heights of a life-style different from that of the majority of their peers. For such persons, *paideia* had always been seen as a preparation for higher things. All that Basil did, in his address *To Young Men,* was to make more insistent and more universal the concept of philosophy. All Christians were called to be adherents of "the sublime philosophy." But "Greek letters," that is, *paideia,* still functioned as it had done. It was a moral and intellectual boot camp in which the flighty young sharpened their minds and toughened their moral fiber before committing themselves, as adults, to the more serious choices associated with the Christian life.[21]

Basil, along with his contemporaries and successors, believed instinctively that religion, like youth, was too fine a thing to be wasted on children. Initiation, now in the form of Christian baptism, was a rite that was entered into only after careful consideration. One had to be sure that it was consistent with the circumstances of one's life and with the deepest inclinations of one's character. Firmus, a notable of Carthage, wrote to

18. Firmus, *Ep.* 43, ed. Calvet-Sébasti and Gatier, pp. 79–80.
19. Gregory of Nyssa, *Oratio catechetica* 28.3: *Patrologia Graeca* 45:46A.
20. A. M. Malingrey, *Philosophia* (Paris: Klincksieck, 1961), 212–13.
21. Basil, *To Young Men* 2.6, in Deferrari and McGuire, *Saint Basil* 4:382.

Augustine, stating firmly that he would not yet take the final step of baptism. Though well-read in Christian literature, Firmus claimed that he regarded Christian baptism as too serious a matter to commit himself to it in a hurry: "The burden of such a great weight cannot be borne by the weak. . . . For he gives assurance of reverence for the faith who, to attain the august secrets of the sacred majesty, approaches its inmost reaches with due hesitation."[22] Firmus intended to wait until God himself made his will plain, possibly, as was often the case, by some dream or untoward event that "warned or struck fear" into the prospective initiate.[23]

Firmus' hesitation annoyed Augustine. It flouted the bishop's firm beliefs about grace and predestination. This grace was sufficient for all circumstances, and given the extent of man's fallen condition, it must be appropriated, through baptism into the Catholic church, as quickly as possible.[24] Yet Firmus' views were normal in the Greek East. Full commitment to Christianity, like commitment to the philosophical life, followed the rhythms of the life cycle. Even young men of serious intent, from believing families, postponed their baptism until after adolescence. Baptism was a form of *engagement* that marked their entry into the adult world. Basil and Gregory Nazianzen were not baptized until they returned from their studies, in their twenties. Others were in less of a hurry. Baptism, for them, took on an *ex voto* quality. It was a gesture of thanks and devotion to a God who had, so far, protected them through the storms of life.[25] It was a public occasion, usually performed before a carefully chosen group of peers. "A bishop shall baptize me . . . and he of noble birth, for it would be a sad thing for my nobility to be insulted by being baptized by a man of no family."[26] Such persons would have been indelibly marked by Greek

22. Augustine, *Ep.* 2*.4, 6, ed. J. Divjak, in *Corpus Scriptorum Ecclesiasticorum Latinorum* 88 (Vienna: W. Tempsky, 1981), 11, 12; *Bibliothèque augustinienne: Oeuvres de Saint Augustin 46B: Lettres 1*-29** (Paris: Etudes augustiniennes, 1987), 64, 68; R. B. Eno, trans., *Saint Augustine: Letters VI (1*-29*)*, Fathers of the Church (Washington, D.C.: Catholic University of America Press, 1989), 20, 21.

23. Augustine, *Ep.* 2*.7, ed. Divjak, p. 14; *Lettres 1*-29*,* 72; Eno, *Saint Augustine: Letters VI,* 23. Compare Augustine, *De catechizandis rudibus* 6.10.

24. Augustine, *Ep.* 2*.7-11, ed. Divjak, pp. 14-19; *Lettres 1*-29*,* 72-86; Eno, *Saint Augustine: Letters VI,* 23-28. This is a classic statement of Augustine's views.

25. This was the case with Synesius of Cyrene, after his return from a mission to Constantinople in 400; Synesius, *Hymn* 1.428-95, in *Synésios de Cyrène: Hymnes I,* ed. and trans. C. Lacombrade, (Paris: Belles Lettres, 1978), 54-56; A. Fitzgerald, trans., *The Essays and Hymns of Synesius* (Oxford: Oxford University Press, 1930), 2:380-81, *Hymn* 3.

26. Gregory Nazianzen, *Oratio* 40.26: *Patrologia Graeca* 36:396B; C. G. Browne and J. E. Swallow, trans., *Select Orations of Saint Gregory Nazianzen,* Library of the Nicene and Post-Nicene Fathers (Grand Rapids, Mich.: Eerdmans, 1974), 7:369.

paideia long before they advanced, through the baptismal pool, to the higher levels of a "sublime philosophy."

In the conditions of the fifth century, these attitudes gave members of the upper classes room for maneuver. They needed time to make up their minds. If they had to conform to the dominant religion, they wished to feel free to do so without seeming unduly hurried. They had not submitted to brute force. Many fifth-century notables must have resembled General Robert E. Lee, of whom his biographer could write that "he was content until he was past forty-five to hold to the code of a gentleman rather than to the formal creed of a church."[27]

For tenacious polytheists, of course, *paideia* acted as a much-needed buffer. Possession of a common culture had always muted tensions between conflicting segments of the governing classes. It now served to veil deep-seated, private divisions between Christians and non-Christians. *Paideia* was shared by both. It was imparted in schools that continued to serve the city as a whole, not solely the dogmatic interests of the bishop's palace. Many bishops, indeed, were careful to patronize rhetors, even those known to be non-Christians.[28] Education provided a much-needed neutral space, eminently appropriate to young men. All but the zealots in the audience, for instance, considered it a serious lapse in good taste when, in late fifth-century Alexandria, a young rhetor ended a funeral oration in honor of his former professor, a Christian, with an attack on the gods. The polytheists present protested: they had not been invited to a display of ancient rhetoric in memory of a common friend to be subjected to such brutally confessional language.[29]

Yet we must remember that the image of a world where the old and the new came together in an effortless, prearranged harmony would not have carried such weight if the eastern empire of the fifth century had been, in reality, as orderly and as undivided a society as the image suggests. In every region, the tacit alliance between potentially conflicting segments of the urban elite was sealed by the fear of alternatives. These elites knew that they lived in a threatened empire. Quite apart from determined enemies on every frontier — on the Danube, the Euphrates, and the Nile — the countryside of Asia Minor and northern Syria was racked by brigandage, based in the Taurus Mountains. In Palestine, the revolt of profoundly disaffected groups, Jews and Samaritans, remained a constant threat.

Nor was the sacralized violence of the monks much to the liking of

27.   D. S. Freeman, *R. E. Lee: A Biography* (New York: Charles Scribners', 1935), 4:502.
28.   Kaster, *Guardians of Language,* 79.
29.   Zacharias Scholasticus, *Vie de Sévère: Patrologia Orientalis* 2:45–46.

many bishops. We frequently find bishops allying with the city's elite to keep monks out of town and to defend the ancient customs of the city. At just the time when Bishop Marcianus presided, in his benign, classical manner, over the church in Gaza, the monks of the region were indignant that the governor and a notable of Gaza, now resident in Constantinople, wished to continue — apparently without a demurrer from Marcianus — night spectacles in the theater and festivals deemed by the monks to be "pagan."[30] When in 434–435 the prefect of Constantinople, Leontius, wished to hold Olympic games in the fashionable suburb of Chalcedon, modern Kadiköy, across the water from Constantinople, the bishop told the outraged abbot Hypatius to mind his own business: "Are you determined to die, even if no one wishes to make a martyr of you? As you are a monk, go and sit in your cell and keep quiet. This is my affair."[31] Altogether, the closing of the ranks of a central core of Christian notables against obdurate non-Christians, on the one hand, and against the radical forces that their more ruthless predecessors had unleashed, on the other, explains the deceptively unruffled consensus of the new eastern empire of the age of Theodosius II.

Miracles and Power

It was largely the spokesmen of that consensus who presented educated contemporaries with an appropriate image of their stormy past. We know in such detail about what happened at the turn of the fourth and fifth centuries because so much was written about it in the ensuing decades. As Alan Cameron has said of Constantinople in the age of Theodosius II: "The dominating literary preoccupation of the age was ecclesiastical history and hagiography."[32]

Christian writers took up again the history of the church where Eusebius had left off, with the reign of Constantine. In 402 Rufinus of Aquileia, a Latin monk and former friend of Jerome's who had lived in Egypt and the Holy Land, translated the *Ecclesiastical History* of Eusebius, bringing it up to his own times in two further books, with the destruction of the Serapeum and the final victory and death of Theodosius I in A.D. 395.[33] He was followed, a generation later, in Constantinople, by the laymen

30. *Barsanuphe et Jean de Gaza: Correspondance* 836, 837, trans. L. Regnault and P. Lemaire (Sable-sur-Sarthe: Abbaye de Solesmes, 1971), 504.

31. Callinicus, *Life of Hypatius* 33, in *Les moines d'Orient*, vol. 2, *Les moines de la région de Constantinople*, trans. A. J. Festugière (Paris: Le Cerf, 1961), 57.

32. Alan Cameron, "The Empress and the Poet," *Yale Classical Studies* 27 (1982): 279.

33. Françoise Thélamon, *Païens et chrétiens au ivème siècle: L'apport de l'"Histoire ecclésiastique" de Rufin d'Aquilée* (Paris: Etudes augustiniennes, 1981).

Socrates (in 439) and Sozomen (around 443)[34] and, later (in 449), by Theodoret, bishop of Cyrrhus, who had already written (in 440) a triumphant history of the monks of his own region, his *History of the Friends of God.*[35]

The shift of attention to the recent history of the church was a political fact in its own right. If, in the words of Joseph de Maistre, the army that is the first to celebrate a *Te Deum* is the army that is deeemed to have won the battle, then the Christian literature of the generation that succeeded the death of Theodosius I can be seen as a *Te Deum* whose triumphant strains solemnly declared the victory of the Christian church over all other religions in the Roman world.

The histories confirmed, in vivid narratives, the Christian representation of their own times, as it had been propounded in preaching and in polemical writings. The monks, of course, received special attention. Simple holy men were portrayed as having reduced non-Christian philosophers to silence at the Council of Nicaea.[36] It was no coincidence, for Sozomen, that the fortunes of philosophers should have reached their nadir under the emperor Valens—when they were hounded down all over the eastern empire on charges of illicit divination and high treason—at a time when the "true" philosophers, the monks of Egypt and Syria, reached their peak, in numbers, holiness, and popular acclaim.[37]

Above all, Christian historians lingered on dramatic moments of confrontation between the two faiths. Rufinus' *Ecclesiastical History* reached its climax with the destruction of the mighty temple of Serapis in Alexandria in 392, followed by the victory of Theodosius I at the battle of the Frigidus in 395 over a western usurper, Eugenius, whose army had placed its faith in statues of the ancient gods.[38]

34.   Detailed studies, such as that of Thélamon for Rufinus, are lacking, but see especially A. D. Momigliano, "Popular Beliefs and the Late Roman Historians," in *Studies in Church History* 8, ed. D. Baker (Cambridge: Cambridge University Press, 1971), 1–18, now in *Essays in Ancient and Modern Historiography* (Oxford: Blackwell, 1977), 141–59; Glen Chesnut, *The First Christian Histories,* Théologie Historique 46 (Paris: Beauchesne, 1977); Lellia Cracco Ruggini, "Universalità e campanilismo, centro e periferia, città e deserto nelle *Storie Ecclesiastiche,*" in *La storiografia ecclesiastica nella tarda antichità: Convegno di Erice* (Messina: Industria Poligrafica di Sicilia, 1978), 159–94; idem, "Imperatori romani e uomini divini," in *Passatopresente* 2 (Turin: Giapichelli, 1982), 9–91; Mario Mazza, *Le maschere del potere: Cultura e politica nella tarda antichità* (Naples: Jovene, 1986).

35.   R. M. Price, *Theodoret: A History of the Monks of Syria,* Cistercian Studies 88 (Kalamazoo, Mich.: Cistercian Publications, 1985): ix–xxxiv.

36.   Gelasius, *Ecclesiastical History,* 2.13.1–15, ed. G. Loeschke and M. Heinemann (Leipzig: J. C. Hinrichs, 1918), 61–64; Rufinus, *Ecclesiastical History* 1.3: *Patrologia Latina* 21:469B–470C; Sozomen, *Ecclesiastical History* 1.18; Thélamon, *Païens et chrétiens,* 430–35.

37.   Sozomen, *Ecclesiastical History* 6.28–35.

38.   Rufinus, *Ecclesiastical History* 2.22–34: *Patrologia Latina* 21:528A–540C; Thélamon, *Païens et chrétiens,* 325–417, 459–72.

The mood of triumph generated at that time is captured in a fifth-century papyrus fragment of an illustrated world chronicle. In its left-hand margin, the patriarch Theophilus is shown standing on top of the Serapeum, clasping the Gospels and framed by palms of victory. In the right margin, the usurper Eugenius, who put his trust in the gods, kneels in defeat.[39] The imperial court, now settled permanently at Constantinople, under Theodosius' eldest son, Arcadius (383–408), and, later, his grandson, Theodosius II, validated the perspective of the church historians. Local events, such as the fate of the temples in Alexandria and elsewhere, were taken up and broadcast to the empire at large as part of the official chronicle of Constantinople. They merged with the solemn life of the "Ruling City," with its imperial occasions and high Christian ceremonies, to communicate, throughout the eastern empire, a sense of the recurrent, unfailing victory of the Christian emperors over ancient gods and restless barbarians.[40]

Altogether, the impression conveyed by many modern scholars, that the fourth century A.D. was characterized by a widespread and fully conscious conflict between Christianity and paganism, derives, in large part, from a skillful construct first presented to the Roman world by the Christian historians of the fifth century. It was they who chose to speak of the previous century in terms of a conflict brought to a rapid conclusion in a series of memorable victories by the Christian faith. In this manner, they imposed a sense of narrative closure on what has been more appropriately termed a "Wavering Century."[41] The pagans must know that there had been a war and that they had been conquered. "The pagan faith," wrote Isidore of Pelusium, "made dominant for so many years, by such pains, such expenditure of wealth, such feats of arms, has vanished from the earth."[42] As the emperor Theodosius II roundly declared in 423, "the regulations of constitutions formerly promulgated shall suppress all pagans, although We now believe that there are none."[43]

It was an image of the times that depended for its credibility on what has been called, in analogous circumstances, an "ideology of silence."[44] Polytheism, in fact, remained prevalent on all levels of East Roman society.

---

39. Thélamon, *Paiens et chrétiens,* 247; a colored plate of the scene with Theophilus standing on the Serapeum forms the frontispiece of Thélamon's book.

40. B. Croke, "City Chronicles of Late Antiquity," in *Reading the Past in Late Antiquity,* ed. Graeme Clarke (Rushcutters Bay, New South Wales: Australian National University Press, 1990), 193.

41. Pierre Chuvin, *A Chronicle of the Last Pagans* (Cambridge, Mass.: Harvard University Press, 1990), 36–56.

42. Isidore of Pelusium, *Epp.* 1.270: *Patrologia Graeca* 78:344A.

43. *Codex Theodosianus* 16.10.22; Chuvin, *Chronicle of the Last Pagans,* 91–92.

44. Charles J. Halperin, *Russia and the Golden Horde: The Mongol Impact on Russian History* (London: Tauris, 1985), 5, refers to medieval Russian relations with the non-Christian nomads.

Called by Greek Christian authors "Hellenism," the old religion of the "Hellenes," traditional polytheism, like Judaism, achieved great prominence in Christian writings of the fifth century. It formed part of a Christian discourse of triumph. The faith of the "Hellenes" stood for the demonic errors of a past that had been irrevocably transcended. But this was a literary construct, an insistent *basso profundo* to the celebration of modern times, associated with the Christian empire.[45] Polytheists themselves were rarely mentioned in official circles.

As a result, our evidence allows us no more than fleeting glimpses of the life of old believers. We know, for instance, of polytheists firmly established in small cities all over the eastern empire. At Athens,[46] at Aphrodisias in Caria,[47] and at the shrine of Menouthis outside Alexandria,[48] we have vivid accounts of non-Christian practice up to the end of the fifth century. In other regions, such as the Bekaa valley of Lebanon and Harran (Carrhae) on the eastern frontier, polytheism was normal up to and beyond the end of the sixth century.[49]

The fragmentary nature of our sources tends to exaggerate the local, and hence the seemingly residual, quality of the practices that they describe. Communities loyal to the old gods tend to be treated, by modern scholars, as isolated pockets of "pagan survival" in a largely Christian empire. Only very rarely is the ideology of silence abandoned, in a Christian source, in such a way that we can see these fragments as part of the greater circle of stubborn and ceremonious resistance to Christianity. Writing to the patriarch of Constantinople in 431 to justify his resistance to Cyril of Alexandria after the Council of Ephesus, John of Antioch insisted that the churches of the East could not afford to be weakened by theological controversies (of the sort provoked by Cyril) if they were "to hold their own against the heathen in Phoenicia, Palestine and Arabia."[50] Brought

45.   P. Canivet, *Histoire d'une entreprise apologétique au vème siècle* (Paris: Bloud and Gay, 1958), 118–25.

46.   Garth Fowden, "The Pagan Holy Man in Late Antique Society," *Journal of Hellenic Studies* 102 (1982): 33–59; Alison Frantz, *The Athenian Agora xxiv: Late Antiquity* (Princeton: American School of Classical Studies at Athens, 1988), 57–92.

47.   Charlotte Roueché, *Aphrodisias in Late Antiquity,* Journal of Roman Studies Monographs 5 (London: Society for the Promotion of Roman Studies, 1989), 85–96; R. R. R. Smith, "Late Roman Philosopher Portraits from Aphrodisias," *Journal of Roman Studies* 80 (1990): 153–55.

48.   Zacharias, *Vie de Sévère,* 14–35; Chuvin, *Chronicle of the Last Pagans,* 106–11.

49.   M. Tardieu, "Sabiens coraniques et 'Sabiens' de Harran," *Journal asiatique* 272 (1986): 1–44; C. Klugkist, "Die beiden Homilien des Isaak von Antiochien über die Eroberung von Bet Hûr durch die Araber," in *IV Symposium Syriacum 1984,* Orientalia Christiana Analecta 229 (Rome: Pontificium Institutum Studiorum Orientalium, 1987), 237–56; Chuvin, *Chronicle of the Last Pagans,* 112–13, 139–40.

50.   *Collectio Casinensis* 287.5, ed. E. Schwartz, in *Acta Conciliorum Oecumenicorum* 1.4 (Berlin: de Gruyter, 1932–33), 210.

out though it was by political calculations, John's admission allows us to sense the extent of the muted landscape usually hidden from us by the glare of Christian sources. Recent work has tended to confirm the picture hinted at by John. The resilience and adaptability of polytheism was an integral, if officially unmentionable, part of the heterogeneity and vigor of the eastern provinces in late antiquity.[51]

Nor was this polytheism invariably local. Accounts of student life in Alexandria and Beirut at the very end of the fifth century show the sons of notables from all over the empire for whom polytheism was still a family religion. Christianity, usually of an ascetic and observant kind, was a novel and disturbing option, attractive to young hotheads among the student body. Families could even be divided. Out of four brothers from Aphrodisias in Caria, one became a monk in Alexandria under the name of Athanasius, two remained prominent local figures in Aphrodisias, and the fourth, Paralios, was sent to complete his studies at Alexandria, on condition that he made no contact with his brother, the renegade to Christianity.[52] It was an upper-class society as open to stormy disputations between upholders of the old and the new religions and as prone to dramatic conversions as was the Elizabethan Oxford of Edmund Campion.

Thus, despite the claims of his defenders in later years,[53] the future architect of Monophysite theology, Severus, later patriarch of Antioch, came directly from a polytheist background. He was touched by Christianity only when he made contact with circles of young zealots in the lecture halls in Alexandria and Beirut.[54] He needed to have the story of Adam and Eve explained to him when he first saw them on a mosaic in a Christian church.[55] Severus' adolescent conversion to a radical—one might say a "fundamentalist"—form of the dominant religion and his subsequent baptism at the shrine of Saint Leontius at Tripolis, near Beirut, were not so very different from the conversion of his older contemporary, Proclus of Lycia, from a religiously neutral career as a Roman lawyer to the ancient

---

51. G. W. Bowersock, *Hellenism in Late Antiquity* (Ann Arbor: University of Michigan Press, 1990), 2–5, 35–40, 72–81.

52. Zacharias, *Vie de Sévère*, 14–16, 37–44; Roueché, *Aphrodisias in Late Antiquity*, 85–86.

53. Zacharias, *Vie de Sévère*, 7–10.

54. G. Garitte, "Textes hagiographiques orientaux relatifs à Saint Léonce de Tripoli II: L'Homélie copte de Sévère d'Antioche," *Le Mouséon* 79 (1966): 335–86; *Homily* 4.1–4, pp. 357–58, trans. p. 374. These parts of Zacharias' *Life of Severus* have been conveniently translated and commented upon in R. A. Darling Young, "Zacharias: The Life of Severus," in *Ascetic Behavior in Greco-Roman Antiquity: A Sourcebook*, ed. V. L. Wimbush (Minneapolis: Fortress Press, 1990), 312–28.

55. Zacharias, *Vie de Sévère*, 49.

wisdom that led him to sail to Athens, "under the escort of all the gods," in order to take up the austere life of a philosopher.[56]

In many ways, the ideology of silence protected such persons. The fifth- and sixth-century eastern empire had its fair share of men of *paideia* in high places who learned to keep their beliefs to themselves. The more devout of these lived in a world that was as much of their own creation as was the mirage of a totally Christian empire proposed by their opponents. At Athens, the philosopher Proclus and his biographer Marinus gave little sign that they lived in the same city as that revealed, in its monuments, to have included ostentatious reminders of the Christian dispensation: a palace for the pious empress Eudocia, the daughter of an Athenian professor, in the agora; a large tetraconch church in the courtyard of the Library of Hadrian; and perhaps even a settlement of Christian monks commanding the pass through Mount Aigaleos, at Daphni.[57]

At Aphrodisias in Caria, Asclepiodotus repaired the dome of the principal bathhouse adjoining the theater in about 480. His honorary statue stood beside his handiwork.[58] "Loaded with honors by the emperors" and "a leader of the town council," Asclepiodotus was a devout polytheist. He married his daughter to a philosopher, his namesake, the doctor and natural scientist Asclepiodotus of Alexandria. The young couple relied on a vision of Isis for the promise of a child.[59]

Asclepiodotus of Aphrodisias knew to which heaven he belonged. His monument, carved in the form of an elegant pyramid, made this plain: "He did not die, nor did he see the stream of Acheron, but in Olympus Asclepiodotus is among the stars—he who also built splendid things for his motherland."[60] And yet all this happened at a time when the temple of Aphrodite, its open colonnades now sheathed with stone to make it a closed Christian basilica, rose above his city as the bishop's new cathedral.[61]

We are in a world where religious groups had come to take advantage of the ideology of silence in order to settle down beneath a "ruling faith."[62]

56. Marinus, *Life of Proclus* 8–10, ed. J. F. Boissonade (Leipzig, 1814; Amsterdam: Hakkert, 1966), 6–8.
57. Garth Fowden, "The Athenian Agora and the Progress of Christianity," *Journal of Roman Archaeology* 3 (1990): 497–500.
58. Roueché, *Aphrodisias in Late Antiquity*, no. 53, pp. 87–88.
59. Zacharias, *Vie de Sévère*, 17–19; Roueché, *Aphrodisias in Late Antiquity*, 88–92.
60. Roueché, *Aphrodisias in Late Antiquity*, no. 54, p. 88.
61. Robin Cormack, "The Temple as the Cathedral," in *Aphrodisias Papers*, ed. Charlotte Roueché and Kenan T. Erim, Journal of Roman Archaeology Supplement 1 (Ann Arbor: University of Michigan Press, 1990), 75–84.
62. Damascius, *Life of Isidore*, fragment 316, in *Damascii Vitae Isidori Reliquiae*, ed. C. Zintzen (Hildesheim: G. Olms, 1967), 251.

They did so in a manner that came closer to the stable, if unloving, relationships that would later characterize the status of Jews and Christians under Muslim rule than to the ideal image of a world without polytheism, propounded by Christian writers and implied in the imperial laws. If such people did not exist, officially, they were nonetheless free to continue their lives largely unmolested: "peaceful Jews and pagans who are not attempting anything seditious or unlawful" were protected by law from Christian violence.[63] Many "Hellenes" continued to follow careers as philosophers and as exponents of *paideia* in high places, in a manner that followed directly trajectories exemplified, for the fourth century, by Libanius and Themistius. If the abundant correspondence of Severianus of Damascus had survived, for instance, we might know the late fifth-century Greek world as well as we know that of Libanius in the fourth.[64]

The career of one such "Hellene," at least, is known to us.[65] Isocasius was a native of Aegae, in Cilicia. He first became famous as a sophist at Antioch. Bishop Theodoret sent him pupils and may have used him, as a distinguished local resident, to help secure the election of his friend, Domnus, as patriarch of Antioch in 441.[66] Isocasius cared for his health in the old manner. Exhausted by work, he retired to seek a dream of healing from the gods, in the rare tranquillity of a seaside shrine, long associated with the wonder-working hero Sarpedon, on the outskirts of Seleucia in Cilicia — modern Meryamlik, with its haunting view of the tranquil coastline of the Mediterranean (now, alas, turned into a housing estate, where the venerable stones of the shrine are rapidly disappearing into the pickup trucks of developers). Christians ascribed Isocasius' cure to Saint Thecla, whose basilica stood on the site and was regarded as one of the principal pilgrimage centers of the Christian world. Their opinion worried Isocasius not in the slightest. Despite a rebuke from Thecla, he accepted his cure without changing his loyalty to the old gods.[67]

It was only when his career took him, at last, to Constantinople, around 465, as *quaestor* of the imperial palace — an important office, eminently appropriate to a man of letters with a reputation for "philosophical" recti-

63. *Codex Theodosianus* 16.10.24 (of 423), repeated in *Codex Justinianus* 1.11.6.

64. Damascius, *Life of Isidore,* fragment 279, ed. Zintzen, p. 225.

65. J. R. Martindale, ed., *The Prosopography of the Later Roman Empire,* vol. 2, *A.D. 395–527* (Cambridge: Cambridge University Press, 1980), 633–34.

66. J. Flemming, ed., *Akten der ephesinischen Synode vom Jahre 449,* in *Abhandlungen der Königlichen Gesellschaft der Wissenschaften zu Göttingen,* Phil.-Hist. Klasse 15.1 (1917): 126.11, trans. 127.16.

67. *Miracles of Saint Thecla* 39, in *Vie et Miracles de Sainte Thècle,* ed. G. Dagron, Subsidia Hagiographica 62 (Brussels: Société des Bollandistes, 1978), 394; cf. *Miracles* 18, 40, pp. 338, 396.

tude—that Isocasius' beliefs became a liability.[68] Accused of polytheism during a riot in 467, he may have narrowly escaped a lynching.[69] What even Christian contemporaries remembered about this occasion was that Isocasius demonstrated a poise and courage worthy of a philosopher. Brought to the court of the praetorian prefect, Pusaeus, his former colleague, Isocasius stood before the judge's curtain, "naked . . . his arms bound behind his back. 'Do you see yourself, Isocasius, in what condition you stand' [said Pusaeus]. And Isocasius said in reply: 'I see, and I am not dismayed. For being mortal, I have fallen upon the misfortunes of a mortal. But you pass judgement on me with pure justice, as you used to pass judgement when sitting at my side.'"[70] It was model behavior in a philosopher when facing the powerful.

In fact, Isocasius' polytheism proved to be his winning card. By allowing himself to be baptized, he defused the anger of the crowd: "He returned to his province beloved by the emperor; [for] he was a man of great prudence and a just judge . . . and helped the people of Cilicia."[71] In a court whose members were convinced that they were able to combine an intolerant official Christianity with a high level of Greek *paideia*,[72] the polytheism of Isocasius had been an open secret to his peers, of relatively little importance until a political crisis revealed that even his belief in the gods was negotiable.

Men such as Isocasius and the tenacious, low-profile polytheism of which he was only one unusually prominent example had no place in the Christian representation of the eastern empire. An ideology of silence protected the official triumph of the church. It screened from view the disquieting complexities of real life in an empire of great religious diversity, much as a millennium later in the same city a similar ideology of silence protected the belligerent Islam of the Ottoman state. The presence of so many persons and practices that could not be mentioned—or mentioned only as if already conquered—acted, in fact, as an accelerator to the elaboration of a more consequential and assertive image of a Christian empire for those who shared, or wished to seem to share, in the new dispensation.

We must always remember this. The fifth-century Christian image of

68.   Jill Harries, "The Roman Imperial Quaestor from Constantine to Theodosius II," *Journal of Roman Studies* 78 (1988): 170.

69.   John of Nikiu, *Chronicle* 88.7, in *The Chronicle of John, Bishop of Nikiu, translated from Zotenberg's Ethiopic Text,* trans. R. H. Charles (London: Williams and Norgate, 1916), 109.

70.   *Chronicon Paschale,* ad ann. 467, in *Chronicon Paschale 284–628 A.D,* trans. M. and M. Whitby (Liverpool: Liverpool University Press, 1989), 88.

71.   John of Nikiu, *Chronicle* 88.11, trans. Charles, p. 110.

72.   Cameron, "Empress and the Poet," 270–85.

the emperor and of the society he ruled never embraced the full reality of East Roman life. The strength of the eastern empire at that time lay precisely in the widespread sense that — unlike the war-torn West — many of its basic institutions had not changed since the days of Constantine and Theodosius I. Taxes continued to be collected efficiently.[73] Cities rose and fell in relative prosperity, expressing their life in the traditional manner, through inscriptions, honorary statues, and public buildings.[74] Bishops and civic notables, as we have seen, had reached a *modus vivendi* that stressed consensus and continuity with past values. As with the representation that placed illiterate monks in sharp opposition to the exponents of *paideia*, the fifth-century representation of emperor and society contained components which, though stressed for the sake of dramatic effect, were readily sacrificed or compromised in real life.

Yet there was much that was new. It may be worth our while to draw attention to some of the more novel aspects of the political imagination of fifth-century Christians. For it is by following these aspects that we can trace the vectors, as it were, of wider changes in East Roman culture and society, which led from the death of Theodosius I in 395, through the Council of Chalcedon of 451, to the very different empire ruled by Justinian from 527 to 565.

One obvious change can be seen in the Christian historiography of the first half of the fifth century. Christian historians did not only celebrate the triumph of the church. In so doing, they brought into even greater prominence the role of the emperor in East Roman society. In the hagiography and ecclesiastical histories of the age, the power of the emperor was no longer presented as tethered by the silken ropes of an upper-class *paideia*. The emperor's power came from on high. It was made intelligible by miracles. The personal devotion of individual rulers, not their *paideia*, was held to bring felicity to the empire, in the form of the blessing of God. An abundance of miraculous happenings and of wonder-working persons, associated with the reigns of individual pious emperors, was the surest sign of that blessing.[75]

73.   A. H. M. Jones, *The Later Roman Empire* (Oxford: Blackwell, 1964), 1:202–8; 2:1064–68.

74.   Roueché, *Aphrodisias in Late Antiquity,* 60–120; J. Ch. Balty, "Apamée au vie. siècle: Témoignages archéologiques de la richesse d'une ville," in *Hommes et richesses dans l'Empire byzantin: ive.–viie. siècles* (Paris: P. Lethielleux, 1989), 79–89; Robin Cormack, "Byzantine Aphrodisias: Changing the Symbolic Map of a City," *Proceedings of the Cambridge Philological Society* 216 (1990): 26–41; Hanna Geremek, "Sur la question des *boulai* dans les villes égyptiennes aux ve-viie siècles," *Journal of Juristic Papyrology* 20 (1990): 47–54; M. Whittow, "Ruling the Late Roman and Early Byzantine City: A Continuous History," *Past and Present* 129 (1990), 3–29.

75.   Chesnut, *First Christian Histories,* 182–88; Mazza, *Le maschere del potere,* 291–302;

Theodosius I, for instance, was said to have achieved a miraculous victory at the battle of the Frigidus, gained through his own prayers and those of the far-distant Egyptian holy man, John of Lycopolis (Siut).[76] Above all, the heart of the emperor was shown to be swayed to piety and to the stunning, fully public miracle of mercy by the repeated interventions of "true" philosophers, courageous bishops, and holy monks. No ecclesiastical history of the age was complete without a vivid scene of confrontation that emphasized the successful *parrhésia* of monks and bishops in their dealings with the emperor.[77]

Nothing of this, in itself, was new. Many Christians of the fourth century had wished to see the politics of the empire in just such a light. The writings of Eusebius of Caesarea clearly illustrate widespread expectations. The imperial power could hardly have been presented in more starkly supernatural terms than in Eusebius' *Oration* and *Life of Constantine*. Yet the very circumstantiality of the fifth-century historians betrays a shift of emphasis. In Eusebius we meet Constantine with his eyes raised firmly to the heavens.[78] He took little notice of his subjects as individuals. Rather, he preached at them endlessly, in sermons and in solemn laws.[79] In the tradition of Origen, Eusebius presented the emperor as a vibrant soul come down to earth to act as the herald of the true religion in the Roman world, "calling in a great voice that all can hear."[80]

Eusebius, however, wrote in Caesarea, at a considerable distance from his hero. His *Life of Constantine* was a tentative book, "an experiment in hagiography."[81] By the fifth century a Christian emperor could be taken for granted, and not least by residents of Constantinople, like the historians Socrates and Sozomen. What now mattered was how a Christian emperor fitted into his empire. It was through stories that emphasized the shared piety which bound the emperors Theodosius I and Theodosius II

Lellia Cracco Ruggini, "Il miracolo nella cultura del tardo impero: concetto e funzione," in *Hagiographie, Culture et Sociétés, ive.–xiie. siècles* (Paris: Etudes augustiniennes, 1981), 161–204.

76.   Rufinus, *Ecclesiastical History* 2.32–33: *Patrologia Latina* 21:538C–540B; Augustine, *City of God* 5.26.

77.   See, for example, the treatment of Basil and Ambrose in Theodoret, *Ecclesiastical History* 4.6, 16–17, and 5.17.

78.   Eusebius, *Life of Constantine* 4.15.

79.   Ibid., 4.24, 29.

80.   Eusebius, *In Praise of Constantine* 2.4, trans. H. A. Drake (Berkeley: University of California Press, 1976), 86. See Averil Cameron, "Eusebius of Caesarea and the Rethinking of History," in *Tria Corda: Scritti in onore di Arnaldo Momigliano*, ed. E. Gabba (Como: New Press, 1983), 77–88, and Mazza, *Le maschere del potere*, 238–47.

81.   T. D. Barnes, "Panegyric, History and Hagiography in Eusebius' *Life of Constantine*," in *The Making of Orthodoxy: Essays in Honour of Henry Chadwick*, ed. Rowan Williams (Cambridge: Cambridge University Press, 1989), 110.

to their Christian subjects, rendering them accessible to Christian spokesmen and susceptible to Christian sentiments of mercy and of pious zeal, that writers of the fifth century gave flesh and bone to the towering but distant figure of a Christian emperor, as first sketched by Eusebius.

It was the flesh and bone of access to the imperial power that came to count in the fifth century. A groundswell of confidence that Christians enjoyed access to the powerful spelled the end of polytheism far more effectively than did any imperial law or the closing of any temple. The sense that the representatives of the church could touch the levers of power on every level of the imperial system ensured that the "unyielding languidness of ancient Mediterranean communities" turned slowly but surely in the direction of Christianity.[82] Let us look briefly, then, at a few examples of this new confidence at work.

Many philosophers became bishops. Lay historians of the church, such as Socrates and Sozomen, reveal an ecclesiastical world in and around Constantinople in which idiosyncratic transitional figures abounded. Sisinnius, later bishop of the stern Novatian sect in Constantinople, had been taught philosophy by none other than the mentor of Julian the Apostate, the magnetic Maximus of Ephesus.[83] "Sisinnius was accustomed to indulge himself by wearing white garments, and by bathing twice a day in the public baths. And when someone asked him why he, a bishop, bathed himself twice a day, he replied: 'Because you do not give me time for three baths.'"[84] Others retained their ancient, rugged image. At Tomi, a crucial garrison city on the Black Sea, Bishop Theotimus continued to wear the long, shaggy hair of the professional philosopher. He was known to the local Huns as "the god of the Romans."[85]

None of this is surprising. Philosophers, after all, had tended to be local notables of high-minded, indeed profoundly religious, dispositions. They already possessed the social position and the type of culture that made them useful to the Christian communities. Synesius of Cyrene fits easily into this pattern of local notables and philosophers turned bishops.[86] He had studied under Hypatia, though an early death spared him knowledge of

82. Van Dam, "From Paganism to Christianity," 3.
83. Socrates, *Ecclesiastical History* 5.21.
84. Socrates, *Ecclesiastical History* 6.22, trans. A. C. Zenos, in *Library of the Nicene and Post-Nicene Fathers* (Grand Rapids, Mich.: Eerdmans, 1979), 2:152.
85. Sozomen, *Ecclesiastical History* 7.26.
86. The studies of Jay Bregman, *Synesius of Cyrene: Philosopher-Bishop* (Berkeley: University of California Press, 1982), and S. Vollenweider, *Neuplatonische und christliche Theologie bei Synesios von Kyrene,* Forschungen zur Kirchen-und Dogmengeschichte 35 (Göttingen: Vandenhoeck and Ruprecht, 1985), lack the historical dimension that has been handsomely provided—if with differing conclusions—in T. D. Barnes, "Synesius and Constantinople,"

his mentor's brutal murder. When he visited Constantinople in 397–400 on an embassy on behalf of his city, he knew how to style his relations with the powerful in terms of the ancient, philosophical ideal. Affecting the "rustic" candor of a philosopher,[87] Synesius set about lobbying high-placed officials in order to obtain tax relief for his native Cyrene. It was a tiresome business, but in the course of it he wrote two brilliant contributions to the vigorous pamphlet war that raged incessantly, if discreetly, along the fringes of the court: the *De regno* and the *De providentia: The Egyptian Tale*.[88] He did his duty by his city in the old-fashioned manner. Synesius later looked back with satisfaction on those years. His native intelligence, supplemented by a happy ability to interpret his own dreams, had enabled him to act as a philosopher should. He had been successful "in the management of public office in the best interest of the cities, and . . . more undaunted than was ever any Greek in a position of intimacy with the Emperor."[89] Back in Cyrenaica, talents whose deployment in Constantinople had been more a matter of wishful thinking than of reality were soon called upon by the Christian church. In 410 the clergy and notables of the region nominated Synesius as bishop of Ptolemais.

Synesius may well have grown up as a devout Christian.[90] The only "conversion" that his election and eventual consecration as bishop of Ptolemais, in early 411, imposed upon him was a drastic change in his life-style and the need to show a greater measure of caution in his intellectual pursuits. As the nominee of the formidable patriarch of Alexandria, Theophilus, to a key see in the furthest province of the patriarch's ecclesiastical empire, Synesius knew that Theophilus (or whoever might succeed him as patriarch) could yet prove to be a dangerous neighbor. Only a decade previously the

---

Greek, Roman and Byzantine Studies 27 (1986): 93–113; J. H. W. G. Liebeschuetz, "Synesius and Municipal Politics of Cyrenaica," *Byzantion* 55 (1985): 146–64; J. Long, "The Wolf and the Lion: Synesius' Egyptian Source," *Greek, Roman and Byzantine Studies* 28 (1987): 103–15; Denis Roques, *Synésios de Cyrène et la Cyrénaïque du Bas-Empire* (Paris: C.N.R.S., 1987); Lizzi, *Potere episcopale nell'Oriente Romano*, 33–111; J. H. W. G. Liebeschuetz, *Barbarians and Bishops: Army, Church and State in the Age of Arcadius and Chrysostom* (Oxford: Clarendon Press, 1990), 105–38, 228–35; and Alan Cameron and Jacqueline Long, with Lee Sherry, *Barbarians and Politics at the Court of Arcadius* (Berkeley: University of California Press, forthcoming), chap. 2.

87. Synesius, *De providentia* 1.18, in *Synesius Cyrenensis: Opuscula*, ed. N. Terzaghi (Rome: Istituto Poligrafico, 1944), 105; and *Patrologia Graeca* 66:1253C; A. Fitzgerald, trans., *The Essays and Hymns of Synesius* (Oxford: Oxford University Press, 1930), 2:306.

88. Liebeschuetz, *Barbarians and Bishops*, 106–7, 253–72.

89. Synesius, *De insomniis* 9, ed. Terzaghi, p. 176 [c.xiv], and *Patrologia Graeca* 66:1309A; trans. Fitzgerald, *Essays and Hymns* 2:349.

90. Bregman, *Synesius*, 60–163; Roques, *Synésios de Cyrène*, 302–3; Liebeschuetz, *Barbarians and Bishops*, 141.

patriarch had cowed the monks of the Nile delta and had reached out as far as Constantinople to topple John Chrysostom.[91]

Synesius had to be sure where he stood with such a man. His *Letter* 105 was a public document, written to his brother, for the attention of Theophilus and the *scholastikoi,* the educated church lawyers, of Alexandria.[92] In it, Synesius deliberately played on his personal reluctance to abandon views that he held as a philosopher. By doing so, he sought to guarantee his official position as bishop of Ptolemais. Theophilus was put on the spot. If he wanted Synesius as a colleague, he must accept him as he was.

Precisely the issues which Theophilus was likely to use against Synesius, should their relations sour, were spelled out for a clear ruling. Synesius told the patriarch that he intended to continue to live with and to sleep with his wife.[93] He would maintain "philosophical" views on the resurrection of the body.[94] The views propounded by Synesius bore a marked resemblance to opinions associated with the teachings of Origen, who had denied that the physical bodies of the dead would be reconstituted. Theophilus had denounced these views as so many "patches from the worn out garment of the philosophers" and had instigated a savage witch-hunt against suspected Origenists that had devastated the monasteries of Nitria and Kellia in 400.[95] On that occasion Theophilus had used the smear of "Origenism" in a more than usually cynical manner.[96] That was

91. A. Guillaumont, *Les "Kephalaia Gnostica" d'Evagre le Pontique,* Patristica Sorbonensia 5 (Paris: Le Seuil, 1962), 59–80, is the best summary of the controversies in Egypt at that time. We can expect a complete study of the Origenist controversy in Elizabeth A. Clark, *The Origenist Controversy: The Cultural Construction of an Early Christian Debate* (Princeton: Princeton University Press, forthcoming).

92. Synesius, *Ep.* 105: *Patrologia Graeca* 66:1488D; ed. A. Garzya, *Synesii Cyrenensis Epistulae* (Rome: Istituto Poligrafico, 1979), 190; A. Fitzgerald, trans., *The Letters of Synesius of Cyrene* (Oxford: Oxford University Press, 1926), 202. For the legal meaning of *scholastikos,* see Roueché, *Aphrodisias in Late Antiquity,* 76–77.

93. Synesius, *Ep.* 105: *Patrologia Graeca* 66:1485A; ed. Garzya, p. 187; trans. Fitzgerald, p. 199. John Chrysostom had recently deposed the bishop of Ephesus for having, among other things, taken his wife out of a convent to complete unfinished family business; Palladius, *Dialogus de vita Johannis Chrysostomi* 13:48.

94. Synesius, *Ep.* 105: *Patrologia Graeca* 66:1485BC; ed. Garzya, pp. 188–89; trans. Fitzgerald, p. 200. The classic statement remains that in H. I. Marrou, "Synesius of Cyrene and Alexandrian Neoplatonism," in *The Conflict of Christianity and Paganism in the Fourth Century,* ed. A. D. Momigliano (Oxford: Clarendon Press, 1963), 147–48.

95. *Paschal Letter* of Theophilus (of 401), cited in Jerome, *Contra Johannem Hierosolymitanum* 7: *Patrologia Latina* 23:360C, and *Paschal Letter* 9–10 (of 402), translated by Jerome, *Letter* 98.11: *Patrologia Latina* 23:800. Peter Brown, *The Body and Society: Men, Women and Sexual Renunciation in Early Christianity* (New York: Columbia University Press, 1988), 381–82; see also T. Orlandi, *Shenute: Contra Origenistas* 356, 392–97 (Rome: C.I.M., 1985), 32–33, 38–41.

96. Socrates, *Ecclesiastical History* 6.17.

all the more reason to fear that he might use it again against Synesius.

Reading Synesius' courteous but unyielding manifesto, the patriarch could not say that he had not been warned: "Let the beloved of God, the right revered Theophilus, knowing the situation and giving me clear evidence that he understands it, decide on the issue . . . [for] he will not leave himself any grounds on which hereafter to sit in judgement on me, and turn me out of the rank of the priesthood."[97]

Secured in his position by this maneuver, Synesius settled down to the exercise of *parrhésia* as a Christian bishop. He attempted to organize his colleagues to face down the governor of the Pentapolis.[98] Having spent much of his time as a lay notable deploring the inertia of the military men who defended Cyrenaica against the nomads, he now found himself, as bishop, manning the walls of Ptolemais.[99] As a bishop, he was at least as successful as he would have been had he remained a civic notable. He deployed the same methods: letters to friends at court, appeals to the ancient glory of the city, and skillful invectives were more useful to him than was the novel power of excommunication.[100] Despite hectic activity, Synesius seems to have died a disillusioned man, heartbroken by the death of his sons and oppressed by a growing sense of political isolation.

On the other side of the Nile delta at Pelusium, Synesius' younger contemporary Isidore, a priest of ascetic leanings, was equally busy. Pelusium, the crucial port through which the commerce of the Red Sea was distributed to the Mediterranean, was closer to the center of affairs than was the distant Cyrenaica of Synesius. Isidore's letters are correspondingly more buoyant. They fill eight hundred columns of the *Patrologia Graeca*. He wrote to welcome and edify governors.[101] He instructed the local intelligentsia on every conceivable topic, ranging from the virtue of poverty to the deportment of women, and from the miracles of Apollonius of Tyana (whose life he said he had read with care) to the origins of the hippodrome and the fact that

97. Synesius, *Ep.* 105: *Patrologia Graeca* 66:1488BC; ed. Garzya, p. 190; trans. Fitzgerald, pp. 201–2.

98. Synesius, *Epp.* 57, 58: *Patrologia Graeca* 66:1384A–1404A; ed. Garzya (41 and 72), pp. 52–70, 127–29; trans. Fitzgerald, pp. 127–43. Roques, *Synésios de Cyrène,* 191–202.

99. Synesius, *Constitutio* and *Catastasis: Patrologia Graeca* 66: 1565A–1577A; ed. Garzya, *Synesii Opuscula,* pp. 283–93; trans. Fitzgerald, *Essays and Hymns,* pp. 360–68.

100. J. H. W. G. Liebeschuetz, "Why Did Synesius Become Bishop of Ptolemais?" *Byzantion* 56 (1986): 188–91; idem, *Barbarians and Bishops,* 228–35; Lizzi, *Potere episcopale nell'Oriente Romano,* 85–116.

101. Isidore of Pelusium, *Epp.* 1.47, 208, 290; 2.15, 25, 120; 5.40: *Patrologia Graeca* 78:211B, 313B, 352D–353A, 468A, 473BC, 560C–561A, 1352B. Cf. *Ep.* 1.35: *Patrologia Graeca* 78:204C, to Theodosius, and *Ep.* 1.178: *Patrologia Graeca* 78:297B, to the praetorian prefect, Rufinus. See R. Delmaire, "Notes prosopographiques sur quelques lettres d'Isidore de Péluse," *Revue des études augustiniennes* 34 (1988): 230–36.

Noah had eaten salad in the Ark.[102] Writing to high officials and well-placed friends, he hounded an unpopular governor all the way to Constantinople.[103]

In all this, Isidore cultivated a reputation for *parrhésia*. He put the *dux* Gelasius in his place, for instance, by telling him that while pride was a sin, the poor *dux* need not fear succumbing to it, "being, as you are, ill-born and poor, unintelligent, uneducated, ungainly."[104] Isidore lived with one foot in the desert and the other firmly planted in his city. With a man of so sharp a pen, who had an opinion on everything for everyone, there was little need to turn to a non-Christian philosopher for information and free speech.

Further up the Nile, in the countryside of Egypt, the same situation prevailed. One usually thinks of the formidable monastic leader Shenoute of Atripe as if he lived on a different planet from that of his older contemporaries Synesius and Isidore.[105] Shenoute might go for evening strolls with the prophet Jeremiah. But when he emerged from the White Monastery at Sohag, close to Panopolis (modern Akhmim), his letters and addresses showed a man with similar, down to earth concerns. He also despaired of the incompetent outsiders who were sent from Constantinople to defend Upper Egypt against the terrible tribes of the South.[106] Like Synesius, he gave his blessing to those who did a proper job by killing barbarians.[107] When he preached before governors and their retinues, ancient Greek praise of justice, control of anger, and humanity, the well-used coin of local notables hoping against hope for soft government, obtruded beneath the seemingly exotic, Coptic veneer.[108]

---

102.   On poverty, see Isidore of Pelusium, *Epp.* 2.146, 2.168: *Patrologia Graeca* 78: 592A–601B, 620CD; on women, 2.53:496C–497A; on Apollonius of Tyana, 1.398:405B; on the hippodrome, 5.185:1436C; on Noah, 1.69:229B.

103.   Isidore of Pelusium, *Epp.* 1.158, 462, 483, 485–86: *Patrologia Graeca* 78:288D–289A, 436D, 445B, 445D–448A.

104.   Isidore of Pelusium, *Epp.* 1.99: *Patrologia Graeca* 78:249C.

105.   J. Timbie, "The State of Research on the Career of Shenoute of Atripe," in *The Roots of Egyptian Christianity,* ed. B. A. Pearson and J. E. Goehring (Philadelphia: Fortress Press, 1986), 258–70.

106.   Shenoute, *Letter* 21, ed. J. Leipoldt and W. E. Crum, *Corpus Scriptorum Christianorum Orientalium 43: Scriptores Coptici 3* (Leipzig: O. Harassowitz, 1898), 68; trans. H. Wiessmann, *Corpus Scriptorum Christianorum Orientalium 96: Scriptores Coptici 8* (Louvain: L. Durbecq, 1953), 37–38.

107.   Besa, *Life of Shenoute* 105–8, ed. J. Leipoldt and W. E. Crum, *Corpus Scriptorum Christianorum Orientalium 41: Scriptores Coptici 1* (Leipzig: O. Harassowitz, 1906), 51–52; trans. D. N. Bell, *Besa: The Life of Shenoute,* Cistercian Studies 73 (Kalamazoo, Mich.: Cistercian Publications, 1983), 74–75; P. du Bourguet, "Entretien de Chénoute sur les problèmes de discipline ecclésiastique," *Bulletin de l'institut français d'archéologie orientale du Caire* 57 (1958): 114, 121.

108.   P. du Bourguet, "Entretien de Chénoute sur les devoirs des juges," *Bulletin de l'institut français d'archéologie orientale du Caire* 55 (1956): 87, 91.

Shenoute was a patron and spokesman in the grand manner. He linked Upper Egypt to Alexandria and thence to Constantinople. It could be believed that the imperial court had summoned him with the honorific title of *Tekparrésia,* "Thy *parrhésia.*"[109] It was said that a grain of wheat which he had picked up from the pavement of the imperial palace kept the monastery's millstone spinning for days during a time of famine.[110] In reality, as many as twenty thousand refugees from a Nubian invasion had camped outside the White Monastery. Shenoute's report of the incident is surprisingly detailed. The four bake houses of the monastery worked ceaselessly, producing "now 18, now 19, now 20" baskets of loaves a day: 8,500 *artabae* of grain alone had been consumed. In the name of Christian care of the poor, Shenoute had undertaken the feeding of the equivalent of a whole town for three months. It was what an old-fashioned *tropheus,* a "nourisher" of the community, had once been expected to do.[111] The more tangible miracle of an imperial tax exemption for the lands of the White Monastery soon followed. It was an entirely appropriate, and traditional, return for a public service undertaken by a private person, whose scale and careful self-advertisement were worthy of the great urban benefactors of earlier times.

Shenoute was remembered in Egypt as the figure who mediated between his region and an unimaginably distant court. If part of the virtue of the imperial cult had been, in the words of Glen Bowersock, that "it succeeded in making multitudes of citizens of far-flung regions feel close to the power that controlled them," then fifth-century legends of the kind generated by the activities of Shenoute played a similar role under a Christian ruler.[112]

Yet further to the South, in the frontier district of Syene, the bishop, Appion, petitioned the emperor directly, to place more troops in the region under the bishop's command in order to protect the churches and the populations that sought refuge around them: "Your philanthropy is accustomed to reach out the right hand to all who beseech you . . . and so I throw myself on the ground, before your divine and spotless footprints. . . . And if I obtain this, I shall raise up to God the customary prayers for your perpetual power."[113] Appion got his way. The *dux* of the Thebaid, the mili-

109. Besa, *Life of Shenoute* 54, ed. Leipoldt and Crum, p. 30 (a variant of the manuscript); trans. Bell, p. 58.

110. Besa, *Life of Shenoute* 17, ed. Leipoldt and Crum, p. 16; trans. Bell, p. 47. Cf. *Life* 139, ed. Leipoldt and Crum, pp. 61–62; trans. Bell, p. 81.

111. Shenoute, *Letter* 22, ed. Leipoldt and Crum, pp. 69–70; trans. Wiessmann, pp. 38–39.

112. G. W. Bowersock, "The Imperial Cult: Perceptions and Persistence," in *Jewish and Christian Self-Definition,* ed. R. F. Meyer and E. P. Sanders (London: S.C.M. Press, 1982), 3:182.

113. D. Feissel and K. A. Worp, "La réquête d'Appion, évêque de Syène à Théodose II," *Oudheidkundige Mededelingen uit het Rijksmuseum van Oudheiden te Leiden* 68 (1988): 99.

tary commander of the region, received a copy of the petition, endorsed by Theodosius II in his own hand.[114] We know of Appion's petition only through the chance discovery of a papyrus. There must have been many like it from all over the empire.

In the early empire the elites of the Greek cities of Asia Minor had incorporated the cult of the emperor into their traditional religious observances, as a sign of their determination to "create a positive relationship with the center."[115] In the changed circumstances of the age of Theodosius II, the way to a "positive relationship with the center" was seen to pass on an increasing number of occasions through the Christian church. The protestations of loyalty and the pertinacious lobbying of Christian bishops, such as the distant Appion of Syene, ensured that the godlike power of the emperor was experienced as effective for good in their own localities. It was this process that turned an empire whose emperor had happened to be a Christian, as was the case for much of the fourth century, into the unambiguously Christian empire that we associate with Byzantium.

The growing confidence of Christians that they controlled access to the imperial power and could interpret its workings to their advantage was highlighted by the demoralization of their most vocal opponents. The true tragedy of the world revealed to us in the pages of an old believer such as Eunapius of Sardis (who wrote his *History* and *Lives of the Philosophers* at the very end of the fourth century) lies in the fact that he described men and women who no longer felt that they could make sense of the exercise of power. The trenchant study by Kenneth Sacks, "The Meaning of Eunapius' History," has made plain this aspect of the end of polytheism in the Greek East.[116] At a time when miracles, publicly performed and publicly proclaimed, were held to register the decisive impact of Christian bishops and holy men on the exercise of the imperial power, Eunapius and his circle observed nothing but power out of control. The ancient restraints of *logoi* no longer bound an increasingly tyrannical court. His *History* was marked, in the words of Sacks, by a "pervasive distrust of autocracy."[117]

The inability of the gentry of Sardis and its region to "create a positive relationship with the center" dispirited Eunapius more deeply than did even the rise of Christianity and the destruction of the temples. It formed the central theme of his *History*. A gallery of portraits of local governors sent down from Constantinople, preserved in the fragments of his *History*,

114. Feissel and Worp, "La réquête d'Appion," 99–100.
115. S. R. F. Price, *Rituals and Power: The Roman Imperial Cult in Asia Minor* (Cambridge: Cambridge University Press, 1984), 206.
116. Kenneth S. Sacks, "The Meaning of Eunapius' History," *History and Theory* 25 (1986): 52–67.
117. Ibid., 67.

show him to have been a man of the fourth century, still anxiously concerned to gauge the intentions of the powerful in terms of the unwritten constitution of *paideia*. In most cases, he concluded, *logoi* had done little to control the "rough hewn nature" of the ruling class.[118] He ended his *History* with stories of the shameless sale of provincial offices at the imperial court and a memorable scene in which a delegation from Sardis was browbeaten in the court of the praetorian prefect at Constantinople.[119]

Eunapius, of course, wrote at a time when the laws of Theodosius I, the destruction of the Serapeum, and the ravages of the Visigoths in Greece induced a peculiar sense of foreboding. Not every old believer shared in the consequential alienation from power that Eunapius and his circle regarded as the hallmark of the true philosopher. Some still regarded imperial service as a birthright and a duty. Later in the fifth century Severianus of Damascus wished to live the philosophical life. But he began to dream that he was seated on a moving mountain, driving it with reins. It was a sure sign that he coveted the high coach of a provincial governor.[120] He left the philosopher's school to embark on a career in imperial service.

Yet Eunapius' sad mood was there to stay. Philosophers no longer expected to impinge on public life. When it came to be written at the end of the fifth century, non-Christian hagiography made *il gran rifiuto*. Far from being a means to power, as was the case in the Christian hagiography of the fifth century, the miraculous became, instead, a consolation for its absence.

The stories recorded in Marinus' *Life of Proclus* (written after the philosopher's death in 485) and Damascius' *Life of Isidore* (written around 520) reveal the hopes of men and women who had turned their backs on the social world where Christian holy men such as Shenoute of Atripe were demonstrating their supernatural gifts through dramatic, public confrontations with the invisible power of the demons and with the visible rage of imperial officials.[121] The miracles recorded in these books rarely record a dialogue with the powerful. They do not show governors and emperors giving way to an inspired *parrhésia*. Quiet courage in the face of a hostile government, not successful intervention, was all that could be expected of a man of culture. Denounced as a polytheist, the philosopher Hierocles

118. Eunapius, *History*, fragment 35, in *The Fragmentary Classicising Historians of the Later Roman Empire*, ed. and trans. R. C. Blockley, ARCA 10 (Liverpool: Francis Cairns, 1983), 52.

119. Eunapius, *History*, fragment 72, ed. Blockley, pp. 116–18.

120. Damascius, *Life of Isidore*, fragment 278, ed. Zintzen, p. 223.

121. Shenoute, *Letters* 16, 19, 23–24, ed. Leipoldt and Crum, pp. 38–39, 63, 84; trans. Wiessmann, pp. 18–19, 35, 43–47.

stood up from the flogging inflicted upon him by the prefect of Constantinople, wiping the blood from his back with a tag from Homer.[122]

The old believers, rather, looked out to the still immensity of the universe. Out there, beyond society, the gods, whose statues lay shattered and desecrated on earth, still shone with untarnished radiance in the refulgent temple gallery of the stars, far above the heads of the black-robed monks and bishops, whose vulture shades cast an ever-lengthening shadow across a faithless world.[123] The *kosmos,* the *mundus,* the glittering universe associated with the fixed stars would survive, "glowing in the vigor of eternity"; only Christians dared to call that divine realm "time-bound and of brief duration."[124] For men such as Eunapius, miracles came as messages from an untroubled and abiding region. They dropped to earth as fine and insubstantial as the rays of the dawn star.

The deadly, confrontational quality that had come to characterize Christian hagiography was noticeably lacking in these accounts.[125] By framing amulets to heal diseases and by performing secret rites to ward off drought and earthquake from his beloved Attica, a man such as Proclus was not concerned to grapple, through the noisy, theatrical rite of exorcism,[126] and through spirit-filled acts of *parrhésia,* with the dark forces that upheld East Roman society. Rather, he participated, through theurgic rites, in the continuous, providential care of the gods, as they played with discreet and lighthearted ease in the lower reaches of a beautiful universe. Such miracles were recorded with due reticence. They were the last lapping of the waves of a sun-stilled ocean of pure spirit against the narrow shoreline of the sensible world.[127]

122.   Damascius, *Life of Isidore,* fragment 106, ed. Zintzen, p. 81; see Martindale, *Prosopography* 2:559–60.

123.   Plotinus, *Enneads* 1.8.51; see H. D. Saffrey, "Allusions antichrétiens chez Proclus," *Revue de sciences philosophiques et théologiques* 59 (1975): 553–63, and P. Hoffmann, "Simplicius' Polemics," in *Philoponus and the Rejection of Aristotelian Science,* ed. R. Sorabji (London: Duckworth, 1987), 72–76.

124.   *Consultationes Zacchaei et Apollonii* 1.1, ed. G. Morin, Florilegium Patristicum 39 (Bonn: P. Hanstein, 1935), 8.

125.   Peter Brown, "The Rise and Function of the Holy Man in Late Antiquity," *Journal of Roman Studies* 61 (1971): 80–101, now in *Society and the Holy in Late Antiquity* (Berkeley: University of California Press, 1982), esp. 122–29.

126.   Plotinus, *Enneads* 2.9.14; Damascius, *Life of Isidore,* Epit. Phot. 56, ed. Zintzen, p. 82; now excellently studied, for the case of St. Martin of Tours, in Aline Rousselle, *Croire et guérir: La foi en Gaule dans l'Antiquité tardive* (Paris: Fayard, 1990), 109–208.

127.   Marinus, *Life of Proclus* 28, ed. Boissonade, p. 24. Philosophers were thought by Christians to be able to intervene in the "lower world" of matter. See Anastasius Sinaita, *Quaestiones* 20: *Patrologia Graeca* 89:524–25; for miracles as "play" in a Christian text, see Severus of Antioch, *Homiliae Cathedrales* 27: *Patrologia Orientalis* 36:556–67. On theurgic rites, see Anne Sheppard, "Proclus' Attitude to Theurgy," *Classical Quarterly* 32 (1982):

It would only be in the intimate, domestic friendships of the circle of their colleagues, students, and wives and in their dreams—when the gods visited them with gentle familiarity—that the last philosophers felt at ease. They created for themselves an old-fashioned and studiously nonabrasive world held together by *homonoétiké philia,* by the indissoluble kinship of like minds.[128] They wished to imagine no other. At a time when the art and literature of the Christians had filled the imaginative universe of early Byzantines with invisible protectors, with saints, and with mighty angels decked out in the full panoply of official costume, as developed at the hierarchical court of Constantinople,[129] the philosopher Proclus dreamed as if he were still a man of the ancient city. Asclepius had visited him one night: "Just as in the theater, orators pronounce panegyrics of great men, the god stood up, and with a gesture of the hand, and in a dramatic tone, uttered these words: 'Proclus, glory of the home-town.'"[130] It was a time-honored gesture, which many leading figures would still have received on solemn occasions in their cities in the fifth century. The memory of it was enough to make the old philosopher burst into tears. "Voices of the mind," Proclus' dreams came to him from a world beyond his times: "Echoes from the first dawn of our creation."[131]

All that Eunapius of Sardis had hoped to provide, in his *Lives of the Philosophers,* was a "moral survival kit for pagans."[132] The heroes of later polytheism were to be as pure from the taint of power as their lightly

212–24, and Gregory Shaw, "Theurgy: Rituals of Unification in the Neoplatonism of Iamblichus," *Traditio* 41 (1985): 1–28.

128.   Fowden, "Pagan Holy Man," 55–58. See Damascius, *Life of Isidore,* fragments 22 and 49, ed. Zintzen, pp. 26, 41; and A. Smith, *Porphyry's Place in the Neoplatonic Tradition* (The Hague: M. Nijhoff, 1974), 94.

129.   Peter Brown, *The Cult of the Saints* (Chicago: University of Chicago Press, 1981), 62–63. For contemporary Christian awareness of this tendency and its risks, see Severus of Antioch, *Homiliae cathedrales* 72: *Patrologia Orientalis* 12:83; A. Van Lantschoot, "Fragments coptes d'une homélie de Jean de Parallos contre les livres hérétiques," in *Studi e Testi 121: Miscellanea Mercati* (Rome: Vatican, 1946), 320, 325; and C. Mango, "St. Michael and Attis," *Deltion tés Christianikés Archaiologikés Hetaireias,* ser. 4, 22 (1984): 39–43. A Christian vision may be dated to within a generation by reference to court protocol; see J. Bremmer, "An Imperial Palace Guard in Heaven: The Date of the Vision of Dorotheos," *Zeitschrift für Papyrologie und Epigraphik* 75 (1988): 82–88. By contrast, the use of the language of hierarchical relations could be a subject of jokes among cultivated non-Christians: see *The Philogelôs; or, Laughter-Lover* 76, trans. B. Baldwin (Amsterdam: J. C. Gieben, 1983), 14. Greeted by a priest of Sarapis, who said, "May the Master be merciful to you," a *scholastikos* replied: "May the Master be merciful to *you* . . . for *I* am a free man."

130.   Marinus, *Life of Proclus* 32, ed. Boissonade, p. 26; see Roueché, *Aphrodisias in Late Antiquity,* 125–36.

131.   K. P. Kavafy, *Poiémata* (Athens: Ikaros, 1958), 8.

132.   Sacks, "Eunapius' History," 66.

incarnated souls were pure from the taint of matter.[133] Only a saint, Eunapius had implied, could be a good emperor.[134] Since the death of Julian, no such saints were likely to appear. Eunapius' Christian contemporaries, by contrast, had grasped the nettle of the autocracy. A Christian emperor did not need to be a saint. (Ambrose had as few illusions as did Eunapius about the sensuality and ill-temper of Theodosius I.) An emperor needed only to know when to listen to saints — to the bishops and monks whom Eunapius so cordially feared and despised. In the stark words of Lellia Cracco Ruggini, the Christian hagiography of the fifth century was "the voice of Hope," and that of Eunapius, with his unrelieved sense that power corrupts and that absolute power had corrupted absolutely, was "the voice of Fear."[135] Christian writers and Christian leaders shared none of Eunapius' doubts about the autocracy. They were enthusiastic theorists of monarchy by divine right. But they did more than that: they combined with effusive loyalty to the imperial system in general effective strategies for confronting and mitigating its power in the localities. It is to this that we must turn.

Bishop and City

When we consider the role of the bishop in the cities of the eastern empire, we must be careful to define precisely the areas of fifth-century society that were affected by the bishop's rise to prominence. Many areas were not. Thus, as long as the collection of taxes depended on collaboration with the existing local elites, the bishop's role in one essential aspect of imperial government remained peripheral. On the serious issues of taxation and justice, the empire remained irremediably profane. The right of sanctuary, for instance, was strictly controlled. In "fleeing to the church," late fourth-century persons would not have been guaranteed safety by the mere fact of being within the walls of a holy place. They had to seek out the bishop or his clergy. The bishop then had to intervene on their behalf with the governor. It was a test of personal authority and of diplomacy such as any other notable — the non-Christian rhetor Libanius, for instance — might have had to undertake on behalf of a client.[136] There was no guarantee that the bishop would succeed. At precisely the time when Theodosius I demonstrated his piety in a series of laws against polytheism, the rights of Christian churches to offer sanctuary for fiscal debtors remained

133. Ibid., 65.
134. Eunapius, *History,* fragment 28.1, ed. Blockley, p. 42.
135. Lellia Cracco Ruggini, "The Ecclesiastical Histories and the Pagan Historiography: Providence and Miracles," *Athenaeum,* n.s., 55 (1977): 118.
136. H. Langenfeld, *Christianisierungspolitik und Sklavengesetzgebung der römischen Kaiser von Konstantin bis Theodosius II,* Antiquitas 1.26 (Bonn: Habelt, 1977), 107–200.

strictly curtailed.[137] A few years later, armed guards entered Ambrose's basilica and snatched an offender out from among the bishop and clergy, among whom he had taken cover.[138] Only two decades later was the sacred nature of the church building itself deemed to confer protection on a fugitive.

The newly discovered letters of Augustine show that the bishops of Africa, for all their access to the western emperors on theological issues, carried little weight with the government when it came to taxation. The bishops were anxious for news of the arrival of an imperial agent to announce amnesty for those who had taken shelter in the churches after a tax revolt in Carthage in 426.[139] But the occasional amnesty was a gesture that a Christian prince could afford in relation to a major Christian city such as Carthage. In the provinces, by contrast, the tax machine worked relentlessly. Augustine complained that bishops who intervened with the tax collectors found themselves liable to prosecution for obstructing "the public necessities." Only a few could find sanctuary: "All the others, the greater number by far, who are found outside the churches, are despoiled in their persons and property, while we can only groan, having no power to help them."[140]

In the Middle Ages Ambrose's relations with Theodosius I were remembered as a high moment of philosophical restraint on the anger of the powerful. In medieval moral treatises, classical memories dating from the age of Augustus now attached themselves to the confrontation between Ambrose and Theodosius: "Others have ordered that a ruler should recite the twenty-four letters of the alphabet before acting, as the emperor Theodosius should have done [before ordering the massacre at Thessalonica] when he was excommunicated by Saint Ambrose for rashly causing so much blood to be spilled."[141] Yet the moments when Ambrose had played to perfection the role of philosopher to the irate emperor Theodosius were few and far between. The system was not changed by such encounters. Ambrose ended his life disillusioned by his inability to control the unbridled *avaritia*, the land-grabbing and amassment of private fortunes, associated with the high

---

137. *Codex Theodosianus* 9.45.1 (A.D. 392) and 2–3 (A.D. 397 and 398); see Liebeschuetz, *Barbarians and Bishops*, 151–52.

138. Paulinus of Milan, *Life of Ambrose* 34.

139. Augustine, *Epp.* 15*2, 16*2, 23A*1, ed. Divjak, pp. 84, 86–87, 121; *Lettres 1*–29*, 264–66, 270–72, 370–72; Eno, *Saint Augustine: Letters VI*, 115, 119, 166.

140. Augustine *Ep.* 22*.3, ed. Divjak, p. 115; *Lettres 1*–29*, 350; Eno, *Saint Augustine: Letters VI*, 157.

141. Johannes Pauli, *Schimpf und Ernst* (1520), cited in J. C. Schmitt, *The Holy Greyhound* (Cambridge: Cambridge University Press, 1979), 67; he refers to Augustus and the philosopher, *Epitome de Caesaribus* 48.14–15.

officials in charge of taxation in northern Italy.[142] Preaching at Turin in
the 400s, Bishop Maximus was no more optimistic. The "protection of
the people" required the bishop to "raise his voice to a shout."[143] Administrators and tax collectors were unimpressed. They turned up every Sunday, finely dressed for church. Behavior appropriate for a monk or clergy-
man, they said, was not to be demanded of a tax official.[144]

It was, rather, on the local level, as "controller of crowds," responsible
for the peace of the cities, that the bishops consolidated the advantages
that they had first gained at the end of the fourth century. When the patriarch
John of Antioch excused himself for having arrived late for the Council
of Ephesus, it was sufficient to claim that he had been detained in Antioch
in order to quell riots associated with a time of famine.[145] In the early
sixth century another patriarch of Antioch, the controversial Severus, wrote
bluntly to a colleague: "It is the duty of bishops like you to cut short
and to restrain any unregulated movements of the mob . . . and to set themselves to maintain all good order in the cities, and to keep a watch over
the peaceful manners and customs of those who are fed by them."[146]

The imminent threat of urban violence formed the backdrop to the ecclesiastical struggles of the period, from the Council of Ephesus in 431
to that of Chalcedon in 451. In their frequent mutual accusations of the
use of force, each side highlighted the new resources of popular support
on which a bishop could draw: bath attendants, pallbearers, hospital orderlies, longshoremen, peasants from the estates of the church, and bands of
monks. Syrian abbots were accused of recruiting able-bodied young men,
potential prizefighters, for their monasteries, and occasionally, overseers of
the church poor would appear, ominously distributing cudgels.[147] For the
imperial commissioners, the phrase *kindunos kai stasis,* "danger and revolt,"
was so much a piece of the bureaucratic jargon of the age that it passed,
directly transliterated, into Syriac.[148] Its appearance on an official report

142. Paulinus, *Life of Ambrose* 41.
143. Rita Lizzi, *Vescovi e strutture ecclesiastiche nella città tardoantica* (Como: New Press,
1989), 202–3.
144. Maximus, *Sermon* 26.1–2, ed. A. Mützenbecher, *Corpus Christianorum* 23 (Turn-
hout: Brepols, 1963), 101.
145. Nestorius, *Bazaar of Heraclides* 2.1 [372], in *Le Livre d'Héraclide de Damas,* trans.
F. Nau (Paris: Letouzey and Ane, 1910), 239.
146. E. W. Brooks, *The Sixth Book of the Select Letters of Severus Patriarch of Antioch*
1.9 (London: Willis and Nugent, 1903), 46.
147. T. E. Gregory, *Vox populi: Popular Opinion and Violence in the Religious Controversies of the Fifth Century A.D.* (Columbus: Ohio State University Press, 1979); A. Vööbus,
History of Asceticism in the Syrian Orient, vol. 3, *Corpus Scriptorum Christianorum Orientalium*
500, Subsidia 81 (Louvain: E. Peeters, 1988), 204.
148. Nestorius, *Bazaar of Heraclides* 2.1 [373], trans. Nau, p. 239; Flemming, *Akten
der ephesinischen Synode,* 20.14.

usually signaled a politic withdrawal of the authorities (usually on theological issues) in the face of the threat of upheaval in distant and murmurous Christian cities.

The vacillation of the government in handling the ecclesiastical controversies of these years shows that the traditional "license of the *plebs*" had taken on a new meaning. It was no longer a license that could be contained, on the local level, by being treated as part of the dialogue between the *plebs* and their traditional "nourishers," the town councillors. As orchestrated by the bishops, the license of the *plebs* stretched beyond the city. Through a bishop such as Cyril of Alexandria, the Christian population of a city could feel that they spoke directly to the court. Their *phônai,* their voices, organized in rhythmic acclamations and recorded in shorthand as they were uttered, bypassed the town council. They were forwarded immediately to Constantinople, to be read by Theodosius II himself.[149]

In a study of newly discovered inscriptions that record public acclamations at Aphrodisias in Caria, Charlotte Roueché has drawn attention to the increased tendency in the fifth century to use chanted slogans as a form of political and theological decision-making.[150] Such acclamations carried with them an aura of divinely inspired unanimity. In them, the crowd expressed a group *parrhésia,* tinged with supernatural certainty. They could address the governor directly, by chanting to him en masse in the theater or on the occasion of his arrival, with the certainty that their acclamations were formally recorded and would then be forwarded to the emperor.[151] It was a studiously melodramatic device, with a long past history of use in circuses, hippodromes, and other places of public assembly. Its increased prominence in the fifth century left very little room for the traditional function of the civic notables, which had been to keep local grievances within the narrow confines of the city.

The Christian church took full advantage of this new form of political pressure. Its great basilicas with their spacious courtyards provided weekly parade-grounds for the use of slogans. The liturgy itself owed much to the secular tradition of chanted acclamations.[152] The sermons of the bishops were interspersed with euphoric chanting by the congregation. Leaders of the claque in church often emerged as skilled agitators in the theater, as did Hierax, cheerleader for the sermons of Cyril of Alexandria.[153]

The Christian *plebs* quickly came to sense the power of acclamation in

149. Nestorius, *Bazaar of Heraclides* 2.1 [373], trans. Nau, p. 239.

150. Charlotte Roueché, "Acclamations in the Later Roman Empire: New Evidence from Aphrodisias," *Journal of Roman Studies* 74 (1984): 181–99.

151. Ibid., 188, 196–98.

152. E. Peterson, *Eis Theos: Epigraphische, formgeschichtliche und religionsegeschichtliche Untersuchungen* (Göttingen: Vandenhoeck and Ruprecht, 1926), 166–79.

153. Socrates, *Ecclesiastical History* 7.13.

the city at large. In Carthage, for example, fiscal officials were vetted by a form of popular acclamation.[154] By the early fifth century the Catholic *plebs* had a voice in that procedure. Augustine defended one such official, Faustinus, before the Christian congregation in Carthage. He was thought to have become a Christian only in order to be sure of their support.[155] For Horapollon, a non-Christian teacher in Alexandria, it was disturbing to know that, at the Sunday liturgy, the Christian people had chanted against him, calling him Psychapollôn, "destroyer of Christian souls."[156] In the changed conditions of the use of acclamation in public life, such chants could only too easily spill out from the basilica and impose their message directly on the emperor and his officials.

To take one example: the attempt of Jews to gather again in Jerusalem, to celebrate the Feast of Tabernacles in 438, was met by a massive demonstration outside the palace of the empress Eudocia, then residing in the Holy City. First, an official delegation from Jerusalem—clergy, officials, leaders of the Jews—went to meet the empress at Bethlehem. Bearing olive branches, they appealed for tolerance. But they were soon cowed in Jerusalem itself by acclamations engineered by the Syrian monk Barsauma. The cheerleaders set up the chant of "'The Cross has conquered'; and the voice of the people spread and roared for a long time, like the great noise of the waves of the sea, so that the inhabitants of the city trembled because of the noise of the shouting. . . . And the events were announced to the emperor Theodosius."[157] With such incidents we have come a long way from the ceremonious and allusive styles of persuasion with which men of *paideia* were supposed to cast the ancient spell of words on receptive governors.

These spectacular forms of group pressure characterized the life of major cities. But the eastern empire depended also on the continuance of its small towns. Their fate varied greatly from region to region in the fifth century. One development, however, appears to have been widespread. In the smaller cities of the provinces, the town councils, always precarious, further lost their cohesion and social function. The social differences that had already divided the urban notables in the later fourth century became unbridgeable in the course of the fifth. The inner circle of notables, the *prôteuontes,* who collaborated most closely with the imperial government, stood apart. They now formed a province-wide nobility. They maintained

154.   Codex Theodosianus 11.7.20; see François Jacques, *Le Privilège de la Liberté,* Collection de l'école française de Rome 76 (Rome: Palais Farnèse, 1984), 424.

155.   Augustine, *Sermo "Morin"* 1: *Patrologia Latina Supplementum* 2:657–60.

156.   Zacharias, *Vie de Sévère,* 32.

157.   F. Nau, "Résumé de monographies syriaques: Vie de Barsauma," *Revue de l'Orient chrétien* 19 (1914): 121, 124–25.

the urban facade of the capitals of their province. It was in the provincial capital, the *métropolis*, that the nobility assembled. At Aphrodisias in Caria, they demonstrated their new importance and their continuing intimacy with imperial officials in yet another impressive spate of inscriptions and public buildings.[158] But these men felt little or no loyalty to the smaller cities of their region. In these, protection, law and order, and the maintenance of a vestige of civic pride devolved increasingly on the bishop and clergy.

Cyrrhus, the see of Theodoret, was a tiny city compared with the great *métropolis* of Antioch. It was as its bishop that Theodoret "nourished" Cyrrhus. He mobilized the local holy man to petition for a remittance of tax arrears.[159] He invited the local gentry to take part in the solemn dedication of new churches, whether they were Christian or not.[160] He repaired the aqueducts and bridges of the city and rebuilt its porticoes.[161] Cyrrhus was "a little city," whose ugliness Theodoret claimed to have "covered over" by lavish spending. Without its bishop, the city might have become little more than a large village. Yet even Theodoret was accused, by his enemies, of spending too much of his time in the *métropolis,* visiting Antioch regularly and lodging beside the patriarch's cathedral.[162] The accusation hurt. Hence in long letters of self-defense Theodoret publicized his benefactions to the city of which he had become bishop. He also wrote with evident enthusiasm, in his *History,* of bishops who, like himself, acted as the defenders of their cities. The bishop of Erzerum (Theodosiopolis), for instance, constructed his own catapult, known to the locals as "Saint Thomas," and presided over its firing from the walls.[163]

All over the eastern provinces, the Christian bishop came to be held re-

158. Roueché, *Aphrodisias in Late Antiquity,* 34; Liebeschuetz, "Synesius and Municipal Politics of Cyrenaica," 157–58; J. F. Haldon, "Some Considerations on Byzantine Society and Economy in the Seventh Century," *Byzantinische Forschungen* 10 (1985): 75–112.

159. Theodoret, *Ep.* 42, ed. Y. Azéma, *Théodoret de Cyr: Correspondance 2,* Sources chrétiennes 98 (Paris: Le Cerf, 1964), 112.

160. Theodoret, *Ep.* 68, ed. Azéma, p. 148.

161. Theodoret, *Ep.* 81, ed. Azéma, p. 196; cf. *Ep.* 79, ed. Azéma, p. 186. At the same time, Bishop Plancus of Gerasa rebuilt a bath; C. H. Kraeling, *Gerasa: City of the Decapolis* (New Haven, Conn.: American Schools of Oriental Research, 1938), no. 296, p. 471. In the sixth century Bishop Marcianus of Gaza repaired the bath and porticoes; Choricius, *Oratio* 7.52, pp. 127–28; see also Anna Avramea, "Les constructions profanes de l'évêque d'après l'épigraphie et les textes d'Orient," in *Actes du xie. Congrès international d'archéologie chrétienne,* Collection de l'école française de Rome 123 (Rome: Palais Farnèse, 1989), 1:829–35.

162. Theodoret, *Ep.* 139, in *Théodoret de Cyr: Correspondance 3,* ed. Y. Azéma, Sources chrétiennes 111 (Paris: Le Cerf, 1965), 146. Flemming, *Akten der ephesinischen Synode,* 114.31; cf. 86.20.

163. Theodoret, *Ecclesiastical History* 5.36.

sponsible for the defense of law and order. In the reign of Justinian, it was the bishop of Hadrianoupolis (near modern Eskipazar, a little off the main road between Istanbul and the Black Sea port of Samsun) who received imperial edicts against banditry and communicated them to the local landowners, assembled in the audience chamber adjoining his basilica.[164]

At Jerash in modern Jordan (Gerasa), Bishop Paul built a special prison for those awaiting trial. By so doing, he intervened in a manner characteristic of the age. He facilitated existing forms of criminal practice. Prolonged imprisonment before trial had not been sanctioned by Roman law. Libanius had denounced such imprisonment in 386 as an abuse by which the powerful terrorized the lower classes.[165] In building a prison sometime in the early sixth century, the bishop of Jerash acted "to the advantage of the city." He institutionalized, by claiming to render more humane, what had begun centuries before as an illegal form of constraint upon the poor and had come to be accepted as normal in his own time.[166]

Sunkatabasis: Divine Condescension and Imperial Power

Yet the rise of the bishop to local prominence was not based simply on successful collaboration with his peers, the civic notables. However it might show itself in practice, the bishop's claim to act as "lover of the poor" had edged to the fore a new imaginative model of society. It was a model that ignored the ancient distinctions between citizen and noncitizen and between city and countryside.[167] It pointedly brushed aside the ceremonious dialogue of the civic notables with the urban population, gathered as the traditional *démos* in theaters and hippodromes. The care of the poor emphasized, instead, a very different, more basic bond of solidarity. The poor were nourished not because they were the fellow citizens of a specific city, but because they shared with great men the common bond of human flesh. The rich man was to treat the beggar who lay "like a broken potsherd" at his door as a fellow "son of the earth." The poor man was not

164.   Denis Feissel and Ismail Kaygusuz, "Un Mandement impérial du vième siècle dans une inscription d'Hadrianoupolis d'Honoriade," *Travaux et Mémoires* 9 (1985): 409–10; see W. Müller-Wiener, "Bischofsresidenzen des 4.–7. Jahrhunderts im östlichen Mittelmeerraum," in *Actes du xie. Congrès international d'archéologie chrétienne* 2:651–709.

165.   Libanius, *Oratio* 45.4 (III.361), in *Libanius: Selected Works 2,* ed. and trans. A. F. Norman, Loeb Classical Library (Cambridge, Mass.: Harvard University Press, 1977), 162; Roger A. Pack, "Studies in Libanius and Antiochene Society under Theodosius" (Ph.D. diss., University of Michigan, 1935), 70–96.

166.   P.-L. Gatier, "Nouvelles inscriptions de Gérasa: Le prison de l'évêque Paul," *Syria* 62 (1982): 297–305.

167.   Evelyne Patlagean, *Pauvreté économique et pauvreté sociale à Byzance* (Paris: Mouton, 1977), 17–35.

a fellow citizen; he was the rich man's brother in mortality.[168] "He whom we look down upon, whom we cannot bear to see, the very sight of whom causes us to vomit, is the same as we, formed with us from the self-same clay, compacted of the same elements. Whatever he suffers, we also can suffer."[169]

Poignant though such appeals to a common flesh might be, the poor were viewed from a great height. Christian gestures of compassion to the poor served to emphasize the enduring and vertiginous quality of the chasm that separated the highest from the lowest classes of society. All men stood before God as the poor stood before the powerful on earth—as helpless beings, in need of mercy. To care for the poor was to "bow down" from a distant eminence. It was apposite that the mosaic pavement of a church building at Jerash should bear an inscription from the Psalms: "Bow down Thy ear, O Lord . . . for I am poor and needy."[170] It was a sentiment which any believer could express. The whole population of Egypt every year sent up to heaven "the groans of the poor" for the rising of the Nile.[171] It was as the "poor" that they hoped to gain the ear of a distant God.

A society seen in terms of such stark cleavages could be spoken of, with increasing appropriateness, in terms of the archaic, precivic world of the Old Testament. The absorption of the Bible by Christians brought the social imagination of an ancient Near East, that knew nothing of the classical city, into the fifth-century present. When the monks of Shenoute's White Monastery chanted the Psalms, King David himself was said to have stood among them—a royal figure, dressed in the robes of an emperor.[172] The cry of the poor to the powerful, that echoed through David's Psalms, was not out of place in late Roman Egypt. Civic life was a recent arrival in that ancient land. Contrasts of wealth and power, reminiscent of an ancient Near Eastern society, as this was mirrored in the Old Testament, were taken for granted. By using the Bible, Shenoute spoke a social language that his contemporaries could understand. His letters of rebuke to governors (unlike his sermons of welcome) were *catenae* of citations from the Old Testament. To ignore them was as much an act of sacrilege as to ig-

168. Romanos Melodes, *Hymn* 30.11.4, in *Romanos le Mélode: Hymnes 3*, ed. J. Grosdidier de Matons, Sources chrétiennes 114 (Paris: Le Cerf, 1965), 290.

169. Jerome, *Letter* 77.6: *Patrologia Latina* 23:694.

170. H. I. Marrou, *Patristique et humanisme* (Paris: Le Seuil, 1976), 95; Thomas Sternberg, "Der vermeintliche Ursprung der westlichen Diakonien in Ägypten und die Conlationes des Johannes Cassianus," *Jahrbuch für Antike und Christentum* 31 (1988): 203, is less certain that the room in question was a center of distribution to the poor.

171. L. S. B. MacCoull, "SPPXV.250ab: A Monophysite Trishagion for the Nile Flood," *Journal of Theological Studies*, n.s., 40 (1989): 130.

172. Besa, *Life of Shenoute* 91–92, trans. Bell, pp. 68–69; ed. Leipoldt and Crum, pp. 44–45.

nore the voice of the prophets that spoke through them. When told that he had angered a governor by his *parrhésia,* Shenoute protested: "I have said nothing except what is written in the Scriptures, indeed, rather, in the *Psalms.*"[173]

Increasing recourse to the language of the Old Testament showed that the myth of the city could no longer veil crushing asymmetries of power. The brittle privileges and self-respect once associated with the notion of citizenship had slipped away. Townsmen and peasants alike learned to approach the great on bended knee. Both categories were equally members of the "poor" by comparison with the power of their masters. Even justice itself had become a form of almsgiving. When a good governor was praised, in Christian terms, as *philentolos* and as *philoptôchos,* a lover of God's commandments and of the poor, his power was imperceptibly invested with a more *de haut en bas* quality than previously. He was not obliged to show *praotés,* gentle courtesy, to a select group of men of *paideia,* as natural leaders of the community. All classes were equal under him, as recipients of a compassion modeled on that of the overpowering position of the rich man in relation to the abject poor.[174] And before the emperor, as before God, all subjects were poor. On arriving at Constantinople, even a self-respecting local notable would find himself a *ptôchos,* a beggar dependent on the favor of the imperial majesty.[175]

Hence the use of a language in relation to the imperial power that echoed the pathos of Christian appeals for compassion towards the poor increased at that time. A mystical solidarity was supposed to bind the emperor, despite his godlike majesty, to all his subjects. He shared with them the common frailty of human flesh. In the words of advice offered by the deacon Agapetus to the emperor Justinian, "The Emperor is honored by bearing the image of God, but the image of [mortal] clay has been worked into this, so that he might learn that he is the equal in nature to all other persons."[176]

Appeals to the shared humanity of an emperor and those he ruled had deep roots in the political thought of the ancient world.[177] It was, how-

---

173.   du Bourguet, "Chénoute sur les devoirs des juges," 90, 94. Shenoute, *Letter* 24, ed. Leipoldt and Crum, p. 88; trans. Wiessmann, p. 44.

174.   L. S. B. MacCoull, *Dioscorus of Aphrodito: His Work and His World* (Berkeley: University of California Press, 1988), 100.

175.   Dorotheus of Gaza, *Instructions* 2.34, in *Dorothée de Gaza: Oeuvres spirituelles,* ed. L. Regnault and J. de Préville, Sources chrétiennes 92 (Paris: Le Cerf, 1963), 196.

176.   Agapetus, *Expositio Capitum Admonitionum* 21: *Patrologia Graeca* 86:1172A.

177.   I. Ševčenko, "A Neglected Byzantine Source of Muscovite Political Ideology," *Harvard Slavic Studies* 2 (1954): 173, is important on the image of the emperor that such a tradition conveyed.

ever, a commonplace that took on a new charge of meaning in the fifth century. The heavy rhetoric of compassion for the shared flesh of the poor endowed the theme of imperial power with dramatic overtones. The emperor was to show *sunkatabasis,* condescension, to his subjects, as the rich stooped to hear the cry of the poor and as God himself had once stooped to join himself, through his Incarnation, to the impoverished flesh of the human race. It is, perhaps, no coincidence that the first generations in which the inhabitants of the imperial capital had to face the permanent and overwhelming presence among them of a godlike autocrat were marked, in Constantinople and elsewhere, by vehement Christological debates (associated with the councils of Ephesus and Chalcedon, in 431 and 451) on the precise manner in which and, above all, on the precise extent to which God had condescended to join himself to human beings in the person of Christ.

The central issue of the Christology of the period was how to combine fellow feeling with the exercise of absolute power. In the words of Pope Leo, Christians must think of the joining of the divine and human in the person of Christ in such a way that "the bending down of compassion" does not imply a "failing of power."[178] A God incapable of suffering and raised above his creatures in inaccessible majesty had bent down to earth. In the person of Christ, he had freely identified himself with human flesh. He had become a fellow "son of the earth," a kinsman of the human race. He had taken on human flesh in the womb of the Virgin Mary. Mary's human flesh, first taken from her womb and nourished in Christ through long suckling at her breast, bound God to humanity.[179] "What action could be more humbling to the emperor of the universe than to come freely to share in the poverty of our flesh?"[180] This shared flesh was the one, frail hope of all Christians: "Look only at the cause of His mercy, the body that He borrowed from us. / Learn the cause of His favor, His hunger and thirst like our own."[181]

---

178. Leo, *Tome 3,* in *The Seven Ecumenical Councils,* trans. H. R. Percival, *Library of the Nicene and Post-Nicene Fathers* (Grand Rapids, Mich.: Eerdmans, 1974), 14:255; analyzed in Jaroslav Pelikan, *The Emergence of the Catholic Tradition* (Chicago: University of Chicago Press, 1971), 258.

179. Averil Cameron, "Virginity as Metaphor: Women and the Rhetoric of Early Christianity," in *History as Text: The Writing of Ancient History* (London: Duckworth, 1989), 190–91. For the bond between mother and son, based on the womb and on three years of suckling, see J. Horn, "Untersuchungen zur Frömmigkeit und Literatur des christlichen Ägyptens: Das Martyrium des Viktor, Sohnes des Romanos" (Ph.D. diss., University of Göttingen, 1988), 214, 217, 232.

180. Gregory of Nyssa, *Oratio de Beatitudinibus: Patrologia Graeca* 44:1201B, cited at the Council of Ephesus, *Collectio Casinensis* 59 [xvi], ed. Schwartz, p. 44; A. J. Festugière, trans., *Ephèse et Chalcédoine: Actes des Conciles* (Paris: Beauchesne, 1982), 239.

181. Isaac of Antioch, *On the Incarnation of the Lord,* lines 272–73, in *S. Isaaci An-*

The early Byzantine icon of Mary as Mother of God, with the infant Christ seated in majesty on her lap, as if still bound to her womb, receiving, as a gentle reminder of human kinship, the touch of her hand upon his knee, was an image that conjured up a poignant wish for solidarity.[182] If God and humanity could be seen to be bound together in so intimate a manner, by the shared flesh of the Virgin and her child, then the invisible thread of fellow feeling for a shared human flesh that linked the emperor to his subjects and the rich to the poor might yet prove as strong. In this way, the Christological controversies of the fifth century centered obsessively on the nature of the *sunkatabasis,* the awesome condescension of God in stooping to identify himself with the abject poverty of the human condition.

We can sense, in the charged issue of God's condescension through the incarnate Christ, the impalpable weight of a whole society's deepest hopes and fears for its own cohesion. In a world more deeply divided than before — between the rich and the poor, the weak and the powerful — a sense of the shared frailty of human flesh offered, at least, a lowest common denominator of solidarity. The emperor and the powerful must observe that minimal restraint upon their actions. As a result, the language of power in early Byzantium came to be suffused with the melodramatic tones of a contemporary Christological debate, whose most serious agenda had been the attempt to spell out the exact mode of God's identification with human nature and, so, the extent of his openness to his distant human subjects.[183] Shenoute, for instance, would read the story of the Passion of Christ with tears streaming down his face. In great sermons and letters of rebuke, he wrote to the powerful that they also should learn to bend as Christ had bent: they also must forgive the insubordination of their inferiors and must show mercy to the poor, to petitioners, and to their own servants.[184]

In so doing, Shenoute, and many like him, used the high-pitched lan-

---

tiocheni opera omnia, ed. G. Bickell (Giessen: W. Keller, 1873), 44; S. Landersdorfer, trans., *Ausgewählte Schriften der syrischen Dichter,* Bibliothek der Kirchenväter (Munich: J. Kosel, 1913), 136.

182.   This is clearly seen in the case of the Mary icon of the Pantheon, in H. Belting, *Bild und Kunst: Eine Geschichte des Bildes vor dem Zeitalter der Kunst* (Munich: C. H. Beck, 1990), 141. As the conveyor of humanity's prayers, the Virgin's hand that makes physical contact with Christ is gilded in this icon. See also J. F. Haldon, *Byzantium in the Seventh Century: The Transformation of a Culture* (Cambridge: Cambridge University Press, 1990), 422–24.

183.   *Sunkatabasis* is well characterized in J. Grosdidier de Matons, *Romanos le Mélode* (Paris: Beauchesne, 1977), 269–70, 283.

184.   Shenoute, *Letters* 31, 34, ed. Leipoldt and Crum, pp. 95, 104; trans. Wiessmann, pp. 54, 59. See D. N. Bell, "Shenoute the Great and the Passion of Christ," *Cistercian Studies* 22 (1987): 291–303.

guage of a high-pitched society. God remained the Emperor of Heaven, and the emperor was very much God on earth. His bending was all the more stunning because it was so very rare. It was a power wielded, now, with *sunkatabasis,* with condescension. *Sunkatabasis* assumed an imperial office set in the cliff face of majesty. It lacked the overtones of a discreet and low-keyed appeal to a common code of deportment, based upon a common upper-class culture. The emperor no longer yielded to the philosopher because he shared with him the same restraints imposed by an elegant and ennobling *paideia.* He yielded to his bishops and to holy men because even Christ himself had yielded, to become a man like those he ruled. Swathed in majesty, the emperor made plain, not that he shared a culture with his upper-class subjects, but, rather, that despite all appearances to the contrary, he shared a common humanity with all Christians.

It is with an image of Christ-like imperial power, destined for a long future in the Christian Middle Ages, that we can end this book. We have entered a different world from that with which we began, among the men of *paideia* of the fourth century A.D. The changes that we have described are vividly summed up in Coptic legends of the later fifth century. In these we see the emperor and the exercise of his power refracted into bizarre, postclassical shapes.

In a conflation of the story of the Riot of the Statues at Antioch with that of the massacre of Thessalonica, we learn that Theodosius I had once wished to burn the city of Siut (Lycopolis) to the ground because of a riot in the circus.[185] The terrified citizens flocked to their local hermit, John of Lycopolis. His advice was hardly a surprise. They must stage a good *adventus* for the imperial commissioner. "When he arrives, go out to meet him, bearing the Gospels and crosses, swinging incense-burners and carrying branches of palms and olives. Keep moving before him until you have brought him close to the city."[186] Then the commissioner was to be led to John, to pay a governor's visit of respect to a holy person, before his final entry into Siut.

Everything passed off successfully. John healed the commissioner's son and reminded him that "we are all in need of the mercy of Christ." The commissioner agreed to report back to Constantinople. But just to be certain, John set off for the capital. He arrived instantly, in a cloud of light

185. Paul Peeters, "Une vie copte de S. Jean de Lycopolis," *Analecta Bollandiana* 54 (1936): 363; and W. Till, *Koptische Heiligen-und Märtyrerlegende,* Orientalia Christiana Analecta 102 (Rome: Pontificium Institutum Orientalium Studiorum, 1935), 147; Lellia Cracco Ruggini, "Poteri in gara per la salvezza di città rebelli: Il caso di Antiochia (387 d.C.)," in *Hestiasis: Studi di tarda antichità offerti a Salvatore Calderone,* Studi tardoantichi 1 (Messina: Sicania, 1988), 284–90.

186. *Le Synaxaire Arabe Jacobite: Patrologia Orientalis* 3:323–26.

that hovered over the imperial *consistorium*. John's hand emerged, giving the sign of blessing to the emperor and profferring a petition. Only when the petition was duly subscribed (as Theodosius II had subscribed the petition of the bishop of Syene) did the hand withdraw and the cloud head back to Egypt. The emperor's judgment was all that a new age could desire: the circus and all pagan places of public assembly were to be destroyed, but the Christian city, grouped around its churches, was to remain.[187] Such a legend reflected the dreams of persons for whom "a positive relationship with the center" had remained a matter of vital importance, but in whose hearts the ancient city had been allowed to die.

It is by following such themes, from the fourth into the fifth century A.D., that we can begin to recapture a little of the scale and the excitement of the transformation that goes under the deceptively simple title of the rise of Christianity in the later Roman Empire.

187. Ibid.

Index

and its gods, 76; proper use of wealth, 83
town hall, 20, 43, 44, 105, 115
Trajan, emperor, 13
Trastevere, Rome: house of Symmachus burned by mob, 80
travel: distances, 9; fluctuation with seasons, 10; battle with, 10, 17; one month to reach Antioch from Constantinople, 9, 16; fear of, 14; by sea shorter than by land, 15; and transport of provisions, 17; visit of cities, 21; of letters, 47; of emperor, 68; mule-cart, horseback, on foot, 118
Trier, 9
Tripolis (Trablus, Lebanon), 130
tropheus ("nourisher"): good notable as, 82, 141
Troy (Turkey), 122
Turin (Italy), 148
Turkey, 5, 15
Tyana (near Niğde, Turkey), 139

Vaggione, R. P., 98n
Valens, eastern emperor: resides in Antioch, 12n; instigates treason trials, 12n, 64, 127; morose, ill-educated, 68; appealed to by Themistius, 68–69; orders death penalty for Nicene Christians, 69; description of crisis ascribed to his reign, 104n; confronted by Basil of Caesarea, 112, 135n
Valentinian I, western emperor: praised for not imposing religious beliefs, 7; and trials for sorcery in Rome, 12n; edict on "concord" of governors and provincials, 33; anger of, 60; confronted by philosopher, 65
Valentinian II, emperor, 98, 104, 111, 112
Valentinian heretics: church of, destroyed at Callinicum, 108
Valerian, emperor, 35
Van Dam, R., 14n, 24n, 121n, 136n
Van Esbroeck, 67n
Van Lantschoot, A., 145n
Vatican, Rome: cemetery of, gathering place of beggars, 91
venatio, wild beast show, court likened to by Ammianus Marcellinus, 11
Vera, D., 20n, 40n
Verona (Italy), 110

Veyne, P., 65n, 82n, 92n
villa, fortified, 23
violence: murder of Hypatia, 5; shown by imperial government, 7; in punishments, 10; and politics, 11; of monks, 20, 107–8; stoning of tax-collectors, 27; power shown by, 43, 48, 50; of military men, 50; domestic, 51–52; in law court, 52–53; extended to petty notables, 54; and rage, 54; as human lapse, 55, 112; popular violence, 81, 87, 88; against temples and pagans, 89, 114, 119, 120, 127; religious, 90, 132; against synagogues, 108, 115; urban, 148
Virgil, 39
Virgin Mary: as "Theotokos," 15; and Christ's flesh, 155; icon of, as Mother of God, 145
Visigoths: use Christian monks, 72; Theodosius and, 103; ravage Greece, 143
Viventius, urban prefect of Rome: flees city during papal election, 81
voice: control of, 48, 49, 58; quality of well-tuned, 49; shout, 50
Vollenweider, S., 136n
Vööbus, A., 95n, 148n

Wadi Natrun (Egypt): hermitages of, 73
Waha, M. de, 98n
Walker, W., 93n
Wallace-Hadrill, A., 19n, 58n, 88n
Wallis Budge, E. A., 14n
Ward, B., 73n
wealth: displayed in churches, 95, 121; private, 147
Wells, S., 68n
Wenger, A., 74n, 94n
Wes, M. A., 54n
Westerink, L. G., 117n
Whitby, M. and M., 133n
White Monastery (Sohag, Egypt), abbot Shenoute, 140; refugees fed at, 141; king David appears to monks of, 153
Whittaker, C. R., 58n, 82n
Whittow, M., 134n
Wickham, L. R., 16n, 17n, 116n
Wiessmann, H., 140n, 141n, 143n, 154n, 156n
Wilken, R. L., 91n
Williams, R., 135n